Dinner for One

How Cooking in Paris Saved Me

SUTANYA DACRES

Dinner for One

How Cooking in Paris Saved Me

PARK
ROW
BOOKS

PARK
ROW™
BOOKS™

Recycling programs
for this product may
not exist in your area.

ISBN-13: 978-0-7783-3303-6

Dinner for One: How Cooking in Paris Saved Me

Park Row Books
22 Adelaide St. West, 41st Floor
Toronto, Ontario M5H 4E3, Canada
ParkRowBooks.com
BookClubbish.com

Printed in U.S.A.

To everyone who has come out on the other side of a love lost.

Dinner for One

How Cooking in Paris Saved Me

L'être ne recherche que soi

A travers le multiple choix

De l'amour et de ses orages.

O Désir, sompteux voyage

Vers notre fascinate image

Qui nous exalte ou nous déçoit!

—C'est à soi-même qu'on veut plaire

Sur le coeur brûlant qui nous plaît

Ou, dans l'ivreese et la colère,

Ne sachent si l'on aime ou hait,

Par la volupté l'on espère

Mourir, et ne mourir jamais!

—Anna de Noailles, "L'être ne recherche que soi,"
from *Les Forces éternelles*

It is ourselves we long to find

From within the countless binds

Of love and all its storms.

Oh, Desire, sumptuous journey

Toward our own enthralling image

That disappoints or glorifies!

—It is ourselves we aim to please

Resting on the burning heart of another,

Where, in rage and ecstasy,

Whether we love or hate we can't remember,

Through our lust we hope, we seek

To die, and live forever!

Prologue

The day I reached my breaking point started out like so many others since my husband had left four months earlier—wake up, get ready and leave my apartment as quickly as possible. Decently sized by Paris standards, the 463-square-foot apartment faced south, overlooking a shared courtyard, with double-door windows that spilled sunlight into the bedroom and living room. At the time, remnants of The Frenchman—let's call him TFM for short—dotted the space like stains of a past meal on a rumpled tablecloth. Every morning a yellow mirror from his childhood bedroom reflected empty eyes and dark under-eye circles. A family heirloom chest purchased by his father now held all the documents that confirmed my existence as a legal resident of France. A mammoth bookshelf in the living room built by TFM our first weekend living together housed his books, intermingled with mine. His energy lingered in the space.

As I dressed—pulling on a black shirtdress, slipping my feet into caramel-colored sandals, dabbing pink blush on my cheeks and coloring my lips MAC Ruby Woo red—I had no reason to think that the day would be such a turning point for me. After he moved out, feelings of hopelessness and loss quickly became familiar friends, and I had turned to constant *apéros*, the French version of happy hour, to ensure that I didn't have to find myself alone, and sober, in what used to be my marital apartment. A full social calendar and big smiles gave the impression that I was somewhat in control of the tornado that recently touched down in my life, but that couldn't have been further from the truth.

I headed out in the early afternoon to meet my relatively new friend Tiffanie at the Jeu de Paume museum, a space dedicated to modern and postmodern media in the Jardin des Tuileries. Parisian by birth, Tiffanie and I met during my years working at one of the big four advertising agencies in Paris. We were both experiencing intense transitions—me from being married to newly single, and she was moving away from the advertising world to answer her true calling as a visual artist—but our methods of transitioning differed wildly. Tiffanie had a purpose, plan and goal, whereas I chose late nights, partying and denial. I refused to face how my pain was suffocating me.

After we wandered long enough through the morose photography exhibitions of Sabine Weiss and Josef Sudek we treated ourselves, with a bit of nudging on my part, to a bottle of rosé in the Jardin des Tuileries. As a good wannabe Parisian, I made sure to have the bottle on hand to enjoy after our day at the museum. That was simply what one did. It was a sunny Saturday, and I had no obligations; I was on a mission to *profiter de la journée*. We settled into the gardens' iconic green chairs side by side, people-watching and sipping our wine, cackling with laughter, giving my spirit brief respite from my divorce, my shame, my feelings of worthlessness.

Eventually, we hopped on the metro heading north. The destination was Sunset, a New York-style cocktail bar in the Montmartre neighborhood of Jules Joffrin. Walking up the stairs out of the metro station, using our hands to shield our eyes from the still-beaming late-afternoon sun, I noticed a concerned expression on Tiffanie's face.

"Is everything okay?" I asked.

Looking at me for confirmation, she responded, "We're only going to have one bottle, right?"

I smiled, threw an arm around her shoulders. "Yes, one. I promise."

At Sunset we were promptly seated in an ideal people-watching spot *en terrasse*. Unlike the typical Parisian rattan bistro chairs that line so many sidewalks, the seating at Sunset was a mix of long wooden tables and benches that forced you to sit next to strangers, where you couldn't help but eavesdrop on their conversations. My status as a regular meant that I was treated like a local celebrity, and the staff knew what I liked.

"And for you ladies," the young, wiry Senegalese waiter said, presenting us with a cold bottle of Côtes de Provence rosé, the condensation dripping off its sides, as soon as we sat down. Unbeknownst to Tiffanie, the wine fest was about to begin. A few hours and several empty bottles of wine later, most of which I drank, I was looking around to get the waiter's attention to order another.

"The last one," I said to Tiffanie, but we both knew that was another empty promise.

My eyes met the waiter's, but before I could give him the universal signal for another round, Tiffanie yawned. Stretching out both her arms to their full length, she slurred, *"J'en peux plus."*

She'd had enough, and I knew that her saying it in French meant that there was no convincing her to stay. The language of our friendship was English, so her switch to French signaled that she was too intoxicated to put any further effort into speaking my mother tongue. "I can't anymore," she repeated in English to make sure that I understood that there would, in fact, not be one last bottle. "I have to go home," she said while gathering her belongings.

I had just caught my second wind and didn't want to leave; the abundance of wine temporarily relieved the heaviness of my new reality. I wanted to bathe in it, stay forever, but I followed suit. We drunkenly kissed each other on the cheek and parted ways, beginning my crooked five-minute walk back home.

The cobbled street that led from Sunset to my apartment bustled during the day, lined with a butcher shop, a bakery, a greengrocer and a fishmonger's shop. But it was deserted at 7 p.m. as I stumbled onto it, trying to keep my balance and not fall over. I had achieved my goal—I was completely off my face, and the next morning I would be so hungover, with a pounding head and body, feeling like a block of cement had been dropped on it the night before, that I wouldn't be able to think, that I could bury any attempt at introspection while feeding my insatiable need to forget. A few minutes later I was in front of my limestone Haussmann apartment building, attempting to enter the correct *digicode* and failing at every try. Eventually, I managed to enter the correct sequence of numbers and pushed open the black wrought iron door that leads to a courtyard. I was relieved that I didn't have to force small talk with any neighbors, especially the retired busybody of the building who tends to the makeshift flower garden in the courtyard when he's not adorning the hallway with passive-aggressive notes that outline his latest grievance such as suggesting that hosting parties in a *salle de fête* would suit him better than in the comfort of ones own home or my personal favorite, when he complained about boisterous laughter permeating the buildings walls and reminded everyone that quiet hours begin at 10 p.m. The makeshift flower garden was the only thing about the apartment building that continued to bring me joy; the memories that lay within its walls did the opposite. After going through another door I began the climb up the navy blue spiral stairs to my front door. I opened the door, crossed the threshold into my apartment and, like clock-work, stripped myself naked and fell into what felt like a familiar alcohol-induced deep sleep. Removing all of my clothes upon entering my apartment was a recent habit, as if with each layer of clothing removed so, too, were reminders of the night's sins.

When I woke up I felt abnormally parched and hungry. I rubbed my heavy eyes, reached for my glasses and pulled myself off the couch. With both hands holding my head, I stumbled naked into my tiny red-and-white-tiled kitchen. I swung open the refrigerator door and bypassed a bottle of wine before taking out a glass bottle of water and a bowl of moldy strawber-ries. After quenching my thirst, I looked at the strawberries with disgust. Even hungover I wasn't going to eat those. Out of the corner of my eye, I noticed that the Parisian sky had a magical, cotton-candy, summer-evening glow. It wasn't the usual fresh azure morning sky dotted with cumulus clouds that puts a new day in motion. *Interesting*, I thought.

"It's probably going to rain," I said aloud to no one. I opened the window to let in crisp morning air but was met with con-fusion. The smells circulating the courtyard were not the day-break scents of coffee, toast and croissants. Instead, the aroma of tomatoes, onions and garlic wafted past my nose. I heard glasses clinking together. I was perplexed. I looked around, panicked and ran to the living room where I began frantically searching for my cell phone. I found it and looked at the time. It was only 9:30 p.m. That was when the realization that it was only a few hours after I'd returned home and I wasn't hungover but still very drunk, washed over me.

My body slowly sank into the hardwood floor of my living room, my back curved like a half-moon, my face buried in my palms. I started crying. The deep shame that had been bubbling beneath the surface finally erupted. I had an out-of-body mo-ment and, as I saw myself sobbing on the floor, shaking, still naked, it was clear that I could no longer hide from myself. On the outside I looked like I was doing a good job of getting over my marriage. I went to work every day. I was sad, but not too sad. My conversations didn't revolve around the demise of my marriage, and the random hookups signaled that I was moving on. But behind the fake smiles and the "I'm fine" lies, I was ashamed. I felt like an unlovable failure, and I was allowing that shame to destroy me.

Just three years earlier I was a newlywed living in my own romantic comedy. I was married to a Frenchman whom I met at a bar in New York City, and he made me quiver when he said my name. He opened up my world to another way of living— we took trips to far-flung locations like Egypt and Sri Lanka, we danced and we hosted dinner parties. There was that one time in Stockholm when we lay together side by side in our hotel room, eating junk food and watching terrible TV shows, and we couldn't have been happier. We were a team; I was his and he was mine.

I was convinced that our love was ironclad. In my mind we defied the confines of race; mine Black, his white. The constraints of religion didn't stand a chance; mine Christian, his Jewish. Our nationalities and cultures were a second thought; I an American-Jamaican woman from the Bronx and he a French-Jewish-Algerian man from Paris. We created a deep bond despite an ocean physically separating us and a six-hour time difference dictating how often we were able to speak to each other in real time; overcoming those obstacles strengthened and solidified our desire to build a life with each other. It was us against the world and we would move through life's ups and downs with ease and grace, together.

On our wedding day in 2013, I was proud that we had survived a three-year long-distance relationship, and the grand prize was everlasting love. Until 2016, when almost three years after we said our "I dos" in the *Mairie du 15e*, the city hall of the fifteenth arrondissement, my picture-perfect Paris life crumbled to bits like a flaky croissant. As I lay naked and crying on the living room floor of our Montmartre apartment, I asked myself, *How did this become my life?*

The answer was that I was suffering from more than just a broken heart. A series of dangerously indulgent weekends led me to an all-time low. My spirit was crushed, and finding comfort in self-destructive behavior that I thought I had left behind in my graduate school days was clear evidence of a lack of love and concern for myself. The pain was all-encompassing—I couldn't see past it and wasn't sure if I ever would be able to.

What I didn't know at the time was that the very aromas that had woken me up and brought on my lowest hour—of garlic, roasting tomatoes and searing onions, the smells of dinnertime in Paris—also promised to be my salvation. I replenished my spirit by making dinner for myself, and myself alone. The practice of cooking for one brought me so much good. I stopped punishing myself and replaced self-harm with kindness and compassion.

Making solo dinners gave me the courage to not succumb to my divorce, but to transform through it. From the darkness of divorce and a love lost came a deeper understanding of who I am and a love of myself that I didn't know was missing, but I am forever grateful that I discovered and wholly embraced them.

ACT 1

One

THE HARTFORD CHRONICLES

"You really need to pay more attention to detail, Sutanya," Nancy, my colleague and proxy manager, griped for the umpteenth time. There were spelling errors found in every piece of marketing material that I worked on—webinar invitations, company-wide newsletters and even the most basic emails—because my focus was elsewhere. It was 2009; I was twenty-four years old, a year and a half into a master's degree program and working as a marketing assistant at a midtier insurance company. Devising an exit strategy out of my job and suburbia commanded my focus and brainpower almost all the time. I couldn't imagine this being the climax of my life, something that someone like Nancy could never understand.

In her early thirties, Nancy was just about a decade older than I was and deep in the trenches of adulthood. She had sensible shoulder-length dark brown hair that probably never saw the stroke of hair dye, and intense dark brown eyes that always conveyed a sense of worry and anxiety. Her work uniform consisted of some variation of dark slacks, a nondescript solid-colored dress shirt and sensible shoes. I, on the other hand, wouldn't balk at wearing fishnet stockings under a black miniskirt on a Tuesday and a multicolored shift dress on Wednesday. We couldn't have been more different, yet we were tasked to work closely together. Her obvious die-hard fandom of Casual Corner aside, Nancy was spectacular at her job. Sharp, witty and supremely organized, she could've been a bigwig marketing executive in New York City or Boston, but the suburbs of Connecticut were her home and she never left.

I was intrigued by the fact someone with so much potential could be satisfied with a simple suburban life. Didn't she want more? Wasn't she curious about what the world outside the suburbs in Connecticut could offer? How was she not frustrated? I understood the pull towards a life in the suburbs, the allure of ample space, very green grass and frequent barbeques in the summer can't be denied, it just wasn't for me. The idea of completely succumbing to the ease of suburban life riddled me with angst, but I didn't know if extracting myself from its grip was the smartest thing to do.

The collapse of Lehman Brothers and the global financial system a year prior in 2008 sent the world economy into a tailspin, so for now Connecticut made sense. I was enrolled in graduate school, holding on to a steady job by a thread and a prayer and living in an affordable apartment with good friends. I wanted to believe that there was something bigger out there for me but it wasn't clear what the bigger thing was. The only thing I did know for sure was that I didn't want to be a Nancy.

With my corporate job, graduate school course load and silver Honda Accord, the cloud of suburban purgatory loomed menacingly above me. I was on the fast track toward a life that was tolerable, but far from satisfying. West Hartford, Connecticut, was supposed to be a temporary stop, but six years after first stepping foot onto the campus of the University of Hartford as

an undergraduate, I was still there. The New Yorker in me became comfortable with the ease and predictability of suburban
life. The rent was cheap, the neighborhoods were *The Truman
Show*-esque and the people scarily cheerful. Yet, I was yearning to return to big-city life. I missed the sirens, I craved its di-
versity and I longed for the spontaneity of not knowing where
my day would take me.

During the weekends I would often carve out time to escape
to places far away from Connecticut. It started with fashion
blogs; I was able to see how women in San Francisco, London,
Paris and my home city of New York were stepping out boldly,
stylishly, into the world. From there, I stumbled upon the blogs
of American women living in Europe. Some of the bloggers were
my age, others just a few years older, yet they were living lives
that were foreign to mine. They had to communicate in different
languages, learn new social codes and try to assimilate to their
adopted cultures in order to survive. There was no monotony—
simply waking up every day was an adventure. They were in
love with European men who treated them as if they were the
center of the world. They were living real adult lives; not me.
I became hooked the more I read about these women and their
seemingly perfect lives, and I began fantasizing about what a life
in Europe would look like if the chance presented itself.

From my IKEA desk, a glass of wine on the left and half of a
joint in the ashtray on my right, I would bring my chair closer
and lose myself in their blog posts. I laughed as they recounted
their latest innocent language blunders. I felt sad when they
shared the details of an argument they had with their partners
and felt relieved when, at the end of the blog post, I learned that
they made up. They always made up.

Every day as soon as the clock struck 6 p.m., I urgently peeled
out of the parking lot of my job and, if I didn't have any graduate school obligations, drove over Avon Mountain toward the

brick Georgian Revival building in the West End of Hartford where I lived with two roommates, Gabbie and Joli.

Gabbie juggled several jobs—working at the Bloomfield Public Library, babysitting for a family a few towns over and even sometimes waking up at 4 a.m. to plow snow in the height of the winter. Jolie spent her days at a vintage consignment store while trying to jump-start her styling career. We each earned just enough to pay the ridiculously cheap rent of three hundred dollars each for the spacious three-bedroom, 1500-square-foot apartment we shared. Our third-floor walk-up had high ceilings, original early-twentieth-century crown moldings and built-ins, a walk-in pantry in the kitchen, a balcony off the back of the kitchen and an original claw-foot tub in the bathroom. A medley of flea market finds, garage sale treasures and burgeoning artists' first pieces of work was my reentry into a magical oasis of early twenty-somethingness.

The dynamics of our relationship were akin to sisterhood. We bickered, argued and made up, often. We shared clothes and grievances. But most importantly, both of them were from Connecticut and more attuned to suburban life, which helped to calm me. Gabbie was raised in the Hartford area and our shared Jamaican heritage made our bond fast and deep. Joli was Ecuadorian by way of Montreal, Canada, and, like me, desperately wanted to escape the doldrums of suburbia. Our shared immigrant backgrounds also served as a connector. Like me, from an early age, they toggled between two cultures. The culture at home and the one we experienced and witnessed every day outside our homes. When you grow up as a child of an immigrant, or you're an immigrant yourself, code switching becomes as second nature as breathing. On one hand it means you're adaptable and flexible, but at other times it can become quite difficult to form an identity. It's hard to know who you are when blending in and making others comfortable is your way of functioning in the world.

The constant struggle to find the balance between the two

worlds we were raised in while attempting to design a unique way of life that matched our desires and likeliness was pronounced and ever present. But together we created a feeling of home and safety that allowed the mutability of our identities and being in our early twenties to manifest itself in different shapes and paths until we found what was right for us.

It was around this time that I began self-medicating with the ironic combination of cooking, exercise, weed and partying. In rare moments of lucidity this behavior surprised and worried me, but not enough for me to stop. Overexercising gave me a sense of control; the weed made me numb to my deep feeling of restlessness; the cooking gave me the illusion of leading a responsible and healthy life; and the partying, well, I was 24. That's probably the one thing I did best.

When I was at my gloomiest, it became common for Gabbie to let out an audible gasp upon entering our apartment, switching on the lights and finding me sitting in the complete darkness in our living room in a comatose-like state from overindulging in weed—and waiting for the time to pass. Sometimes the only light in the living room was a muted episode of *Family Guy* on the television.

"Sutanya! What are you doing?" Gabbie would ask.

"Huh, what?" I replied, barely shaken from my haze of melancholy. I would carefully choose my words to make my behavior seem not so destructive. "I exercised and like, now I'm just chillin'."

"You need to cut the shit," she said on more than one occasion when she had enough of being startled by my despondent presence on an almost daily basis.

For most of our friends, Friday nights meant two-for-one shots, late-night bar hopping and, if they were lucky, clandestine hookups. But not us. Fridays were a sacred day of the week. We got all the other shenanigans out of the way earlier in the week or held off until Saturday. For Gabbie, Joli and me, Friday evenings were our night. The only day of the week we would reserve for each other and cook dinner.

My go-to meal was orzo pasta salad. The small bits of pasta mixed with red peppers, feta, cherry tomatoes, corn and Dijon mustard felt sophisticated, yet unstuffy. Something the American women abroad "friends in my head" bloggers would surely approve of. Gabbie was almost always on wine duty, Joli in charge of the music and I always tasting and adjusting, adding a hint of smoked paprika if needed and always too much olive oil. Our magical family dinners always ended with us cackling late into the night. During the seasons when the weather was particularly sweet, we ate outside on the wooden balcony off our kitchen, lights haphazardly strung across its railings, in oversize T-shirts, red wine-stained teeth and lips, roaring with laughter and reveling in our youth. On those nights my life in Hartford didn't seem so bad. The dopamine-fueled optimism of youth filled my body and mind during those fleeting moments of happiness, but it never lasted long enough.

A few months later on Christmas morning, a chorus of curses escaped my mouth as I sped down the Merritt Parkway, furtively glancing at the hickeys on my neck in the rearview mirror. I couldn't believe what I was seeing. I was on my way to church in the Bronx to celebrate the holiday with my family. Would I even be allowed to step foot in the house of the Lord?

I grew up in a religious household. My mother found solace in church and its accompanying community when the trials of marriage and raising children in a foreign country became overwhelming. I wasn't as religious as my mother hoped I would be, but fourteen years of Catholic school education, countless Sunday school sessions and many evenings and weekends spent at choir practice leave their mark. I had faith, believed in God and most importantly, knew that my mother, and possibly God, would not be pleased with my new accessories.

If I hadn't found myself the night before at Christmas at Killarney, an annual holiday party hosted by friends, I would've been in the Bronx on Christmas Eve as planned. The Christmas at Killarney Christmas Eve-eve celebrations grew from a small gathering among friends to the premier Hartford holiday party before everyone left for their respective homes and towns to experience forced regression back to childhood for up to three days maximum, if they were lucky.

"Do you really have to leave tomorrow morning?" Gabbie asked the day of the party. I was sitting cross-legged on her bed, wearing my favorite sweatpants and hoodie combination, watching her pull off and try on everything that was on the clothing rack that served as her closet, feeling content that I wasn't partaking in any of it. Glass-paned French doors opened onto Gabbie's room, welcoming guests into a bohemian wonderland filled with books, countless tchotchkes, or as she liked to describe them, *treasures from all the places she loved*, and various wall hangings that ran the gamut from reproductions of Impressionist masterpieces to a disco ball.

"Yes," I responded firmly. "I promised my mom I would be in a pew on Christmas Day, and I want to beat the traffic and—"

Gabbie cut me off. "This is the last time we're going to see each other in 2009!" she pleaded. "You've been having a rough year and you need to relax more." I assumed she conveniently forgot all of the marijuana-aided relaxation techniques I frequently indulged in, but I let it slide. "You've never been to this party, and it's the best part of the year!"

I wasn't swayed. I needed to be in the right state of mind when I walked into church on Christmas morning and launched into a conversation with God. I desperately needed a one-on-one and potential intervention with Him because I had no idea what the hell was going on. Like my mother, being in a church gave me a sense of calm and clarity. Two things I desperately needed. I found comfort in believing that there was something greater than I was out there in the mysterious universe, and that greater being's mission was to guide me along the right path. At times when the path didn't seem as straightforward as I envisioned, I fell back on my faith and belief in God to pull me through. My faith would come in handy years later when my life was actually falling apart.

Frustration mounting and patience waning, Gabbie began demanding I go to the party. "Why are you staying home by yourself when *both* Joli and me are going? It doesn't make any sense!" I ignored her and turned my focus to an open book that was on her bed. "What are you gonna do? Stay here and smoke weed until you fall asleep?"

I looked up at her. The last line stung because it was true. "Come on, Gabs. That was a low blow," I responded. I opened my mouth to continue my protest, but nothing came out. She'd won, and she knew it. I was going to the party. I looked down at my lap and heard her say, "You should wear this." She tossed a beige mini wrap dress on my lap. "It always looked really good on you," she said.

After a less than five-minute drive, the three of us pulled up in front of a shabby two-family house in Gabbie's Toyota Corolla. From the sidewalk I could see people spilling out of the first-floor apartment and immediately regretted my decision. I stepped out of the car and smoothed out my dress over my knees. I needed something to do with my limbs besides getting back into the car and speeding to our apartment. I was on the brink of grabbing Gabbie's keys out of her hands when the door of the apartment swung open.

It was Bridgette, one of the hosts of the party and one of the three roommates who lived there. "Hiiiii, guysssssssss, welcome, welcome."

The apartment had a curiously upscale hipster-brothel-chic aesthetic. Red was the dominant color theme of the night. Red wine already stained Bridgette's pink lips; red lights greeted us; red curtains draped the windows; and a faux crystal chandelier decorated with red string was the main centerpiece.

Under the red lights of the party with my red Solo cup filled with Yellowtail red wine, I bounced from conversation to conversation in search of the most interesting one. I was annoyed at myself for succumbing to peer pressure and trying to find a way out the door when out of the corner of my eye, I noticed a man with dark and thick wavy hair watching my every move. Most of the men at the party didn't care to update their skater-boy uniform for the occasion, whereas his navy blue blazer with an emblem on the chest pocket, crisp white Oxford shirt and round tortoiseshell glasses signaled that he wasn't from around these parts. He was standing alone in the corner, looking just as bored and lonely as I was.

Sympathetic to his plight, I smiled at him and held up my red Solo cup in his direction, my attempt at sharing long-distanced cheers. Understanding and accepting my invitation, he made his way over to where I was standing. We fell into an easy conversation after admitting we both didn't know many people present and were hard-pressed to come up with a good reason to be at the party. Our body language eased as the time passed, from side-by-side observing the crowd and making jokes, to face-to-face and immersed in each other's every word. We discovered that we shared curiously similar mutual interests. I learned that he spoke French and was a history teacher. He learned that I studied French during my high school and undergrad years and my career goal when I was a teenager was to become a history professor, but instead I was working toward a master's degree in communication. He broke a moment of silence by asking about a recent exhibition at The Wadsworth Atheneum Museum of Art. I wasn't used to talking about art exhibitions with the men

I met at these parties, or in Hartford in general. I was used to half listening to them talk about how many Jager Bombs they downed the week before at the Pigs Eye Pub—downtown Hartford's eminent bar for binge drinking and indulging in reckless behavior. The lonely intellectual wanted to know more about the art scene in Hartford and started shooting off questions.

After answering some of them I said teasingly, "I didn't think there would be a pop quiz tonight." He blushed, first in his cheeks until his entire face was flushed red. "It's Saturday. You don't have to be a teacher tonight," I said with a smile.

"Sorry, I can't help it," he said with his eyes cast down, looking into his cup. I laughed and gave him a friendly tap on the arm and moved closer to him, eliminating the last bit of space between us. Our friendly banter quickly turned flirtatious with every refill of my Solo cup. This lonely intellectual stranger piqued my interest.

He seemed different from other men I met during my years in Hartford. He had a European sensibility about him that matched the descriptions of the men that the American women abroad bloggers gushed about. Had I found a European-American man that lived in New England? I made a note to ask him about his background before we parted ways that night. As people became increasingly drunk and belligerent, we decided that my bedroom was the best place to continue our conversation. We didn't quite finish that deep conversation. The tension that was building at the party gave way to a passionate night that sent shock waves through my body and made me feel desired in a way I hadn't in a long time.

I woke up the next day, Christmas Eve morning, reaching for a warm body next to me, but there wasn't one. The lonely intellectual stranger was gone, but he left two reminders of his presence—his phone number on my bedside table, which I saw immediately, and another that snuck up on me.

I walked out of my bedroom toward the kitchen to make a cup of coffee before settling into the couch and sharing the details of the evening, but Gabbie's face stopped me dead in my tracks, eyes wide and mouth agape with awe. She slowly covered her mouth with her hand. Something was wrong, very wrong.

"Go look in the mirror," Gabbie instructed. I passed Joli and her sleep-fogged eyes as I walked to the floor-to-ceiling mirror in the foyer and there they were. I screamed.

"What the fuck are these?" I yelled, pulling my V-neck T-shirt as far down as possible. I walked to the mirror as if I was going to walk through it and counted each one. I needed to get a better view.

"They're not that bad," Gabbie responded to calm me down while rubbing my back. "Look, it's okay. Ain't nothing a little concealer can't fix."

I glared at her and sat on the floor in front of the mirror. Still counting each one in bewilderment. "Three? He really had to leave three?"

"At least you know he's into you," Gabbie said with a chuckle.

I wasn't in a joking mood. "Now is not the time, Gabbie! I don't care! Look at my neck."

"Shit, that's a lot of hickeys," Joli chimed in as she walked past me and back into her room.

We both ignored her, and Gabbie continued, "He obviously doesn't want you to forget him."

I started coming around to Gabbie's theory. I did like him, and the chemistry was there. "Should I call him?" I asked eagerly.

"No! Definitely don't call him."

"Why?" I asked.

Gabbie tilted her head to the side, pursed her lips together and looked at me.

I wanted to call him, but I followed Gabbie's advice this time. I find little interest in playing games when attraction, partnership and commitment are on the line. I always felt the best type of romances grew from reciprocity, but according to the modern rules of dating I was living in the nineteenth century because being up front and honest about my feelings was the last thing I needed to do. I usually found myself playing along and the results were always disastrous.

After much debate and negotiation, Gabbie and I agreed that an easy breezy flirty afternoon text message that acknowledged the night before without coming off as too needy, while managing to make it clear that I want to see him again, but without sounding like I don't have a life, was most appropriate. After several drafts I sent.

Hey! Hope you got home okay. Last night was fun. Let's hang soon? It's rare that I meet French-speaking history buffs in Hartford haha.

Gabbie didn't approve the question mark or my inability to not be earnest, but I was happy with the message I sent because it was me. Despite the menacing hickeys on my neck I couldn't help but smile to myself when flashbacks from the night before spontaneously popped into my mind. I believed my Christmas gift came two days early. I lay on my bed with both hands behind my head and a broad smile on my face. I was experiencing my own Hartford Christmas miracle. I questioned if this was a sign that I shouldn't be in a rush to leave so soon. I did enjoy watching *The Truman Show* after all.

When my BlackBerry buzzed, I was thinking about what a life in which I was the owner of a New England suburban home with a picket fence and station wagon would resemble. It wasn't what I thought I wanted, but my seemingly auspicious meeting with the lonely intellectual the night before led my mind to wander. I looked down and smiled when I saw he responded. I flipped over, legs in the air, snuggled into my bed and ready to read what I expected to be a text message about planning a date after the holidays. After reading the text message, I immediately jumped off my bed and ran into Gabbie's room.

"Motherfucker," I said as I shoved my phone in her face.

She took the phone out of my hand. "Oh, fuck," Gabbie muttered.

His message thanked me for a great night and reassured me that I was a wonderful young lady, but he was in an open relationship and I should never contact him again. While I doubted the truth around his open relationship—I figured I was either meant to be a moment in time or he was in a relationship—I had no choice but to respect his wishes. I gripped the phone with anger. I felt duped by him but mostly frustrated with myself. Why did I expect more from him than what he presented? When we were lying in my bed with our legs haphazardly strewn across each other, I hadn't asked if this moment meant anything or if there was a possibility that it could mean something because I hadn't thought it needed to be. Our meeting felt serendipitous.

In hindsight, the possibility of being in a relationship—giving in to another distraction and something that seemed easy and the right thing to do—almost bamboozled me into staying in a city and living a life that was slowly chipping away at my essence. Before bed that night I made a vow to myself that 2010 was going to be my year. I would focus on myself. No more messing around with Hartford and its bullshit. I needed to get out because I knew deep down within myself that if I stayed one more year, I would never leave. But there were also more pressing matters on my mind. What was I going to do about these hickeys before Christmas morning?

I survived church and Christmas lunch and dinner with my hickeys seemingly going unnoticed. If they did catch anyone's eye nothing was said. My uniform of turtlenecks, scarves and bulky sweaters did not leave any room for double takes or intrusive questioning.

The physical reminders of the casual sex that happened a few days before didn't bother me as much as the pattern of these encounters. I went on dates, had dalliances, one-night love affairs, one-sided crushes and heavy flirtations, but none of those nights spent sharing bottles of wine in cozy bars or hours lying side by side in the park ever transformed into a long-lasting, serious relationship. In the moment they felt exciting, freeing and rebellious but ultimately, they were soulless. Engaging in casual sex was an attempt to fill a void rather than identify what was truly ailing me and my disheartening experience with the lonely intellectual lit a fire under my ass.

I was on a mission to create a timeline and plan that would get me back to New York City by the end of that year. Little did I know that my intensifying desire for something to shake me and uproot me would appear in the form of a French man wearing a gray sweater.

Two

A CAFÉ NAMED FANELLI

The night after Christmas was cold and rainy, but I felt energized for the first time in months. I was ready to create my detailed plan to take my life into my own hands and not allow fuckboys anywhere near me, when my phone buzzed. It was a text message from my friend Audrey.

Are you home?

Audrey had been the resident assistant during my undergrad years and had softened the culture shock of living in the suburbs during the early months of my freshman year. She was from Long Island, not quite New York City, but that felt closer to home than the quiet streets of West Hartford. When I had arrived at the University of Hartford, she saw straight through my frantic energy and took me under her wing, and I didn't leave her side. I had been immediately drawn to Audrey's laugh. She laughed from deep within her belly, with all of her teeth on display for everyone to see, and it was one of the purest expressions of joy I've ever had the privilege of witnessing. In the years that followed her graduation and my stagnation in suburbia, our meetups were relegated to my infrequent visits home.

I usually looked forward to our yearly catch-up, but I wasn't in the right headspace during this quick visit home. I also couldn't bring myself to ignore her text message.

Yep! And Merry Christmas! I responded to her.

When are you going back? she asked.

Tomorrow! I'm just dipping in and out. I knew what was coming next and I was dreading it.

What are you doing tonight? Let's meet in the city and grab drinks, she said.

I rolled my eyes at her suggestion. I was plotting and manifesting.

I think I'm gonna stay in tonight, but you can come here if you want! I suggested.

Negative, she replied in seconds. I never see you. You're never home! Come on, she continued. The peer pressure was mounting, again. She was so insistent that it felt like our friendship was on the line if I didn't agree to see her.

I could've put up more of a fight and stood my ground, but I didn't. I figured whatever was waiting for me in Manhattan couldn't be worse than the emotional roller coaster of the past forty-eight hours, so I gave in and we met at The Mercer Kitchen in SoHo.

My lack of enthusiasm about lugging myself to The Mercer Kitchen was obvious in my sartorial choice for the night. When I walked into the restaurant and removed my jacket Audrey looked me up and down as I stood in front of her barefaced in faded black leggings, an oversize cream sweater, chunky scarf and a curly afro that was multiplying in size right in front of her eyes due to the moisture in the air. If she could've, she probably would've suggested that I kept my jacket on. Saying that I didn't put any effort or thought into my outfit was an understatement. This was not a fun night out; the purpose was to see an old friend without losing focus on what mattered to me the most at this moment in time—my exit strategy.

As I tucked into my margherita pizza, Audrey's belly laugh reminded me of why I gave in to her bullying. I was happy to be with her; her positive energy was infectious. She filled me in on the latest happenings in her life and I did the same. I tried to steer the conversation toward work, my roommates and my plan to move back to New York City, but Audrey wanted the juicy stuff. She wanted to know who I was kissing on, crushing on and, she hoped, sleeping with. I evaded her questions as much as possible until I couldn't anymore. I pulled down my scarf, revealing the faded but still very present hickeys on my neck.

Audrey squealed and wanted to know more. "Who were they from? When did it happen? Where did it happen?" The rapid-fire questions fell out of her mouth, and wine-covered spittle landed on my face. I wiped my face as she eagerly waited for all the details.

What should have been a high-pitched, laughter-filled recount of a wild night was a monotone, pessimistic retelling of a sad tale. I couldn't force humor where there was none.

"Damn, girl," she said sympathetically when I got to the open relationship part of the story.

"It's okay," I responded, trying to convince myself, and her. "I'm happy it happened now. It just proved that I need to stay focused," I added. "So 2010 is going to be all about me. I'm focusing on myself—no men, no dating and no distractions. It's all about me."

We raised our glasses to my declaration. This was the second time I had said it aloud, and it was starting to feel feasible. I believed that I could do it.

Outside the restaurant rain was beating down, which was not very conducive to a night of barhopping. As I pushed open the heavy black doors, Audrey said, "Let's get one last drink."

"Oh no, no," I said.

But Audrey was ready for a battle. "Come on! You never want to go out."

"I'm not even dressed to go out, Audrey. No, it's not happening. And the weather is shit. I'm driving back to Connecticut tomorrow. I'm not in the mood."

"We don't have to go far." She was ignoring me. She really wanted to have this last drink.

"Fine, but not too far," I said, giving in for the third time in less than a week. I made a silent vow to work on not succumbing so easily to peer pressure.

Elated, Audrey said, "Okay! Let's go there," pointing to a red vintage neon sign on the corner of Prince Street and Mercer Street. Fanelli Café, it read.

It wasn't familiar and too closely resembled the dive bars that I frequented in Hartford. I wasn't thrilled. "Really? There? We're going to what's probably the last dive bar in SoHo?"

"Yeah, it looks cool!" she yelled over her shoulder. She was already halfway across the street with me trotting along behind her, furious with myself. I didn't know that I was walking into a New York City landmark. Since opening its doors in 1847, New York characters—from locals to artists, performers and even tourists—have passed through Fanelli Café, leaving traces of their magic for other patrons to revel in, and sometimes experience themselves.

My glasses fogged up as soon as we entered the overly crowded bar. What lay behind the old wooden door and frosted glass was a sharp departure from the sleek and measured vibe of The Mercer Kitchen. A gleaming mahogany bar ran from one side of the room to the other and small tables placed together transformed fellow patrons into unsuspecting third-party participants of the conversation *du jour*. The bar retained an old-world charm that felt uniquely European. I wasn't thrilled to be there, but I was no longer in a rush to leave.

I stood at the entrance, shaking off some of the excess rain from my coat, when I looked up and saw the only two available seats were next to two men gesticulating passionately, their voices drowned out over the music and crowd. As we got closer to them I heard unmistakable French that was loud and slurring. *Drunken tourists*, I thought to myself with an eye roll.

Before sitting down I grabbed Audrey's hand and whispered in her ear, "We're not talking to those French guys. Okay?" It was more of a command than a suggestion.

"Yeah, sure." They were the least believable words out of her mouth. I had little patience for men after my experience with the lonely intellectual, especially French men. My preconceived notion of a French man was a charming, chain-smoking, wine-drinking master seducer. I had no interest in investigating the validity of that stereotype.

Audrey's smile reached megawatt status the short walk from the entrance to the bar. I was more solemn and glared at her in hopes that she would remember our agreement.

"Can we sit here?" I asked the French men, with an unnecessarily aggressive tone.

"Of course," the shorter and drunker of the two responded in accented English. If I had any doubt that they were French, it was dispelled in the way the "s" in the word "course" transformed to a "z" when he said it.

The other member of the duo was dark haired, wearing black thin-framed glasses and a thick gray turtleneck. He was the quieter one of the two and simply observed the interaction while sipping his beer. He left the stage wide open for his friend to be the showman.

"Thank you," I replied with more softness in my voice. I felt the quiet friend's eyes on me, but I ignored his gaze.

Audrey and I settled into our seats and I knew that this was going to be an unusual night when the man who was slouched over behind the bar stood straight up to reveal his full height, which I estimated to be about six-four, and walked toward us to take our order. Bob, I later learned his name to be, was a Canadian, by way of Eastern Europe, former heavyweight boxing champion who manned the bar during the weekends. His bald head shone as brightly as the mahogany on the bar. He was built like a stainless-steel commercial refrigerator, wide and solid, but had a little belly that made it clear that he enjoyed life.

"What are you girls drinking?" His mischievous eyes didn't break contact with mine while he waited for an answer. I don't remember exactly what I ordered, but it was cold enough to quench my suddenly parched throat.

Two drinks later I said to Audrey, "Okay, I'm going to the bathroom but we're not going to talk to them." I was certain Audrey would strike up a conversation with one, if not both, of the French men. She noticed my ears perk up several times since we'd been there as I became increasingly curious about them, especially the showy friend. They spoke perfect English, seemed quite at ease around loud and brash Americans and were having a spectacular time. But I squashed any temptation to speak to them.

"What am I gonna say?" Audrey responded innocently.

"Actually, why don't you come with me?" I suggested.

"I'm not going to the bathroom with you, Sutanya. You're being ridiculous," she replied. I made one last ditch attempt to control the situation by turning around and pulling my index finger to my lips, the universal *be quiet* sign.

When I was finished in the bathroom, as I made my way back to my seat, I heard Audrey's belly laugh. She was talking to the Europeans.

"This is my friend that speaks French!" she excitedly exclaimed while holding out her hand toward me.

"What are you talking about? I don't speak French," I snapped at her through clenched teeth. I wanted to be angry with her, but I couldn't. Deep down inside I wanted to talk to them. And I did speak French, just very poorly.

To my surprise I fell into an easy conversation with the dark-haired quiet observer, but it felt too similar to the beginning of my night with the lonely intellectual. The familiar carefree feeling put me on high alert. I couldn't fall for another man's charms, especially a French man. I tried to build up a defense by pretending to suddenly lose interest or give curt answers to his questions, but he easily broke past every roadblock. He was enjoying a cold beer, not wine, but did excuse himself several times to smoke his Philip Morris cigarettes. So far he confirmed one out of the three stereotypes I had about French men. I wondered how long it would take for him to drop the bomb about his girlfriend or better yet, his wife.

The more I spoke to him the more intrigued I became. He smelled warm and spicy like a fragrant citrus cider. His dark brown eyes that turned slightly downward were a mix of sadness, mischief and warmth. He had a slight lisp that I assumed was a consequence of speaking a foreign language and I found it endearing. He knew how to hold a conversation about something other than how wasted he was the night before.

Over the course of a few hours I learned that he was from Paris but currently in graduate school in Nantes, a humdrum city a few hundred miles southwest of Paris. He was visiting New York City with his mother, sister and Thomas, who was his best friend and heavily flirting with a group of older American women two seats down from us. He shared funny stories about his family. He talked about the recent passing of his father with honesty and vulnerability. He made and held eye contact when he spoke to me. He asked probing questions, and most importantly he was interested and interesting. Within a few hours I was smitten. I allowed myself to live in the moment and be charmed. In twenty-four hours I would be back in Hartford and in two days he would be back in Europe, where both of our realities would resume. But for now I could fantasize.

I found myself deep in his world and he was in mine when at midnight the alarm on my phone went off, signaling that I had to leave.

"I have to go," I said regretfully.

"Why?" he asked with confusion.

"I have to catch the Metro-North train back to my parents' place," I responded while hastily throwing on my jacket and grabbing my black leather pocketbook.

"But I thought the metro ran all night in New York?" he asked. We were both standing and for the first time I noticed the full breadth of his height. He was looking down while questioning me.

I could've stayed and taken a cab back to the Bronx, but I chose not to. Although I wanted to stay, I didn't allow myself to. After my experience with the lonely intellectual a few days prior, I was leery of charming men with thick, dark hair.

I turned to Audrey and announced, "I gotta go." Without giving her the time to come up with a witty response, I looked up at TFM. "The subway does run all night but I'm not taking the subway. I'm taking the Metro-North, a commuter train, back to the Bronx and I have to go all the way to Grand Central to catch it."

We looked at each other in silence, not knowing what to do next. *Should I kiss him?* I thought. *I want to kiss him.*

"But we can become Facebook friends, right?" I suggested instead of pulling his face into mine. It was the more reasonable course of action. We whipped out our phones and connected digitally.

As I turned to leave the bar, he said, "Let me walk you to the door, at least." I looked at him without saying yes or no. With his hand on the small of my back he led me toward the door.

"It's raining like cats and dogs!" he said then chuckled to

himself. "I love that American expression. It's so ridiculous." He was stalling, and I really had to leave.

"It's okay. I have an umbrella," I replied, showing him my big black Mary Poppins-esque umbrella.

"Are you sure you'll be all right?" he asked in a concerned tone.

"Yep, I'll be fine. I'm a big girl," I said, smirking.

"All right, then. It was nice meeting you."

I noticed his hands were in his pockets and he was gently rocking back and forth on his toes. I was analyzing this body language while another moment of charged silence grew between us. Was he nervous? Did he want to kiss me? *I wish he would kiss me.*

"Same here!" I said. "If I'm ever in Europe one day I'll let you know!" A sprinkle of false hope never hurt anyone. After exchanging kisses on the cheeks, he opened the door and I ducked out of the restaurant and into the pouring rain.

"Gabbieeeee," I yelled as I dropped my bags in the center of the foyer.

Her room doors slowly opened. "What? What's up?" she asked.

"You're not gonna believe what happened yesterday." I told her everything about meeting TFM and we proceeded to go through his Facebook profile in great detail.

"Oh wow, you really like this monsieur," Gabbie said.

"Yeah, but he lives in Paris," I said wistfully.

"Nothing wrong with making new friends," she said.

"I can't send him a Facebook message?" I was simultaneously dissuading myself and asking Gabbie for permission.

"Why not? What do you have to lose?" she responded.

I was taken aback by her encouragement, but she was right; I had nothing to lose. So with her help I crafted the perfect message and hit Send. Within three months of sending the first Facebook message, from my bedroom in Hartford to his in Nantes, our correspondence grew from infrequent exchanges to a steady stream of ongoing conversation where we talked about everything and nothing. Our meeting and subsequent email exchange sent a pleasant jolt of freshness into my otherwise mundane life.

When you're single, relatively young and pretending not to want a relationship and to fall in love, but in reality you do kind of want all of those things, you get tired of hearing, "It'll happen when you least expect it." That was why meeting TFM was a sneak attack in every way possible. I could've never foreseen that our daily conversations would've led to a spur-of-the-moment decision to take a post-graduate school trip to Paris that set my life on a completely different path than I had ever imagined.

Three

<u>PENPALSHIP</u>

The attraction I felt the night I met TFM retained its thrilling quality and grew with every email I received from him. My curiosity about him wasn't far behind. Who was this man engaging in a transatlantic conversation with a woman he met once at a bar in New York City? From his emails I gleaned that we were living parallel lives: both trudging along in graduate school—he was studying something that had to do with business—both trying to figure out the next steps in our lives while living in cities that didn't match our personalities or life goals, and we were both bored. In addition to learning about the practicalities of his day-to-day life, I discovered that he was a dreamer, a traveler and intoxicatingly charming, funny and witty. In almost every email there was always a moment when I laughed out loud.

Charm aside, one of TFM's most meaningful qualities was his ability to listen without judgment. When I shared my irritation about working at the insurance company he didn't dismiss my feelings, but he also didn't immediately side with me and join me in bashing my employer. Instead, he took in what I had to say and responded with care, concern and, as always, a sprinkle of wit and humor.

My only advice is results, results, results. Getting results is the only answer; it always is.

Also, even if you despise them, you should take into consideration what they are saying about you. This could actually help you a lot for your future career. To know how people see you in your job is always useful. And you know that you are probably not perfect. So just think about it and about what made them think like that, and how maybe change a little bit your behavior in order to get along better with them. Because you will find people like them all your life. Just learn how to handle them now.

I apologize for playing the wiseguy. I am not saying at all that they are right or anything. I don't even know what we are talking about, actually.

I am just saying that nothing is ever black or white, and truth always lies in the middle. It's better to get criticized than not, I think. At least you know how to improve.

After this paragraph just call me Buddha.

Without knowing it, we were building a friendship, a solid foundation built on comfort, trust and transparency. There was no hint as to whether or not our exchanges would evolve or fade, turning into nostalgic fodder when sharing stories about youthful innocence, but nevertheless his frequent dispatches from France gave my days renewed meaning.

As my comfort grew so did my questions, whether silly or serious. In one email I went from asking him if he considered himself a good dancer to his thoughts on the burqa ban, which was a hot topic of discussion in French society at the time. He indulged me by answering all of my questions, but not without throwing in a few wisecracks that put a smile on my face for days, such as:

> I will reply to your long email soon enough. Don't worry. It's just that I want to do it the right way and that means sending you my genealogical tree and a dental radiography with it.

I shared the drab details of my daily routine peppered with my ambitions and dreams for the future without any overt flirtation, from either of us. There was no ulterior motive; communicating and getting to know TFM from behind a screen encouraged a level of vulnerability that felt liberating. The screen shielded me from his immediate reaction when I shared intimate details about my life and myself. Our distance and the act of writing down my thoughts as opposed to speaking them prevented me from falling into the trap of holding back. My emotional nakedness in front of TFM was new territory that I didn't know I could boldly step into.

I was aroused by his intellect and craved his presence in my life, even if it was digital. I slept with my phone by my side, hoping that the buzz of his email would wake me from my slumber, and in a sleep haze I would read his words and feel that much closer to him. He challenged me intellectually without questioning my intelligence. His self-deprecation didn't stink of insecurity; he questioned himself often and he was genuinely curious about the world and me. At that point in my life, I'd never met someone my age who was so seemingly comfortable with themselves, and that was a part of the magnetism that drew me to him.

I didn't want to admit to myself that our pen-pal friendship was due to more than surface-level boredom and curiosity, but I knew something was different when I sent him a particularly revealing email and several days went by without a response from him. I became so anxious about it that I couldn't focus or concentrate. I got so used to receiving a response within a day or two that when I thought I lost him before he was actually ever really mine, I panicked.

I forced myself not to look at my BlackBerry for the eighth time in thirty minutes as a blank Microsoft Word document stared back at me.

"We're still good for the 4:30 review of the newsletter?" Nancy asked accusingly as she walked past my desk. She caught a glimpse at the cursor blinking steadily on the blank screen in front of me.

"Yep, no problem." I moved my mouse around the empty screen, fully aware of the fact I wouldn't be ready with anything by 4:30 p.m. I couldn't focus on anything but hoping to receive a response from TFM.

"Okay, concentrate," I said to myself. In forty-five minutes I had to walk into Nancy's cubicle and show her a draft of a newsletter that attempted to camouflage corporate ennui with strained excitement. Who cared about an upcoming company-wide PowerPoint presentation, internal promotions and a reminder to update an email signature? Riveting work and exactly why I was in graduate school, I thought. On days like this I often reminded myself that I was lucky to have a steady job during a financial dumpster fire, and with enough tweaking of my résumé I can transform a glorified assistant position into something worthwhile and worthy of a job in New York City.

I managed to type "Housekeeping Details" on the blank screen when the buzz of my phone broke my feeble attempt at concentrating. I grabbed the phone off my desk, hoping it was TFM responding to the email I sent a week ago, but it was a text message from Gabbie.

You wanna go for a drink tonight?

My heart rate dropped as fast as it rose.

Sure, I responded.

Eventually, I managed to add enough exclamation points to banal news about corporate life that even the most cynical reader would be curious about the internal goings-on of a midtier insurance company. My eyes darted across the computer screen while proofreading the newsletter—the last thing I needed was for Nancy to find a mistake—when my phone buzzed. Assuming it was Gabbie again, I didn't look at it and added the final touches to my newsletter. Gabbie had a magical quality about her. Without any hint from me she could sense when I was having a bad day—stressed or anxious—and always sent the perfect text message that made me smile or calmed my nerves. But my heart stopped when I looked at the screen. There, in the inbox, was a message from TFM.

I had one minute to get to Nancy's cubicle, but I wanted to read what TFM had to say. In a recent email he shared his frustration about our pen-pal exchange; he wasn't sure what it meant or where it was going, but he also didn't want to stop. I couldn't help but wonder if this was the beginning of the end. I was relieved to have a sign of life from him and simultaneously annoyed because he left me hanging for five whole days. I was equally annoyed at myself because I was getting worked up about the dynamics and expectations of a pen-pal relationship with a random French man I met at a bar in New York City. I was giving myself a headache. Already late for my meeting, I put my phone on my desk and braced myself for thirty minutes of belittling loosely disguised as encouragement and support. Throughout the entire meeting my mind kept wandering to the email. As soon as I was released from Nancy's clutches, I promptly ran back to my desk.

I opened TFM's email and scrolled and scrolled, quickly realizing that it was an unusually long message for him. I was torn between reading the entire email right then and there, or being late and dealing with the wrath of Gabbie. I was already running late. I printed the email and told myself that I would read it later that night, but as soon as I sat in my car, I knew I couldn't wait. I pulled the multipage email out of my bag and wiggled myself deep into the slightly reclined gray seat of my Honda Accord. After sharing his thoughts on the mixed bag of topics I broached in my previous email—from the representation, or lack thereof, of artists of color in the world's famed museums, French reality television shows, the movie *Julie and Julia* and his post-graduate school plans—he apologized for his late reply in a very TFM way.

My novel was worth the wait btw, wasn't it? I am sorry for the very late reply but I am just not really into pen-friend relationships, actually. I always suck at keeping in touch with my foreign friends, or my French friends when I live abroad. I wonder why I keep emailing you...

It was clear to me why we continued emailing each other. Whether we liked it, or wanted to admit it, our penpalship had evolved in a more profound way than we expected. After exchanging 234 emails in the first 45 days of our correspondence it was only natural that we became regular and reassuring presences in each other's lives that we both wanted and seemingly needed.

I reread his email three more times in the car, savoring every word like it was my favorite meal, until I had my fill of him. His detailed, honest and vulnerable reply made me feel like I was an important part of his life. For me, I was crossing the bridge from stranger to becoming a confidante. With a big grin on my face, I put my car gear in Drive and my journey over Avon Mountain began. I was over an hour late when I finally opened the door to our apartment. Gabbie was in her room, visibly and understandably upset, but I couldn't hide the joy that was racing through my body. She saw my face and demeanor and simply asked, "You got an email from the Frenchie?" with her fore-arms folded across her chest.

"Yesssss," I responded, clutching the door frame of her room. My face was beaming and I was on a cloud that wasn't descending anytime soon. Sensing my dopamine high, Gabbie didn't mention the fact that not only did I flake on our happy hour plans, I also forgot and seemingly didn't care that I forgot. "I'll make dinner for us tonight," I promised her as I glided into my room. I couldn't control my bliss.

The sense of comfort I felt in my exchanges with TFM likely came from the lingering possibility that we would never see each other ever again. It gave me the freedom to truly be myself. I didn't question if I was sharing too much, being too weird, ask-ing the wrong questions, asking too many questions, or respond-ing too quickly. Every exchange with TFM was unfiltered and it was liberating. His responses were positive reinforcement that I could be my whole self in a way that I never had been with any other man before, even if we were just pen pals. I stopped second-guessing myself completely, which is why I did things like create and share an Excel document with music choices that I considered far superior to his. In my email I wrote:

The attached document contains a mixture of chill jams, hip-hop, bossa nova, world, reggae, old-school hip-hop, etc. Pretty much everything, except country. Keep in mind that this is a very small sample of my huge and amazing music collection.

With other men I would've been too scared to be myself. I was always afraid of being "too much." But TFM liked my boldness and stepped up to the challenge. He responded positively, lay-ing out his plan to thoroughly rummage through his old music collection and respond with his selections.

With TFM my light shined as brightly as I wanted it to. I was my most authentic self with him. I didn't hold back; he got it all. And in return he wasn't afraid to share his vulnerabilities either, which was very different from what I was used to with American men I met. They didn't seem to have emotions or know how to express what they were feeling. For example, when his frustration around our purely email correspondence—we spoke only through email, we didn't exchange phone numbers for months and we didn't do any kind of video calling—began to mount he let me know.

It's just something I've been meaning to say for several weeks... I'm just really into real-life interactions and not so much into virtual friendship. Don't get me wrong. I still find our correspondence interesting but idk. I think I am as curious about you as you are about me but it's getting boring and frustrating. I would love to get know you IN REAL LIFE, but yeah, I do find this email exchange a bit useless.

He was able to put words to his emotions and showed me that it was not only okay, but also more interesting, when you brought your entire self to any relationship. Even if the relationship was an unexpected transatlantic penpalship. I didn't have to hide from him; showing up and being authentically me was expected and encouraged.

Serenity washed over me as I lay on my bed, rereading his email for the sixth time. Then another wave of panic set in. I finally admitted how serious my feelings were for him. I had a crush on a French man whom I met once at a bar in New York City, and who lives in Paris. As quickly as I admitted to myself that my feelings for TFM went beyond friendship I came up with a plan. I jumped off my bed and knocked on Gabbie's bedroom door, opened it and popped my head in before she could answer.

"Should we go to Paris?" I asked her.

"Huh?" She looked up from the book she was reading with confusion.

"Well, we're going to be in Europe anyway to celebrate my master's degree, so why not stop in Paris, maybe?"

"Paris, maybe?" she teased. And without skipping a beat, a sly smirk grew on her face and she said, "I'm down."

Purchasing our plane tickets to Paris made the trip official; my exchanges with TFM shifted and took on a different shape. They didn't immediately morph into heavily flirtatious confessions, but nervous excitement was building. Based on his advice my friends and I decided to rent an apartment in Le Marais, a historic neighborhood on Paris's Right Bank and perfectly situated in the center of the city. After sharing this with TFM, in the very end of his next email he slipped in,

I was in Le Marais earlier today. I tried to look around me with the eyes of a tourist and yeah, you're gonna love it!

To which I responded,

I'm not sure if going to Le Marais was out of your way/ daily plans for today but just the fact that you were there and looked at it "with the eyes of a tourist" is so awesome and so sweet. Thank you. Much appreciated.

The growing anticipation around my trip quickly gave way to trepidation about what would happen when I was face-to-face with a man I somehow managed to create an intimate pen-pal relationship with despite only seeing each other once in person. Being true to the transparency of our entire relationship up to that point, I shared my neurosis, and on July 20, 2010, the day before my flight to Paris and seven months after we met, he shared his, too:

No. What's gonna suck is when you'll realize that you exchanged 481 emails with some French [redacted] you can't stand.

Without realizing, the feelings of doubt and worry he shared in those few lines, and previous emails, signaled to me that the feelings of trust and security were mutual. The reciprocity I longed for with men in the past was right there with him. He planted the seed that we were more alike than we were different and we'll always have each other's backs. I was already starting to think that we would make an interesting team, so I responded, saying,

I'll take my chances with the French [redacted] who exchanged 481 emails with a neurotic [redacted] American.

Before landing in Paris on July 21, 2010, I was already in love with the idea of TFM and what he represented to me, which was self-acceptance. The high that I got from his emails made my body tingle and sent my endorphins into a frenzy. On a deeper level I didn't know what our email exchange meant or where our pen-pal relationship was going but I was eager to find out.

I wholeheartedly believed that TFM was the missing piece of the puzzle that was my life. I stopped spending all of my free time self-medicating and feeling sorry for myself. I still hated my job, but at least my personal life seemed to be moving in an interesting direction. The rational part of my brain told me that TFM wasn't someone I could actually date. An ocean separating us posed a significant logistical problem and technically, he was a stranger.

I couldn't have imagined the mark that this trip would leave on the both of us—opening our eyes to the possibility of a future together and putting us on a life path neither of us sought out or dreamt of.

Four

I stared out the window the entire two-hour-and-twenty-minute train ride to Paris from London. Adrenaline and nerves raged through my body. I was going to see a man I had only met once in real life but exchanged over four hundred emails with and had developed feelings for. I worried that TFM may not be exactly as I remembered, and the probability of that potential disaster weighed heavily on me. I tried to calm my anxiety by telling myself that if TFM wasn't the prince charming I envisioned, I still had four days to explore Paris. My efforts to reason with myself proved to be futile considering my grand expectations. I needed our email exchanges to effortlessly transform into satisfyingly rich and savory face-to-face conversations.

After the train ride, Gabbie, my friend Jessica and I piled into a taxi from Gare du Nord, one of Paris's biggest and busiest train stations. As the taxi weaved through traffic to our vacation rental, Gabbie sighed to my right. "It's just *so* beautiful." We chose this neighborhood because of its central location—a stone's throw away from the Seine and walking distance from the city's major museums and must-see sights.

On either side of me, Gabbie and Jessica were taking everything in, and there I was in the middle, uncharacteristically quiet.

"Are you asleep?" Gabbie demanded as she turned to look at me.

"No, it's hard to see outside with you both gawking out the window," I replied.

"You should've slept on the train," Gabbie said, ignoring my sarcasm. No one mentioned TFM, but we all knew that he was on my mind.

"*Et voilà,*" said the taxi driver when we pulled up to the apartment building.

"Is this it?" I asked with suspicion in broken French. The dust-covered small red door in front of me didn't look like it housed the cute, modern apartment that I saw on the rental website. It was tucked between an Italian restaurant and a café that were both eerily empty. I was expecting more elegance and opulence, or at least something that was recently wiped down. We were in Paris after all.

"*Oui, 19 rue François Miron. C'est ça,*" he confirmed.

With a deep breath I turned to the girls and sighed before dragging our bags off the sidewalk. But behind the dusty red door I was delighted to discover a charming courtyard, a cobblestoned secret garden surrounded by ivory-colored buildings on all four sides. I stood wonderstruck by its simple beauty and calm. My anxieties momentarily quelled. It felt like an oasis in the middle of the city.

After lugging our suitcases up what were actually five flights of spiral stairs, not four—I learned that the French don't count the ground floor as the first floor and most buildings do not have elevators—a dark-haired handsome Frenchman relieved us of our bags. "*Bienvenue*, ladies. I hope you had a good journey. Come in, come in." He held his arm out, signaling that we could enter. Once inside, he gave us a tour of the rental. Nestled in the corner of the living room, there was a small, closet-sized room that housed just a toilet.

"The toilet isn't in the bathroom?" I asked.

"No," he chuckled. "In France the toilet is usually in a different room than where you shower. We like to keep those two things separate."

"Oh, makes sense," I replied sheepishly. I felt like a barbaric and uncultured American for even questioning that logic.

From the living room with a toilet, we turned left, and there was a small galley kitchen and a door that led to a small bedroom and a shower. The layout still didn't make sense to me, but we were in Paris. It didn't have to make sense. He went through the details of the apartment, gave us the Wi-Fi codes, the door codes, the keys and emergency phone numbers and his personal cell phone number.

"If you need anything during your stay do not hesitate to call me," he said at the end of the check-in process. "I wish you a great trip!" And with that he was out the door. A brief moment of silence followed before Gabbie, Jessica and I broke out into a unison scream, jumping up and down with glee. We couldn't believe we were finally in Paris.

The first matter of business was finding something to eat. I wanted to see what the fuss around French food was all about, so TFM could wait. French food is often described as the best cuisine in the world and an experience one must have before they die. Like Meryl Streep's iconic sole meunière scene in *Julie & Julia*, I expected to have my own breathtaking experience with French food, so I freshened up and pulled out a vintage red spaghetti-strap halter maxi dress that I bought especially for the trip. The seductive keyhole in the bust of the dress and the low and open back made up for its conservative length. The understated sexy look felt fitting for Paris and, at the time, my interpretation of Parisian chic style. What I didn't know at the time was that wearing bright clothes like a red dress dotted with small gold flowers was the furthest thing from Parisian chic. The trick to Parisian style was to have the same subdued clothes as everyone else so you didn't stand out too much, but one could add their own personal touch, a scarf here, a ring there, a couple earrings on the lobe but nothing too extravagant. I was oblivious to this rule so I happily threw on my dress and we hit the streets hungry and hopeful.

On the prowl for the perfect-looking bistro near the Saint-Paul metro station, I noticed that all of the restaurants had outdoor seating. This wasn't common in New York City or Connecticut, and it captured my attention. I became fond of the idea of being amid the city at all times, even when eating. I imagined that the experience of sitting outside a restaurant while eating allowed a steady flow of energy between you—the person at the restaurant—and the city and the people passing by.

But something seemed amiss as we strolled. We passed at least four restaurants and all of their sidewalk seating was empty. "Isn't it a little weird that there's no one sitting at the restaurants?" I asked the girls.

"Maybe those restaurants aren't that good," Gabbie suggested with a shrug. I wasn't entirely convinced, but it was the most logical answer. My stomach began growling, and I regretted not planning our first Parisian culinary experience. I wanted to bite into a buttery piece of sole or experience a morsel of steak melting on my tongue. We continued our walk, perplexed, until we saw a chef, or maybe he was a line cook, enjoying a cigarette in front of a bistro. That place must be open, I assumed.

Fifteen minutes after sitting down, we were still the only people there and no one came to take our order. I've read about bad customer service in Paris, but I didn't expect to experience it so soon. Eventually, a very slim waiter wearing skinny blue jeans and a button-down shirt, not the classic black slacks and white shirt I was expecting, came to our table and just stood there, staring at us. He didn't say *"bonjour."* He didn't ask *"comment allez-vous?"*

I was the only person in the group who spoke French, and with eight years of studying the language under my belt, I couldn't string a full sentence together. The only thing I was able to eke out was *"carte?"* quickly followed by "menu?"

The waiter sighed, loudly, and replied, *"c'est fermé."*

"Fermé?" I repeated. I knew what it meant, but I didn't understand because the restaurant was obviously open.

"Yes, closed," he responded, his irritation visibly increasing. Seeing the confusion on our faces he continued, "We open again at 7:30, in the evening," sighed and walked away.

This was going to be a long trip. Dejected and starving, we continued our search for lunch, and we were met with a chorus of *"non, c'est ferme,"* *"désolé, c'est ferme"* and *"mesdames, c'est ferme."* I didn't understand why all of the restaurants were closed in the middle of the afternoon in one of Europe's gastronomic capitals. I found it even harder to believe that staff would stay at closed restaurants. I started to wonder if we were being rejected from every restaurant because we were American. We'd been walking around for at least thirty-five minutes and I began taking the refusals very personally. Annoyed and hungry, we stumbled upon an Italian restaurant—not exactly the French bistro I imagined for my first afternoon in Paris, but we didn't have much of a choice.

Five minutes after we had sat down, a waiter comes to our table and says the only French phrase we're now completely fluent in, *"C'est fermé."*

"Pourquoi?" I asked.

The waiter looked at me, confused. *"Pourquoi? Pourquoi c'est fermé?"* he asked.

"Oui. Pourquoi?" I answered with a sly, tight-lipped smile. I

was expecting him to stumble over his words and not be able to come up with a good reason.

Instead, he took a step back, looked me up and down and said, *"Bah, madame, c'est pas l'heure de manger."*

"Huh?" I responded. I wasn't expecting a clear and confident response, and I wasn't sure I correctly understood what he said. *"C'est pas—"*

The waiter promptly cut me off and began explaining in English. "We are not serving food now," he said. "In France, we eat at specific times, breakfast, lunch and dinner. Now is the time between lunch and dinner. No good restaurants are open." I didn't feel like I was in a position to ask for any recommendations, so with my tail between my legs all I mustered up was a weak, *"Oh, merci."*

Now ravenous, we settled for a fast-food Chinese restaurant two blocks from our apartment. "At least it has outdoor seating," I joked to the girls. They were not in a humorous mood. Digging into my noodles with chopsticks I mumbled under my breath, "Welcome to Paris." Little did I know that this was the first of many surprises and emotional roller coasters Paris had up its sleeve for many years to come.

My disappointing first afternoon in Paris left me feeling wrung out and dispirited. The enthusiasm and excitement I had around seeing TFM again after months of emails slowly fizzled out because Paris had already knocked me sideways in her own subtle way, and I wasn't sure I could handle any more. Nevertheless, after a passing moment of internal debate, I knew I had to see him no matter what. I didn't fly across the ocean to back out at the last minute. Shortly after returning to the apartment, I gathered myself, ignoring the feeling in the pit of my stomach that had made its way to below my knees, and shot off a text message.

Hello! It's Sutanya. I'm in your city! I'm using Gabbie's phone, long story. Are you still free to meet while I'm here?

He responded immediately and we agreed to meet the following afternoon at Hôtel de Ville, the main city hall of Paris. Hôtel de Ville was only a seven-minute walk from the apartment and the ideal neutral location for us to meet. If there wasn't a spark, I wasn't too far from my safe space in Paris.

The next day, with a hand-drawn map from Gabbie and ample time for the seven-minute walk, I was on my way. I felt beautiful in my cobalt blue A-line strapless mini dress with identical-colored round buttons down the middle and pockets, paired with strappy tan high-heeled sandals and a chunky multicolored necklace. The look was a definite upgrade from what I was wearing the first time he saw me.

The hundreds of butterflies fluttering around in my stomach gave me a sense of lightness when I turned right onto rue du Pont Louis-Philippe toward rue de Rivoli. On rue de Rivoli I felt myself floating, not walking, toward destiny. The romanticism of my nervousness was quickly squashed by its physical manifestation. I was sweating, a lot. I slowed down my pace but thought I would be late so sped it up again, which led to more sweating. I was stop-and-go for the remaining five-minute walk on rue de Rivoli.

Hôtel de Ville was teeming with people. I worried that I wouldn't be able to see or potentially recognize him. I made a left to walk toward the center of the square that housed the main building, when I saw him. He was sitting on a low concrete wall on the right side of the square, wearing dark blue jeans and a black-and-white-checkered shirt. It was unclear whether we spotted each other at the same time or if I saw him first. Perhaps the electric energy I was emitting forced him to look over in my direction and see me? But in either case, I waved at him and we began walking toward each other.

As we made our way to each other, the people milling around disappeared. The entire city fell silent. He was the only person I saw as the world outside us ceased to exist for a few seconds. I forgot how tall he was and how broad his shoulders were, and I noticed an interesting quirk: he hopped when he walked.

"Hi," I said with a big smile when we were finally face-to-face.

"Hi," he responded with an equally big smile. We hugged and I melted in his arms. It felt like a touch I didn't know I was missing had finally come back to me. When I snapped out of my trance, the city came back to life and the people reappeared, but my body was still warm with his touch.

"Where do you want to go?" he asked. His deep baritone voice made me tingle.

"This is your city. You show me," I responded cheekily.

He led me to a typical French café. As a Parisian, he knew where to find one that was open. Initially, we ordered nonalcoholic drinks but quickly switched to white wine. Our conversation flowed easily like our emails, only better. Instead of imagining how he would laugh at one of my jokes, I heard him do so. I saw the way he pressed his lips together and moved his mouth to the side when he was thinking. I witnessed firsthand how quick on his feet and witty he was. There was no awkwardness, and I was immediately at ease. Everything I felt when I received an email from him was heightened. He was exactly the same in person as he was behind the screen—funny, whip smart, snarky, sarcastic, provocative, curious and kind. I was drunk on endorphins and high on dopamine. Two glasses of wine later, he offered to accompany me to meet Gabbie and Jessica at the Seine, and as we walked side by side, almost holding hands but not quite, I thought to myself, *Shit, this feels different.*

TFM played the role of voluntary tour guide for the rest of the afternoon and the trip. He just kind of stuck around, and we were lucky enough to experience Paris through the eyes of a Parisian. We picnicked at the Eiffel Tower; he took us to Le Showcase, a club under the Pont Alexandre III, one of several bridges that connects the left side of the city to the right. We shared drinks at cafés where we were the only English speakers and ate at restaurants that I was sure we wouldn't have known about without him. And we finally figured out when we could and couldn't eat.

There wasn't anything unfamiliar about what we were eating at the restaurants where we dined, but the flavors danced in my mouth. A tomato is a tomato after all, but I quickly learned that the tomatoes in Paris were different. They were juicy and sweet with the perfect hint of acidity that blended magically with the drizzle of olive oil and pinch of salt that topped them. I experienced *beurre blanc*—a butter sauce made with vinegar and white wine—and I wanted nothing more than to be alone so that I could lick my plate clean. I couldn't get enough of the velvety-sweet tanginess that coated my tongue. I ate and drank to my heart's, and stomach's, content, but never in excess. Like my days spent with TFM, every food experience was more delicious than the last—rich with zesty lushness that left a permanent imprint in memory and on my taste buds.

We were quite the foursome bopping around Paris, but I craved alone time with him. I didn't suggest it because I didn't want to seem like I was ditching my friends, and I wasn't sure if the feelings were mutual. It was unclear whether he wanted to rip off my clothes as badly as I wanted to remove his. I was three days into my trip, and we still hadn't kissed. We spent every day and night together, and he still hadn't made a move.

We were at Favela Chic, a Brazilian restaurant in the 10th arrondissement that transforms into a club at sunset. There was a steady influx of people around us, trying to get the attention of the sole bartender while we waited for our order of mojitos. The crowd forced us so close together that I was convinced he could hear the intensity of my heartbeat. Heat raced through my body as it inched closer to his. With my body pressed against his I got a whiff of the spicy-fruity-woodsy-citrusy fragrance that first made its mark when we met at Fanelli's and I couldn't help but breathe him in. When his eyes met mine I knew that this time I was going to kiss him. I had to stand on my tippy toes to reach his lips and he bent his head down to meet me halfway.

Our first kiss was long and passionate, deep and urgent. With his lean frame against mine, his hands firmly around my waist, and my forearms gently draped behind his neck, we didn't dare let each other go. His kisses flushed me with warmth and my body ached with desire. I didn't want to kiss anyone else ever again. I lost all sense of the world around me and where I was until the bartender yelled something at us that I didn't understand and we ran away like giggling children. We made our way to a semi-isolated corner where we continued making up for all the kisses missed over the past seven months and three days. We took a break to catch our breath when out of the corner of my eye I saw Gabbie speed walking toward us.

"There you are," she exclaimed. "I've been looking all over for you two!" Then she paused, took a step back, studied us and followed up with a question. "Where are both of your glasses?" she asked.

"Glasses?" I responded, while TFM gently caressed the back of my leg.

"Yes, your glasses! And TFM's too!"

I shrugged my shoulders; I miraculously had 20/20 vision and saw clearly that everything I needed in that moment was in front of me. I looked at TFM and we both burst out laughing. Gabbie, taking on the role of the responsible adult, grabbed us by our hands and dragged us into the middle of the club. Miraculously, we found our glasses unscathed on the floor next to the bar where we shared our momentous first kiss.

That was a night of many firsts. Our first kiss, the first time we shared our bodies with each other and the first time it was clear that our feelings went far beyond friendship. We didn't talk about what would happen when I left Paris, because we didn't want the present to end.

My last night in Paris TFM and I spent alone as a twosome. He planned a surprise and refused to give me a hint as to what it could be. I quickly realized that our destination was the Seine, where on its banks he pulled wine, bread and cheese out of his bag. He had the necessary components for a romantic *apéro* on the river. The city was shining on us, especially on me.

In between stuffing my face with cheese and laughing at his jokes, he turned to me and said, "I like that you laugh."

I knew it was a compliment, but I didn't understand it. "What do you mean?"

"Well, you know. You laugh from your belly, like a real laugh. I like it," he answered.

Didn't everyone laugh out loud when something was funny? I didn't know how different I was from the French women of his past and it didn't matter. I found it romantic and reassuring that I was a breath of fresh air to him, as he was to me.

We didn't sleep that last night. We touched each other for what we thought would be the last time; we talked about everything and nothing and smoked his Philip Morris cigarettes while standing naked in front of the bedroom window. We tiptoed around what would happen next, because there would be no next. We decided that ending our pen-pal relationship would be the best and most intelligent course of action. After seeing each other, spending time together and touching each other it was too difficult to think about going back to purely digital communication. We had to stop. The fantasy was coming to an end and my reality awaited on the other side of the ocean. The thoughtful, sweet, kind, funny, smart Frenchman that I was falling for was being deleted out of my life. I was devastated.

The sky gently brightened, blush pink and hazy yellows peeking through the curtains as my departure fast approached. I tried telling myself that this was only a summer fling and that was why we shouldn't stay in touch. This would be a story I'd tell my future daughter(s) and granddaughter(s)—about that time I spent a few days in Paris with a French man to remind them that I had a life before they arrived in mine; about everything I ate; about how instantly comfortable I felt in the city, like I was meant to be here; about the mellow energy of the city and how it influenced me even if it was only a few days. I'll explain what a fun and life-changing experience the trip was, and in particular how TFM boosted my confidence and made me feel alive. I'd take them to the entrance of the apartment where I stayed, telling them that this is where the life-changing trip started, the trip that inspired me to take control of my life by quitting my job in Connecticut and moving back to New York City so that I could finally be happy. After my few days in Paris I grabbed life by the reins and started living again. And, of course, I would encourage them to have a summer fling with a French man.

TFM and I dragged out our goodbyes for as long as we could, but time forced us apart, just like the first time we met. The four of us walked to the taxi stand, Gabbie and Jessica in front, with me and TFM lingering behind. My right arm was wrapped around his waist, my palm resting on his stomach, and he rested his hand on top of mine. I didn't want to appear too affected by what felt like a premature departure, so I tried to make small talk.

"You really should come visit me in New York City when I'm settled," I told him. "As friends, of course," I quickly added.

"Yeah, sure, as friends," he chuckled in response. "You'll forget about me by the time you get home anyway."

"Highly doubtful," I quipped.

At the taxi stand Gabbie and Jessica said their goodbyes to TFM, then ducked into the taxi, giving us a moment alone to say ours. I hugged him tightly and said, "Thank you so much for making this so special."

"The pleasure was mine," he responded.

We kissed one last time. I sat in the taxi, and he closed the door and blew me a kiss through the window. From the rear-view window, I watched him become smaller and smaller until he disappeared. I sat stone-faced, staring straight ahead as we drove to the airport in silence.

To the surprise of no one, while finishing my Euro trip, our digital correspondence continued right where we left off. However, I was pleasantly surprised when four weeks after returning from my trip and two weeks after quitting my job and moving back to New York City, I received an email from TFM that read:

Do you still want [TFM] to visit you in NYC? Because this just got in: he's considering actually doing it. And maybe sooner than you thought.

I read it three times before responding:

Yeah, of course!
Do you really even have to ask?

After hitting the Send button I closed my laptop, joy tickling me under my skin, and thought to myself, *Shit, this* is *different*.

Initially, I was skeptical about TFM's plan to spend eleven days with me in New York City. We spent four blissful days together in Paris, but eleven days in my hometown struck me as excessive. I had just moved back to the Bronx a few weeks earlier and was living with my parents while looking for a job and a new apartment. My stay at home was supposed to be temporary and I didn't expect him to visit while I was in the throes of my transition.

A few days before his visit, while sitting around the kitchen table eating oatmeal, I said to my mother, "Remember that

French guy I told you about? My friend. He's coming to the city in a few days and I told him I'd pick him up from the airport. I'll probably stay the night at the apartment he is renting. I don't want to drive back too late."

To my surprise, she didn't ask any questions. She stopped what she was doing, looked at me, raised one eyebrow and simply said, "Oh." I assume she was intrigued. I didn't talk to my mom about my romantic life, I didn't have any boyfriends in high school and this was the second man I'd ever told her about. She could probably sense that this was different.

The days flew by until I found myself pacing the arrivals terminal at JFK International Airport with nervous excitement waiting for TFM to walk through the doors. When I saw him I wanted to run, but I held myself together and power walked toward him. I didn't realize how much I missed him until he pulled me in and hugged me. In the car drive to his Airbnb we picked up right where we left off.

Our transition from online to offline, distance to closeness, was seamless. The next day I began his introduction to my world through Jamaican food. I bought us beef patties and cocoa bread from a bakery on Flatbush Avenue in Brooklyn. This was his first time eating Jamaican food and I was delighted that his first time was with me and by eating something simple and unequivocally Jamaican. We walked over to Prospect Park where we talked and talked and talked. He met my close circle of friends and although it wasn't planned, I had no choice but to introduce him to my mother.

When I told my mother about his visit, I said that I expected to spend the first night with him and maybe an additional night or two, not his entire eleven-day trip. About six days into TFM's trip my mother's text messages took on a new sense of urgency.

Where are you? Are you okay??? her message read. After responding to her, then calling her to prove that I was alive and well, I turned to TFM and said, "I think you have to meet my mother." Considering the somewhat ambiguous nature of our relationship, I figured it would be less overwhelming to meet one parent instead of both at the same time and the meeting had to be quick and easy, so I decided to take him to her job. We wouldn't have time for lunch or an excessive amount of questions; I didn't want it to be too formal or serious. She simply needed proof that I was alive and not being held against my will.

The first thing my mother said when she met TFM was, "So you're the French man that has stolen my daughter!" We all laughed, and TFM proceeded to charm my mother with his ease of being, wit and intelligence in the same way he did with me.

Our uninterrupted time together in New York City was enough to solidify what I felt in my bones—this was special, he was special and we could be special. Despite spending only four days together months earlier it felt natural to share an intimate space and unlimited time with each other, and that was all the proof I needed.

On the day he was leaving, the energy in the Airbnb felt heavy as he gathered his belongings and packed his suitcase. I couldn't imagine allowing him to step onto the plane back to Paris without expressing the depth of feelings I had for him. Saying our goodbyes at the departure gate and making tentative plans to see each other again sometime in the future wouldn't suffice. Unlike my indecisiveness about leaving Hartford, there was no hesitation around how I felt about TFM and that I wanted to see how those feelings could develop. A year earlier, when I was pleading with the universe to shake up my life, the last thing I expected was a thunderbolt disguised as a French man to appear in my life.

Because our relationship began through written correspondence, using that format to express my feelings for him struck me as the most appropriate and least terrifying. As he puttered around the apartment, gathering his belongings, I opened my journal to write him a letter. I started it with, *Dear TFM, I didn't expect the past eleven days to be so phenomenal* and ended it by saying, *I don't know what will happen after this, but I had to let you know how I feel.* When I finished, I tore the page out of my journal and placed it in an envelope, waiting for the right moment to deliver it. The ideal window of opportunity presented itself while sitting on the couch, face-to-face, savoring our last hour together.

"Here," I said, almost shoving the envelope into his chest.

"What's this?" he asked, using his fingers like tongs to hold the envelope, as if it was an unknown specimen he'd never seen before.

"Just some stuff I need you to know, but couldn't say out loud," I responded.

As he read the letter, I watched a range of emotions take shape on his face—first curiosity, then surprise and finally nothing. He read the letter for a second time, silently mouthing every word with care. When he finished he carefully folded the letter, gently placed it back in the envelope, put it in his back pocket and looked up at me with tears in his eyes. With both hands he pulled my face close to his, looked into my eyes and without exchanging any words I knew this wouldn't be goodbye. It was the beginning.

Nothing made sense about what we were embarking on. We were both in our midtwenties, I recently moved back to New York City and was looking for a permanent job there and he was wrapping up his final year of graduate school and planned to move back to Paris after. We were both on the brink of key life transitions that were typically unkind to relationships born and nurtured in the same city, by people of the same culture— but is there anything rational about falling in love? Especially when you're barreling full force toward a love that would be tested by oceans, time zones, culture and race. Is there anything rational about being emotionally naked in front of someone? Ex-

pecting them to accept and love you despite your twisted imperfections; choosing you every day? Is anyone ever ready for a
challenge that requires nothing less than unbridled authenticity
and sharing your full and true self? I thought I was, so I dove
into a transatlantic love affair with the vigor and determination
of an overly confident, yet misguided, American.

Five

A month and a half after TFM's entrée into my world, it was my turn to explore his. I expected my first trip to Paris to see him to start and end like the romantic comedy I believed I was living. I imagined walking into terminal 2E at Charles de Gaulle International and seeing TFM nervously pacing back and forth while waiting for me. When our eyes would finally meet, I'd drop everything and run into his open arms, followed by a passionate kiss before walking out of the airport, our fingers interlocked.

But when the automatic doors of terminal 2E opened, TFM was nowhere to be seen. I didn't want to believe that he wasn't at the airport, but forty-five minutes after my arrival there was still no TFM in sight. Convinced he stood me up, I walked over to the computer kiosk with two goals in mind—to write him a scathing email banishing him from my life, then find accommodations for a few nights before my premature departure back across the Atlantic Ocean. However, as soon as I logged in to my Gmail account a Gchat window popped up. It was TFM.

TFM: ?

Sutanya: Where are you????

Sutanya: I'm at terminal 2E

Sutanya: I've been here for 45 mins

TFM: I couldn't come

TFM: Because of the strikes

Sutanya: Are you kidding???????????

TFM: I was worried. I kept calling you

TFM: I am so so so so sorry

In the taxi on the way to the Boulevard Raspail address given to me by TFM, I was fuming with anger and disappointment. The lack of effort on TFM's part to get to the airport despite the public transportation strikes felt like an omen. Taking a taxi to the airport would've been a straightforward and easy way to circumvent the transportation strikes. I thought, *am I not worth the minimal effort to him?* For the first time questions stirred in my mind about what I was actually doing, but my rage slowly diminished as the taxi passed through the city center and I fell under Paris's spell and was soothed by her charm. Driving past the packed sidewalk cafés, their tables dotted with white cups of coffee and Parisians sitting side by side, deeply engaged in their conversations, released the tension in my shoulders. By the time the car stopped in front of the limestone building and I spotted TFM outside, leaning against the wall, his ever-present cigarette dangling from his mouth and remorse written all over his face, any doubts that I had quietly retreated to the depths of my sub-conscious. "I'm sorry, baby," he said when he opened the door and kissed me deeply.

He paid the taxi and after having my romantic-comedy greet-ing, I set off to meet the cast of characters who colored his life. This would become my entry into French life and Parisian cul-ture.

The first people I met in TFM's inner circle, and two of the most important people in his life, were his sister, Emma, and her boyfriend at the time, Houssame. Emma looked the part of a Parisian woman, slim and taut in her effortlessly chic dark knee-high leather boots and miniskirt, her wavy dark brown hair sitting gracefully on her shoulders. Her style was expected, it was her personality that caught me off guard. "Hi! It's so nice to finally meet you!" she said with a big smile while kissing me once on each cheek. Her friendly, warm smile was the first thing that threw me off. I had braced myself for the cold shoul-der Parisian women are known for, but she was the complete opposite. She complimented my outfit and made small talk be-fore grabbing me by the hand and confidently leading me into Les Dessous du Panthéon in the fifth arrondissement where all four of us would spend the evening. As I got to know her, in many ways she proved to be the antithesis of what the Parisian woman was in my mind. Houssame, her Moroccan Muslim boy-friend, was an easygoing jokester who liked to push boundaries, like TFM. I knew that TFM's family was special when during a conversation about them he casually mentioned that his sister's boyfriend was Muslim. Housamme's religion and background were never an issue for TFM's Jewish family—they cared more about the person and accepted him without hesitation. His fam-ily's acceptance of Houssame helped me gauge how they would react to me as a Black woman.

We walked into Les Dessous du Panthéon and past the bar directly toward spiral stairs.

"Where are we going?" I asked TFM.

"You'll see," he responded.

At the bottom of the black spiral stairs was an underground dance floor that smelled like sweat and red wine. There were no windows and only one way in and out. I tugged at TFM's shirt to get his attention and yelled over the music, "This is a fire hazard!"

A smile grew across his face and he signaled to Emma and Houssame, who were already dancing toward the fun-size bar in the corner, to come over.

"Tell them what you just said to me," he said.

"Well, this is a fire hazard," I said matter-of-factly.

There was a moment of silence before they all started laughing. The joke was lost on me. My eyes darted from side to side and embarrassment flushed my face. Seeing my discomfort he pulled me in closely and said, "You're so American! It's cute!"

He kissed my forehead and whispered in my ear, *"Tout va bien. Je vais m'occuper de toi.* You're in Paris! Relax and have fun!" He was reassuring me that everything was going to be okay and he would take care of me. After a few furtive glances toward the spiral stairs, I followed his instructions and relaxed. I braced myself for inevitable moments of awkwardness with two of the most important people in his life, which was expected, given the fact that Emma and Houssame were strangers but it didn't feel like they were. They did everything in their power to make me feel included, like speaking English and always checking in to make sure I was okay. At one point Emma and I were alone on the dance floor while TFM and Houssame were at the bar, ordering another round of drinks. When they signaled for us to meet them there, Emma instinctively put one hand behind her back—the universal sign that I should hold her hand so that we don't lose each other in the crowd. There wasn't much of a crowd to get lost in, but her gesture didn't go unnoticed. She could've easily mouthed "let's go" and I would've followed her, but instead, she took my hand into hers and made me feel like the missing piece of their clique. The way the four of us drank, danced and sang at the top of our lungs all night long, like we'd known each other for years, confirmed my sense that TFM came from an open, warm and friendly family. My concerns were unwarranted; I had nothing to worry about.

Fresh croissants, a *pain au raisin* and painkillers greeted me the next morning as I tried to alleviate the fatal combination of jetlag and a hangover.

"Feeling better?" TFM inquired about thirty minutes after my croissant and painkiller cocktail. "We have a lot to do," he continued.

"But I wanna stay in bed a bit longer," I pleaded. He didn't protest, and the itinerary he had planned for the day was promptly forgotten. We spent the morning and afternoon under the covers laughing and talking, elated that we were sharing the same space and bed.

Later that evening we made our way to another bar in the city to meet his group of friends. They'd all been close since high school and still regularly hung out and went on vacations together. Assured after my successful night with Emma and Houssame, I walked confidently toward the couple he waved to. Before he could introduce them, the woman half blurted out, "Hi, I'm Nath! I'm Brazilian!"

"Hi Nath from Brazil," I responded with my hand out, ready to shake hers. She looked at me oddly and didn't respond with her hand.

The curly-haired man standing next to her said, "I'm Chonch. Nice to finally meet you. I apologize for my English."

"Oh, no, please don't apologize. Your English is perfect!" I said with a slight chuckle.

That was something I noticed with a lot of Parisians I met: many of them apologized about the lack of their English language skills while speaking flawless English. I was the one in their country and couldn't string a sentence together in French despite studying it for years; I should be the one apologizing. Almost immediately, Chonch and Nath invited us to their place for dinner before my return to New York City. Besides his family they were the first people to invite me into their circle with the most open arms. We dillydallied in front of the bar, finalizing plans, until a familiar face popped out.

"You guys coming inside?" Thomas asked.

Thomas was TFM's friend who was with him that fateful night at Fanelli's, and this was the first time I'd seen him since then. He was quieter and more sober than I remembered.

"Nice to see you again, Thomas!" I said with enthusiasm that he didn't return. His lackluster response forced me to wonder if I said or did something wrong. Eventually, he warmed up and a stream of people began to pour in, and one by one TFM's social circle became clearer. I immediately thought of the saying "Show me who your friends are, and I will tell you who you are" because like Emma, the women surprised me with their openness and kindness, and the men were easygoing jokesters who wanted to have a good time. They weren't very different from my friends back home and that realization put me even more at ease. While ordering another round of drinks I saw TFM in his element—holding court—happiness beaming off him and everyone around wanting to stand in his light for as long as possible. TFM surrounded himself with people who brought out the best in him, and I fit snugly right in the mix.

"Can I ask you something?" I asked TFM later that night in bed. We didn't stay out too late because we were having lunch with his mother, Annie, the next day.

"Yes," he responded.

"Why didn't Nath shake my hand?" I asked.

"Because it's weird," he chuckled in response.

"Weird? How so?" I inquired now with my body turned to his and my face resting on my palms.

"Well, it's a bit formal, for starters," he said when he turned to face me. "She's a good friend of mine, not your future boss," he explained.

"We're just a bit more affectionate in France," he continued.

"Okay, one more," I said. He didn't respond so I continued. "Why was Thomas so weird with me? Does he not like me?" I asked.

This time he cackled and said, "No, not at all. That's not it. He was afraid you were going to tell his girlfriend about the women that he was flirting with at the bar when we met in New York."

"Girlfriend? He had a girlfriend when I met you guys? Could've fooled me!" I said.

"Oh, and by the way, Nath is not Brazilian. She's French," he added.

"But she said she was Brazilian," I responded.

"It's a bit of an inside joke with our *bande de potes*," he said before further explaining that Nath was born in Brazil and lived there for the first four years of her life because her father worked there at the time and as a result she has a Brazilian passport. But that was it; that was as far as her Brazilian roots went. However, that didn't stop her from owning it with pride and using it as a way to stand apart from her French friends. I found that explanation hilarious. Nathalie was quite the character and I wanted to get to know her.

My first few days were a whirlwind of meetings and emotions; there was a lot to download, journal about and process, but lying in the dark I couldn't help but continuously think to myself, *technically, she is Brazilian, though.*

After some time I swapped out questions about Nath's origins for thoughts about our upcoming lunch at Annie's. I wanted our meeting to be flawless, so I made a mental note to not shake hands when I met Annie. I had to be affectionate.

It was *le grand jour*; we were on our way to Annie's apartment for lunch.

"Do you think she'll like me?" I asked TFM.

"Of course she will. Why wouldn't she?" he responded while giving my hand a quick reassuring squeeze. "Just be you." I had no real reason to be nervous but I remained on edge about meeting his mother. I knew how much TFM loved and respected her and it had been years since he introduced her to a woman he was dating. I was determined to make a positive and lasting impression.

When Annie opened the door to her apartment, it was like seeing an older version of Emma. At just around five feet tall, wearing dark slacks and a V-neck sweater with the sleeves bunched up to her elbows and her hair pulled back into a low demure bun, she, too, fell into the chic Parisian woman category. I pulled her close into me and gave her an American-style bear hug and in an uncharacteristically high-pitched and nasally voice exclaimed, "It is sooo nice to finally meet youuu!"

She didn't hug me back; she stood still. Her eyes, widened with shock, darted back and forth between her son and me, and her arms remained at the sides of her body as if they were affixed there with glue. *"Euuuhhhhh, bonjour,"* she responded with a strained smile before quickly shuffling away.

I was horrified. TFM found this interaction amusing and was trying to hold back his laughter as he took my coat. "Why did you do that?" he asked.

"Do what?" I responded. Although I had an idea of what he was referring to.

"Hug my mom," he answered. "She doesn't know you. Hugging is considered very intimate in France. Next time just kiss her."

Kiss her? I thought to myself. I didn't understand how placing my face onto hers twice in a row while making kissing noises close to her ears was deemed less offensive than an innocent hug. Nevertheless, *don't hug French people or shake their hands* was etched in my brain from that day forward.

At lunch we were all seated at an appropriate distance from each other, I imagine to deter me from giving out spontaneous and unwanted hugs. Despite the language barrier and TFM, Emma and Houssame stepping in as translators for Annie and me, I could tell that she was clever, sharp and curious. At the time, the 2010 midterm elections dominated the news, and I remember agreeing with many of Annie's precise and discerning observations about American culture and its political landscape. Like her son, she was interested in the world around her. She asked questions about my family and wanted to know more about my experience growing up in the Bronx.

Over the course of lunch I learned that there was another foreigner in his family. His cousin Stephane was married to a Finnish woman named Minna and they had two kids. They were next in line for me to meet. I had found the French family version of a mini-United Nations; the makeup of TFM's multicultural, multiracial family felt utopian. Like Houssame's Arabness and Minna's Finnishness, my Black Jamaican-American heritage was accepted as a part of my identity—it wasn't glossed over—but it wasn't a decisive factor. It was obvious that TFM, Emma and Annie were a tight-knit crew bound together by love, admiration and fierce protectiveness of each other. By the end of lunch I was in love with the entire clan. They were caring, warm, intellectually stimulating, funny and unpretentious, and I wanted to be fully welcomed into the fold.

While I was falling in love with his family and friends, we managed to create our own memories, ones we would later share at *apéros*, dinner parties or with the vivacious and tenderhearted Franco-American children I hoped we would have one day.

One evening TFM surprised me with plans to go see a one-man show—in English—at a theater on the Left Bank, followed by dinner at a neighborhood bistro. The evening had all the markings of a *très Parisian* romance. Giddy with excitement I slipped on a little black dress and booties for the occasion, my trusty MAC Ruby Woo coloring my lips. I couldn't wait for our magical evening to begin. After the theater we walked through the zigzagging cobblestone streets, stealing kisses at every chance until we arrived at a quintessential Parisian bistro.

Before walking into the restaurant I caught the scene from the window. I saw a decently populated, dimly lit interior with waiters dressed in black pants, white shirts and black vests scurrying around. The imposing mahogany bar and small round wooden tables packed closely together stood out. The scene made me think of what Fanelli's would be if it were actually in Europe. As we walked to our seat an older gentleman sitting at the imposing wooden bar off to the right commented, *"Oh! Elle est belle, hein?"* He hit on me in front of my boyfriend and did not care one bit. I loved it.

I was too busy taking in the entire scene to pay attention to what TFM said to the waiter, but shortly after sitting we were presented with a bottle of rich and spicy Côtes du Rhone followed by perfectly cooked steak that melted in my mouth. I had to pinch myself to make sure I wasn't dreaming about a movie I was starring in. A cheese platter came next and I dug in without hesitation. The first slice of cheese that I cut was silky, creamy and nutty. I closed my eyes and threw my head back in joy and pleasure. I immediately cut another slice and ate it without any bread. It was that good.

Still enjoying the aftertaste I asked TFM, "What is this cheese? It is so good!"

"This cheese?" he responded while pointing to the platter.

"Yes, that cheese."

"This cheese right here? Are you sure?" he asked again.

"Yes!" I responded, becoming slightly frustrated. "Is it a fucking state secret?" I continued cheekily.

TFM was holding back laughter, but I didn't understand why until he said, "This cheese is butter." He no longer held back and laughed so hard that tears started streaming down his face.

I was mortified. I wanted the floor to open and suck me into the depths of the earth and disappear forever. Instead, we reached for each other across the table and kissed. Red wine and butter stained my lips and a big smile appeared across his. Years later TFM told me that was when he knew there was no turning back and he had no doubts that he was going to fall in love with me. He reassured me that he was charmed by that moment in the restaurant. He said he admired my unabashed enthusiasm around new experiences, especially when it was about cheese that was actually butter, and the fact that I could laugh at myself after my embarrassment wore off. He knew within that moment that he wasn't going to let me go. He would do everything in his power to ensure that "us" lasted forever, and I believed him.

Although there were 3,625 miles and a six-hour time difference separating us, TFM never gave me reason to doubt his feelings and commitment to our relationship. Even when moments of intimate touch were not readily available when they were needed the most, even when the feeling of loneliness and missing each other became too much, his presence was always with me. Gchat, emails, Skype and text messages helped us maintain daily contact; he sent flowers, kept up with emails and found himself in New York whenever he could. He was able to be more present and forthcoming than most of the men in my past, even though those men usually only lived twenty minutes away.

After another trip to Paris a few weeks later, in December, and one failed job in between visits I was desperate to settle into a career-building role. I loved the image of me jet-setting to Paris every few weeks to see *mon amour*, but that wouldn't be possible without any money. I was already living with my parents rent-free, I wasn't going to ask them to also fund a transatlantic romance.

With the New Year, 2011, fast approaching I worked with a recruitment company that placed me in various temporary receptionist positions throughout Manhattan until the career building role presented itself. TFM, knowing that I was applying at various branding agencies in the city, joined my job search, found a consultant position at a leading agency and encouraged me to apply. Impostor syndrome coursed through my veins from the beginning of the application process straight through to the offer, but whenever I wanted to give up he wouldn't have any of it. He was my champion—my biggest advocate—and before every step of the interview process he ended our Gchats by reminding me of that.

TFM: okay babe good luck with the next step

TFM: be confident

TFM: lots of kisses

Despite being in what many consider the prime time of my dating life, with temptations swirling around like forbidden fruit, I didn't consider being with anyone else. I simply didn't want to. Nothing was worth jeopardizing the purity of what TFM and I were creating; I became even more certain that I had found my teammate. TFM had my heart, and I didn't want it back. I trusted that it was in a safe place, never to ache again.

With every trip to Paris I became more integrated in his life. I was included on group emails about parties and vacations that were happening when I was in town. His friends' comments on my Facebook photos and status updates made them feel more like our friends versus just his. His sister, Emma, and I started our own pen-pal relationship. A built-in support group of friends and family began to organically take shape around us in preparation for what was to come next.

After two years of crisscrossing the Atlantic Ocean and acquiring an obscene amount of frequent flier miles, we reached an impasse around the next steps in our relationship. So it felt natural when the idea of marriage began to pepper our conversations. We spoke about it in theory: TFM didn't have any desire to live or work in New York City so I would move to Paris; we both agreed on a secular wedding due to our different religions; we even had a list of potential honeymoon destinations. I just didn't know when or how all of this would happen.

Within a few hours of landing at Charles De Gaulle Airport in June, 2012 I could see that there was something preoccupying TFM. He was curt, on edge and rude. It wasn't uncommon for one of us to be in a surly mood on any given day or evening when talking to each other from our respective cities. Trying to maintain a relationship via Gchat, text messages and Skype calls becomes exhausting, fast. However, any irritation we felt about our distance usually diminished as soon as we were face-to-face. It was strange seeing him in a foul mood even after I arrived. Something was amiss but I couldn't put my finger on it, seeing as I didn't *really* know him. We'd been dating for a few years at this point but most of our relationship happened behind a screen, except when punctuated by our in-person visits, but I didn't know him in his everyday element. So when I was confronted with his unpleasant mood, a very common and expected human disposition, I wasn't used to it and didn't know how to respond. As our relationship evolved our face-to-face reunions were a double-edged sword. On one hand they gave me a sense of relief and satiated my ever-growing desire for him, while simultaneously resembling meeting for the first time. We always needed a few days to get into the groove of being around each other. I began to wonder, *who were we without the screens to buffer our inherent imperfections?*

One perk of a long-distance relationship is never having to witness your partner's various moods. Whenever you're physically together each of you only present your best selves. When you're not bogged down by the day-to-day routine of a relationship you get used to existing, as a couple, in the perpetual state of the beginning of the relationship, when everything is the epitome of perfection.

The morning after my arrival we lay in bed with our legs intertwined. The tension I felt between us was still present. Finally, I asked, "Everything okay?"

"Yeah, why?" he responded.

"I don't know, you seem a little off and—"

"Off?" he scoffed, cutting me off. "What are you talking about? I'm fine."

I knew that was the end of the discussion, so I didn't dig deeper. I lay looking up at the ceiling, trying to decipher what could be causing his mood. He was still relatively new at his company and in his role. Consulting was not an easy job, and now he had to juggle the job and me for the next few days.

After kissing me goodbye, before walking out the door, he looked at me over his shoulder. "Let's have *apéro* on Canal Saint-Martin tonight."

"That sounds perfect," I responded. Things were looking up. I interpreted his *apéro* suggestion as an olive branch: sharing a romantic drink by the water was his way of making amends for his shitty mood.

Canal Saint-Martin, located in the tenth arrondissement, is the less touristy version of the Seine. The typical Haussmann-style buildings that flank the two sides of the canal are void of the loftiness that envelops the neighborhoods that sit along the Seine River. In the warmer months the glimmer from the water bounces off the bottles of wine and beer, dotting the night sky with twinkles of summer joy.

On any summer evening you'll find young, trendy Parisians on the banks of the canal with their cheeses, wines and beers.

On this night in particular it was especially packed. The air was thick and sticky, and the lack of air-conditioning in apartments meant that sitting by the water was the only source of temporary relief. Walking up to the canal with a bottle of wine in one hand and provisions in my tote bag, I scanned the area for the best location that would allow me to have a romantic moment with TFM while people watched and eavesdropped.

"This looks like a good spot," I said to TFM and pointed to a space next to a group of friends of varied races and genders.

"No, let's walk a bit more," he said.

I thought it was weird but I didn't protest and followed him as we moved farther and farther away from the crowd. He stopped at the very end of the canal where the only other people present were old men. I was agitated while laying out the elements of our *apéro*. Rosé from my tote bag, mimolette cheese and a warm baguette I grabbed at the *boulangerie* on the way. TFM had the grapes and goat cheese. Sensing my aggravation, he placed his head on my lap and I began stroking his hair. A potential explosion was defused by tenderness and affection. We'd never had a huge blowout argument before; there was never a reason to and I didn't want our first fight to be in public.

"Do you love me?" TFM asked, looking deeply into my eyes as if he was trying to catch any hint of hesitation that may flicker across them.

"Yes, of course I do," I responded.

He fell silent and looked out onto the canal. *What the hell is going on*, I wondered. He turned around again, my hands still in his hair. "Are you sure?"

"Of course I'm sure," I said. "I love you more and more every day."

He went quiet again, and the meaning of all of this came to me like a flash. I convinced myself that he was going to break up with me. That explained why he chose this semidesolate location, so that no one would see me crying and I would cause less of a scene. I braced myself for his explanation, for him to tell me how difficult this decision was and how much it hurt him.

Instead, he turned around again and looked at me with his slightly downturned eyes and asked, "So why don't you marry me?" and proceeded to pull out a white box from his pocket. In the box was a white gold ring with a solitaire diamond.

I looked at him, looked at the ring, looked at him again and looked at the ring in the box. "So…?" he asked because I didn't give him an answer.

"Yes!" I said. "Of course!" We kissed and I couldn't stop looking at the ring and him. Our love story was reaching new heights.

As soon as we returned to the apartment, I made a beeline to the bathroom and started pacing. I couldn't believe he asked me to marry him and that I said yes. Despite our discussions around marriage, I was taken aback by the proposal. We spoke about marriage as an abstract concept, but with a ring on my finger—the big question asked and answered—the concept transformed into a new reality with practical implications, small and large, that I hadn't thought through yet. Up to this point this was the most life-altering decision I'd ever made. All my previous life choices seemed so inconsequential compared to this.

My left hand felt heavy. I was already feeling the pressure of what the ring symbolized and meant. I kept looking at my reflection in the mirror. "I don't know how to be a wife," I said to the stunned face staring back at me.

TFM, sensing that something was amiss, asked, "Everything all right in there?"

"Yeah, everything's okay," I responded, trying to conceal the panic in my voice. He didn't believe me for a second. He tried opening the door but it was locked from the inside.

"Come on, what's going on? Talk to me," he pleaded.

"I said I'm fine!" The aggression in my voice was a clear sign that I wasn't fine.

"If you don't open the door in five seconds I'm going to break it down," he threatened. I couldn't gauge how serious he was, and I didn't want to test him. I splashed cold water all over my face and finally opened the door.

"I couldn't find any towels," I said. That was my excuse for barricading myself in the bathroom and having a wet face.

TFM wasn't convinced. He stood in the frame of the door with his arms crossed at his chest. He wanted the truth, and he wanted it right then and there. After wiping off my face with a towel, a jumble of emotions that were racing through me spilled out of my mouth at warp speed. I was ecstatic yet frightened, hopeful but at the same time eerily unsettled. From his position on the toilet seat cover—I was sitting on the floor—he held my hand and listened until I was breathless and depleted. He understood, shared that he also felt overwhelmed and shocked that he actually took the leap but he was confident it was the right decision. He reminded me that we were made for each other, and most importantly, we were madly in love. TFM's words calmed my heart and comforted my spirit. He reminded me that we were a team and I started getting excited about what was to come next: planning our wedding day.

Unfortunately, we weren't able to immediately get into the wedding planning bit of things. The first test of the strength of our love and partnership came in the shape of a *fonctionnaire*, a civil servant, and multiple trips to the city hall. The common enemies of all of the expat bloggers were the *fonctionnaires*. From their posts I understood that *fonctionnaires* held some of the most important keys to all foreigners' existence in France, and they had the power to make their lives a living hell if they wanted to. To be legally married in France your ceremony must be held at the local city hall where you live. After the civil ceremony, if you choose to, you can have a religious ceremony or another secular ceremony and celebrate in any other way you like. But before you can start planning all of that you need to get permission and a time and date from the city. A time and date is given to you by the city hall after you've applied in person, with your partner, and your *dossier* is approved.

One month after our engagement we were seated in the city hall's plastic chairs waiting to file our *dossier*. I found the juxtaposition of plastic chairs we were sitting on alongside the opulence of the other buildings' contents humorous. I checked the folder on my lap incessantly to ensure my paperwork was void of any errors.

"Madame Dacres et Monsieur TFM!!" a wiry woman with a thick cardigan hanging loosely off her shoulders shrilled from the other side of the hallway. *"Suivez-moi,"* she continued in a less ear-piercing tone.

We followed her into a small dark room where we sat in front of a white linoleum desk with a soft-spoken young woman behind it. She greeted us and asked us a few questions before going through our *dossier* in detail. After a few minutes she looked up and said, *"Okay, c'est bon pour moi."*

Thinking he didn't hear her right, TFM responded, *"Pardon?* I don't think I understand. Everything is okay?"

"Oui, everything looks good to me," she said. "We will get in touch about the date."

"Merci beaucoup," TFM said and I followed suit.

"I can't believe that just happened. That never happens!" TFM said while pretty much running out of the building. It's almost unheard of in France to have a successful initial meeting with any bureaucratic entity. On average it takes two to three visits with an increasingly large *dossier* before getting anything done.

"We have to celebrate. A glass of champagne is a must!" he said before grabbing me by the waist, pulling me in and kissing me. "We're obviously meant to be," he continued before pulling out his phone and texting Annie and Emma to share the good news.

We chose a café across the street for our celebratory drinks and after clinking glasses I asked TFM, "Why is this such a big deal? She accepted our file."

"You don't understand," he said. I cut him off. "You're right. I don't. Please explain," I quipped. He squinted his eyes and smirked at me. He liked when I was a little bit feisty.

"Well, soon-to-be Mrs. TFM," he started. "The thing you have to understand about French administration is that it's a pain in the ass. Whenever you have to do something administrative it's a nightmare, you never have the right documents, they always want more, they lose things, they give you appointments months apart. It's the worst. But if you want to live in France you have to deal with it," he said before taking a big gulp of champagne.

"But isn't everything electronic anyway?" I naively asked. He guffawed in response and continued explaining the ins and outs of the French administration. In the middle of the lesson his cell phone rang and the expression on his face went from happily satisfied to disbelief. He took a pen and paper out of my bag and started writing something down.

"*D'accord. Merci,*" he said before ending the call.

"Is everything okay? Is someone hurt?" I asked.

"No, it was the city hall," he said. "That was the *fonctionnaire's* manager, our *dossier* is incomplete and a few things were stamped wrong. The woman we saw is a trainee and missed a few crucial things. We have to redo our file and reapply."

We finished our champagne in a less celebratory mood than when we arrived and strategized *dossier* version number two.

One month later we were back again, sitting on familiar plastic chairs when the same lady wearing the same cardigan hurls our names down the hallway. This time in the room waiting for us was an older woman who had a no-nonsense attitude about her. I incorrectly assumed our experience with her would be more straightforward. I knew my *dossier* was bulletproof. After the misleading first experience, back in New York, I enlisted the help of a New York–based French lawyer to help me to create the most comprehensive *dossier* this city hall has ever seen. I confidently slid my bulletproof *dossier* across the desk to her.

A sequence of reassuring head nods from her put me at ease and I squeezed TFM's hand. My relief proved to be momentary when abruptly she stopped inputting our information in her computer. She singled out the English and French versions of my birth certificate and began studying them, then looked at something on her computer screen. She did this for a few minutes without acknowledging our existence or asking any questions.

Finally addressing us, she asks, "Mandeville, Jamaica?"

"*Oui*, that's where she was born," TFM responded.

"*Ah, bon? Ça n'existe pas,*" she said.

"Did she just say the town where I was born doesn't exist?" I asked him.

TFM and the woman went back and forth; he insisted that the town of my birth does exist, and her standing firm in her analysis that I was born in a place that is not actually real. *Is this an SNL sketch*? I thought to myself.

Eventually, a third party, her supervisor, ended the debate by explaining to her, and us, that Mandeville, Jamaica, does exist. It simply wasn't an option in the drop-down menu where she was entering our information. She had to manually add it. After that was resolved, I turned to TFM and we shared a look of relief. Then questions about my Jamaican birth certificate and American passport began filling the room.

I thought that the *fonctionnaires* were the last big obstacle we would face in our relationship for a long time. Trips to faraway locales, big dinners with friends and creating our own perfect French–American bubble was top of mind. We both strongly believed that we were ready for that next step, and after several more trips to the local city hall, we were finally allowed to get married. On March 16, 2013, after three years of wanting nothing more than to be together without any distance, physical or otherwise, we joined forces and became husband and wife. Moving to Paris wasn't my dream but the promise of love called and I knew that any answer other than a resounding *oui* would've led to a lifetime of regret and wondering what if. Naively, I thought marriage was a never-ending celebration.

Six

LES MARIÉS

The *salle de mariage* of the *Mairie du 15eme*, the city hall where we were set to marry, was the most elegantly decorative governmental space I'd ever been in. Stunning Baroque-style oil paintings adorned the walls, two stately chandeliers hung from gold-paneled ceilings and TFM and I weren't the only attendees sitting on red velvet chairs; everyone else's rear ends also had the privilege of being exquisitely cushioned during the twenty-minute ceremony. My regular trips to Paris taught me how to prepare myself for the sometimes overwhelming sensory pleasure the city is known for—the majestic bridges that sit above the Seine connecting the two distinct parts of the city, the handwritten specials on chalkboards in front of cafés and the rattan chairs that beckon passersby to stop and enjoy a cup of coffee, the way on first glance all of the apartment buildings look similar but if you pay close attention you'll discover beautiful distinct features in each of them—but I didn't expect the sensory feast would extend to the *salle de mariage* of a local city hall.

The joyful energy permeating the *salle de mariage* as we made our way to the two throne-like red velvet chairs at the front of the room to begin the ceremony made me feel that at any moment I would lose my gravitational pull. The warmth and buoyant energy of the room enclosed everyone in a bubble of love that filled me with a feeling of lightness. With every step I took closer to the chairs, my feet felt farther away from the ground. At any moment it was possible that I would float away like a runaway balloon at a children's party—full, happy and watching everything from up above. Unbeknownst to me, that feeling was a precursor of how I would experience my initial years in Paris—present but not really, mostly observing the situation instead of living it. I was innocently floating toward a future that would prove to be radically different than anything I'd ever imagined.

The deputy mayor tasked with making our union legal under the eyes of French law wore an oversize gray suit that worked perfectly with his rosy cherubic baby face. TFM told me they met prior to the ceremony in order to build a rapport and give him the opportunity to share a bit of our story in an attempt to make an otherwise mechanical procedure more personal, but I didn't know what to expect. The ceremony began with the deputy mayor stating:

"Je suis heureux de vous accueillir, mesdames et messieurs, ce 16 Mars 2013 dans notre Hôtel de Ville de Paris 15eme afin de célébrer l'union de Sutanya Dacres avec [TFM]. En tant qu'officier de l'état civil, c'est toujours avec grand plaisir que je reçois, sous le toit de la République, les futurs époux qui ont choisi la voie du mariage. Un engagement civique et moral qui suppose pour les époux un respect mutuel et un accompagnement de chaque jour."

And I was pleasantly surprised when he repeated it in English:

"I am happy to welcome you, ladies and gentlemen, today, March 16, 2013, in the city hall of Paris's fifteenth arrondissement to celebrate Sutanya Dacres's union with [TFM]. As an official of the state, it is always with great pleasure that I receive, under the roof of the Republic, future spouses who have chosen the path of marriage. A civic and moral commitment that supposes for the spouses a mutual respect and an accompaniment on every day—"

After his English tease he broke into rapid-fire French and I had no clue what the combinations of vowels and consonants exiting his mouth meant. The anxiety that had plagued me up until that moment began to decimate whenever I snuck a peek at TFM and saw him looking straight ahead, with a broad smile across his face, beaming into our future. Despite his gentle, re-assuring squeezes of my hand, I wasn't completely blind to the fact that he was present that day in a way I couldn't be. So much of my life was changing and his wasn't. I was entering his world and leaving mine behind.

"*Sue, t'es magnifique,*" my soon-to-be sister-in-law, Emma, said earlier that morning when she stood back and admired her work. She evened out my skintone using MAC foundation, dotted my cheeks with pink blush and curled and elongated my eyelashes with mascara. We were all at Annie's apartment, where I stayed the night before the ceremony. I was uncharac-teristically quiet and solemn.

"*Ça va, ma belle?*" Annie asked me as I got up from the chair and was making my way to the bedroom.

"*Oui, oui, ça va,*" I responded, trying to sound as convincing as possible. In the same breath I looked across the room and saw TFM strutting across the living room in his black Givenchy tux-edo. He looked dapper, polished and, most importantly, elated.

I was happy, too, but I ached for a moment alone with my fi-ancé. We planned our wedding in three months while living in different parts of the world because we wanted to get married as soon as possible. Removing the physical distance between us was a top priority and the only thing that stood in our way. When it was finally time for me to fly back to Paris for the wedding a snowstorm caused airline chaos and I arrived only two days before the ceremony. In between a surprise bachelorette hosted by Emma and seeing family and friends, many that flew in specifically for the wedding, we had no time to be with each other. I yearned for a quiet moment with him, where we both would agree that, despite spending the past three years crisscrossing the Atlantic to maintain our relationship, our love could, and would, conquer all. I needed him to gently cradle my face in his hands the same way he did after reading the letter I wrote him at the end of his first trip to visit me. I needed to know that everything we spoke about under the covers when we were physically together was coming to fruition. Our fantasy, what always seemed so impossible, was finally becoming our reality.

But I couldn't bring myself to ask for that bit of comfort. I didn't want to plant any seeds of doubt, about my commitment to him or this next chapter in our lives, in his mind or my soon-to-be family's minds. So I kept quiet and transformed my sullen expression into a wide American smile and made my way to the guest room to finish getting ready as everyone buzzed around the apartment, the energy feeling equally thrilling and suffocating.

As we approached the city hall, on our way to the ceremony, I tugged at TFM's sleeve and whispered through my teeth, "Can we talk for a minute?" He didn't hear, so I tugged again, this time with more force. "We need to talk!" I said, louder. I didn't want to start my first day as a married woman without communicating how I felt.

"Huh?" TFM said, not hearing anything I said. "Look, there's Augustin and everyone else. Let's go say hi."

The time between arriving at city hall and the beginning of the ceremony flew by quickly. I tried to stay as close to TFM as possible by holding on tightly to his hand and found it hard to let go as friends called him over for photos or when his cousin, Stephane, wanted to have a quick chat man to man.

During the ceremony, as the deputy mayor went on and on about the values of marriage within France, which seemed to mostly involve having lots of children, the most surreal moment of sitting on that plush velvet chair was realizing that I was getting married and moving to a country where I barely spoke the language. At the age of twenty-seven, when most of who I am had already been formed, I was voluntarily putting myself through the anguish of creating an entirely new identity. The rush of hormones and chemicals that course through your body when you're falling in love, or in the beginning of a relationship, influences you to do crazy things, but this surpassed anything I'd ever done for love.

I followed TFM's lead the entire duration of the ceremony: when he smiled, I smiled, when he chuckled, I shyly did the same, when he looked around the room so did I. I was being uprooted, TFM wasn't and this was the first time I felt a distance that I didn't expect would plague our relationship in the years to follow. In most marriages the couples are starting from scratch together. We were not. I was entering his world—his country, language and culture—which up until that point led to mostly humorous misunderstandings and faux pas. An insight into our new world of unequal footing couldn't have shone more brightly than when the deputy mayor retold the infamous cheese-butter incident.

The retelling of my innocent American gaffe elicited a big roar of laughter from the French speakers in the room while the clueless English speakers simply followed suit, like I did the entire ceremony. There was an enormous gap between TFM and me, but I was determined to fill it because I didn't want to play catch-up for our entire marriage. At the time I didn't realize the struggle that comes along with a love story that required one person to leave their old life behind and create a new one in a foreign country.

The exchange of rings, the final part of the ceremony, unleashed silent tears of joy and fear. Joy because I was officially married to the love of my life despite so many obstacles. I genuinely felt lucky; it all had happened when I least expected it. Fear because I was married to the love of my life, a French man, in French, and in a few shorts weeks would officially become one of those American women abroad floating toward an entirely different life and future in Paris.

ACT 2

Seven

THE EXPAT SUMMER

A week after the wedding I flew back to New York City alone. The abrupt separation after our wedding was brutal but I thought it was the last time we would have to be apart for an extended period. I had six weeks to leave my job at the branding agency, get a French visa, distill and pack my most precious possessions into suitcases, say goodbye to family and friends and mentally prepare myself for the biggest move of my life. The days and weeks flew by at lightning speed, and before I knew it I was at JFK International Airport with four overstuffed suitcases, mostly filled with shoes, and a one-way ticket to Paris. At the check-in counter I nervously shifted the weight from my left to right foot while biting my fingernails, a habit I've had for as long as I can remember, while my mother inspected my suitcases for the fifth time to make sure they were securely closed.

"These suitcases," she muttered to herself while fiddling with the zippers.

"I think they're fine, Mommy," I responded with a half smile.

"I know, baby," she said, looking up at me with tears in her eyes.

On the ride to the airport I promised myself I wouldn't cry in front of my parents, so I turned away and started playing with my phone. Marriage isn't an uncommon rite of passage and it's one that most parents look forward to, but it usually doesn't involve sending their child off entirely into the unknown. In that moment it felt like the umbilical cord that connected us twenty-seven years prior was being cut again, but this time the instrument used wasn't a pair of sterilized scissors, it was a crisp one-way Air France ticket that represented an entirely new set of dreams, hopes and promises.

After my bags were checked in, with my backpack on my shoulders, we walked side-by-side with our hands around each other's waists until security measures forced us to exchange teary goodbyes. My father walked out of the airport terminal because he was overwhelmed with emotion. My parents understood that my decision to leave wasn't based on a desire to be far away from them. Another kind of love was calling me.

I landed at Charles De Gaulle International Airport for the first time as a French resident in June 2013—the beginning of the sweetest season in France—when the sun sets at 10 p.m. and arresting pink-purple-colored skies lull you to sleep. With my suitcases in a trolley and an official French visa in hand, I jumped into the arms of my husband, ready to love. My French visa was confirmation that I was stepping up to the challenge fully and wholly, without inhibition. I didn't know what I was signing up for and how the next few years of my life would pan out, but I joyously answered love's call with a resounding yes.

Blurry eyed but filled with anticipation about the beginning of a new life with TFM, I couldn't sit still in the taxi on the way to our apartment in Montmartre, a neighborhood that sits on a hill overlooking Paris. Montmartre is usually associated with Basilica Sacré-Coeur, the chalky white church that welcomes you into the neighborhood. Since the Belle Époque, it has been a refuge for artists, bohemians and adventurers looking for escape and acceptance—their tribe. The neighborhood has long been a sanctuary for French and European artists, but also for storied African-Americans like Langston Hughes, Josephine Baker and Ada "Bricktop" Smith, who all moved here to escape racism and segregation back home.

From the taxi I noticed the overcast skies, painting the city with strokes of melancholy that were beautiful yet morose, characteristics that I eventually learned Parisians also possessed. When it rains, the moody grays of the city stir a deep desire for stillness and to just be, appreciating the splendor of the city and everyday simplicities around you…and to just mope a little without judgement.

As the taxi inched closer to our new neighborhood, and home, the city was bustling in a very Parisian way, lots of café loafing and animated conversations. I was taking mental notes of cute restaurants and stores I wanted to pop into during my neighborhood exploration when déjà-vu suddenly came over me, but I couldn't put my finger on why this street felt eerily familiar. Then it hit me. The summer before, in 2012, when I got engaged, I drove through this neighborhood on my way to the airport and made a mental note to explore it after moving.

I discovered the neighborhood while taking the Roissy Bus, a shuttle bus service that takes passengers directly from the center of the city to the airport. It didn't matter that it took almost double the time to get to the airport using the bus instead of taking the RER—the train system that services primarily suburban neighborhoods close to Paris and the two major airports. I opted for the bus for sentimental reasons. The bus ride allowed me to have a few intimate moments with the city before my next visit. The summer of my engagement I paid extra attention to the neighborhoods the bus drove through because in a few short months the city would be home.

I knew the route through the Opéra district, the golden tops of the Opera House twinkling in the early-afternoon light, saying *à bientôt,* never *au revoir.* The streets leading to the highway were indistinguishable from each other until the bus drove onto rue Caulaincourt. I was mesmerized. The tree-lined streets had the air of a small village, not a neighborhood in a major city. I glued my face to the window as the bus followed the curve of the street. I took note of the number of cheese shops, bakeries and cafés that lined the streets, all independent stores with a unique story to share [if you knew how to ask for it]. By the time the bus made a slight left onto rue du Mont Cenis toward Jules Joffrin, a district within the greater neighborhood and the last city scene I would experience before exiting at Porte de Clignancourt, I was spellbound. Fast-forward almost one year later; I was on my way to our new apartment in Jules Joffrin.

When it dawned on me that I drove through this neighborhood the year before, I was at a loss for words. I wondered if it was a funny coincidence or if I subconsciously willed it to happen. In the same way sometimes, deep in the pit of my stomach, I mulled over whether or not I willed this love story, marriage and adventure to happen. TFM was going on and on about the apartment—the small renovations he wanted to do and how we should decorate—when I closed my eyes and silently willed a happy, long and fulfilling marriage. I wanted to use these newly discovered powers for something good.

TFM was proud of the apartment he found and he had every right to be; it was a gem. A blue spiral staircase led up to our apartment. The double-door windows in the living room and bedroom were practically floor-to-ceiling. Courtyard views. The compact kitchen had red-and-white tiling. A minuscule bathroom, where from a seated position on the toilet you could turn on the shower, close the bathroom door and turn on the tap to the sink all without ever getting up. Original hardwood covered the living room and bedroom floors. It was all so perfectly Parisian; it had all of the old-world charm one could ask for. We didn't have much furniture, just the basics—a couch, television and a bed. The bed proved to be the most crucial item that afternoon. That day the giving and sharing of our bodies to each other was highly charged and emotional. We were not only christening our marital bed, we were also christening our apartment, our lives and our commitment to each other.

In my love-riddled mind everything about my final years of discontent in Hartford led to this moment. If I had resigned myself to what I assumed would've been a stable and predictable yet ultimately unsatisfying suburban life, fear and cynicism would've thwarted this fairy-tale romance before it had the opportunity to ripen. At the time, falling in love with TFM and getting married seemed to be the antidote to my restlessness. I convinced myself that the trap of stability in the United States would've foiled any chance of meeting and falling in love with TFM—inevitably leading to the both of us battling years of unexplainable melancholy. I was so high on love that I created an illusion of an indestructible marriage and romance when what I should've done was start making a list of marriage therapists because no marriage is immune to the harsh wake-up calls that you're forced to confront about yourself and your partner as your relationship grows and matures. Especially when you're two young-ish newlyweds who have never lived in the same country.

The weeks after my arrival were a blur. I wasn't working and my job-hunting effort was minimal. Instead, I was living an enchanting summer as a newly minted Parisian. I lingered in sunlit cafés like the Parisians, my face turned toward the sun, soaking up every precious ray like a thirsty flower waiting to bloom. I used this opportunity to immerse myself in TFM's world by familiarizing myself with the neighborhood and deepening my relationship with Emma, my sister-in-law, independent of TFM. Her summer sabbatical before starting a demanding PhD program couldn't have come at a better time. She didn't expect her summer of preparation would include drinking rosé over hours-long lunches with me at the various sidewalk cafés that decorated my new neighborhood, but nevertheless she was a happy and willing participant. She was my main teacher of Parisian do's and dont's and my first taste of Paris that didn't completely revolve around TFM. I was hungry for everything she deemed important to share. I was used to having a strong, supportive network of female friends, and Emma slipped right in when they weren't physically present. She didn't replace those relationships; she was a welcomed addition to the spirited group of women who helped shape me.

Typically, our mornings started with a few laps at a running track in my neighborhood. Emma routinely arrived at our apartment between 9:30 and 10 a.m. and changed into her workout clothes before we headed out. The first time she changed into her workout clothes upon arrival, I assumed she had an early-morning errand to complete before our run. By the fourth time I had to ask.

I let out a nervous chuckle. I didn't want to offend her or come off as judging. I was genuinely curious.

"Emma, can I ask you something?" I asked after we finished our run.

"Yes, of course. You can ask me anything. Do not hesitate." She was always very exact with her vocabulary and full sentences. I heard her use of punctuation when she spoke.

"Ummm, why do you change into your workout clothes when you get to my place?" I asked.

"Is it a problem?" she shot back.

"No, of course not! It's just that you live so close, I don't understand why you wouldn't just wear your workout clothes."

"I would never wear workout clothes when just walking around on the street. It's for a purpose," she said. I didn't understand and she saw it written across my face. "It's not pleasant to walk around all of Paris in your workout clothes," she continued.

"Not pleasant for who?" I asked.

"For the people," she said so matter-of-factly.

"Oh," was all I could muster up but I mulled it over for a while. Where I was from, wearing sweatpants to the store was not viewed as a personal affront to the people you encountered along the way, but it seemed that in order to fit in here I'd have to burn all of the loungewear that had traveled across the ocean with me.

That was my first lesson in the power and importance of visual and sensory pleasure in Paris. Everything needs to be beautiful and evoke some kind of emotion, from the handwritten text displaying a restaurant's daily specials to a man walking down the street in his slim-fit dark blue jeans, crisp white shirt and Veja sneakers. One would think that this kind of pressure to be put together at all times would lead to a culture full of anxious and insecure people, but in fact, it has done the opposite. My time spent in cafés, soaking up the sun, gave me ample opportunity to observe Parisians during their favorite season, when moods were high because *les vacances* were just around the corner. The biggest takeaway I got from my loafing at cafés was that Parisians were very sure of themselves and comfortable in their skin. Of course, this doesn't mean every single Parisian that I saw walking down the street struck me as the most beautiful person in the world, but I did notice that they didn't shrink themselves. Almost everyone walked with their head held high, taking up space and asserting themselves. At that point in my Paris journey I didn't understand the importance of inner pleasure or how to cultivate it, so I admired the Parisians from afar and started walking with my head held a little higher, too.

Parisians aren't perfect mythical beings who have all of the answers to life, but their self-assuredness stood out. My café loafing and hawk-eye observations of everything and everyone around me were teaching me that TFM's self-acceptance—and subsequent acceptance of me—wasn't unique to him; it was a very Parisian way of being. No one is seeking perfection from themselves and those around them. They understand that flaws and shortcomings are a part of the human experience and they own it, and the more that way of being became crystallized in my mind it felt like a release. All of my years in Hartford I expected to be perfect and have everything figured out. Paris was soothing me by teaching me how detrimental that frame of mind is to one's ability to simply enjoy life. Embracing my right to relieve myself from the relentless pursuit of perfection wasn't immediate, but until that happened I was a fervent and loyal student.

After a day of quasi-ethnographic studies at various outdoor cafés and/or restaurants, I enjoyed returning to our apartment high on Paris summer, buzzed off rosé and waiting for my love to come home. On the evenings when the rosé-fueled lunches didn't lead to dinner at the same café where I was perched, I prided myself on making it home in time to have dinner prepared for TFM. I eased into the housewife role—it was temporary, and, ultimately, a part of the larger experience.

During the day I was learning about Paris etiquette with Emma, and in the quiet of the evening I was learning about TFM. Although I wasn't the greatest cook I attempted to show him my love through nourishment. I wanted to catch up on lost time by tapping into something visceral and deep-rooted such as the comfort of food and the sensations it gave. I wanted to know the combination of flavors that made him lick his fingers, and the meal that always made a bad day better.

My first food-related TFM discovery was *tarte tatin*. It's a dessert that reminded him of his grandmother, whom he was very close with, and the special memories they shared. In his opinion his grandmother's *tarte tatin* was legendary; I wanted to try to make it myself. I requested her recipe, asked TFM to translate it and thus began my *tarte tatin* and TFM food education.

When perfectly executed, *tarte tatin* is an elegant upside-down apple tart. It's made by caramelizing apples in sugar and lots of butter then covering the apples with a pastry crust. While baking, the apples continue cooking with the sugar and butter, creating a divine bed of caramel that becomes the silky topping when the tart is finished and flipped. TFM liked eating *tarte tatin* at room temperature with a dollop of cream or ice cream, but I always enjoyed it a few hours after baking, or ideally the morning after, when the caramel takes on a toffee texture and the flavors are deepened. My *tarte tatin* was never as good as his grandmother's—I never expected it to be—but it was good enough for TFM to occasionally crave and request, which was exactly what I wanted.

During those initial first weeks in the city I spent a lot of time eating what I characterize as "I just moved to Paris" food. The types of French food that fell into that category were usually simple dishes to most French people, but the smells excited me and the flavors floored me. I was finally having my Meryl Streep in *Julie & Julia* moments. The pastries in particular sang to me; I had to talk myself out of stopping at the *boulangerie* for a sweet treat every day. *Viennoiseries*, like croissants and *pain au raisin*, were my kryptonite. And I wasn't the only one; I quickly learned that Parisians take their *boulangerie* treats very seriously.

One morning while standing in line, waiting to order a warm *tradition au cereale*, I witnessed a full-on screaming match. A young man, who looked to be in his thirties, wearing a suit, was checking his watch and tapping his foot impatiently while the cashiers took orders and engaged in small talk with regular customers that they knew. Eventually, his impatience got the best of him so he decided to cut the line to place his order. He moved to the front without any subtlety, took one last look at his watch and confidently strode to the front of the register and placed his order. An older man around eighty years old was on his way out, but witnessed the entire thing and decided to speak up. I'm not entirely sure what he said, but whatever he said touched a chord because the line cutter responded aggressively. The old man did not like that. My eyes darted left to right; I couldn't believe the scene that was playing out in front of me.

A cashier came out to usher the old man out, but not before he said one last thing to the young man and hit him on the arm with his baguette! The line cutter left the bakery without his baguette but with lots of bread dust on his shoulder, and the entire bakery erupted in applause. I laughed for hours after the altercation, but I also made a mental note to myself: do not mess with French people and their bread. I soon learned that the lesson I was taught in the *boulangerie* that morning applied to food in general. With that in mind I allowed myself to be guided by the city's culinary delights. I doubted I would be disappointed or led astray.

When I wasn't loafing and eating in Jules Joffrin, I was usually just a stone's throw away in the neighborhood of Abbesses. I didn't have to go far for delicious food. I often passed La Mascotte, a neighborhood landmark since 1889. It has had many lives, first as a hotel when it opened, then a small café and deli and finally a restaurant. Like many restaurants in the city small tables were always neatly lined up in front. If I didn't see the waiters and waitresses, who were dressed in traditional black-and-white uniforms, having a cigarette break before the start of their service, they were engaging in the delicate dance of ducking and dodging each other as they served hungry customers.

La Mascotte specializes in seafood and prides itself on serving the freshest catch, and the prices reflect that. The first few times I passed by I hesitated because I felt it was indulgent of me to spend excessively on lunch when I was unemployed, especially if it was just for myself—I hadn't yet discovered the French principle of pleasure. Instead of stopping I would slow down, taking a visual snapshot of everything I saw and, if I was lucky, I'd get a whiff of the pleasant aroma coming from the *plat du jour* as it was on its way to a lucky customer. Usually, I went unnoticed until one afternoon when my slow stroll caught the eye of an elegant waiter. I saw him flick his cigarette on the sidewalk and out it before sauntering over to me. *Oh shit, he's walking toward me,* I thought to myself. *Should I run? I can't run! Shit!* The internal debate continued until he was standing directly in front of me.

"Hello, may I help you?" he asked in French. I didn't respond. I just looked at him.

"Would you like a menu?" he asked in French. This time I mustered up a response.

"No. I'm just looking," I responded. He heard my accent and asked where I was from. I gave him the CliffsNotes version of my story: I'm from New York City, I just moved to Paris and I love the neighborhood. He insisted that I have something to eat before the end of the lunch service and I continuously politely declined until he said, "It's a beautiful day. Why not enjoy it?" My financial situation aside, I had no reason to not enjoy the beautiful day by having lunch at a café in my new city. After scanning the menu I ordered the cheapest main dish, *Moules à la Normande*—Normandy-style mussels—and a glass of white wine recommended by the waiter.

A few minutes after ordering, the waiter returned with a steaming pot full to the brim with mussels and a side of French fries. I wasn't expecting the mussels to be served in a medium-size pot, but I went with it. The first thing that caught my attention when I opened the pot was the smell. I closed my eyes and was instantly transported to the seaside. I looked down and saw black glossy opened mussels decorated with shallots, garlic and parsley in a sauce that I couldn't pinpoint until I took my first bite. It was a cream sauce made with *a lot* of butter. The silky smoothness of the sauce paired with the delicate sweetness of the shallots, the kick of the garlic and the earthiness of the parsley on the mussel rippled across my tongue. They were all very simple ingredients but like the tomatoes during my trip to Paris a few years prior, the way they were cooked allowed each ingredient to stand out. Each ingredient played its role with none overpowering the other; what they brought to the dish was respected to ensure you were delighted with the most flavorful and delicious meal. I was so captivated by this simple yet devastatingly good dish that I didn't notice the involuntary expressions that came across my face. I assume I looked satisfied because as I was leaving, the waiter said, "No regrets?" with a smirk on his face. "No, none," I responded with a big smile. After that meal I decided, like the Parisians, I would slow down and give myself the permission to enjoy what was around me. I didn't start eating at restaurants every day, but a few times a week I allowed my taste buds the pleasure of being transported by the beauty of Paris's culinary simplicity.

Surprisingly, despite the full-on How to Be Parisian 101 lessons that consumed my life, I didn't miss New York City. I loved that in my new life I woke up every morning next to my husband, birds singing in my courtyard and the buttery scent of fresh croissants wafting through the air. My growing identity as the American wife of a Frenchman living in Paris felt comfortable. It didn't feel like I was giving up anything. I was still very much myself; I was simply adding another layer to my story, to our family history. I was ready to conquer Paris.

I relished in Paris's significantly slower rhythm. Most businesses didn't open until ten in the morning and the day could not start without a *café-clope*—the sacred coffee and cigarette morning routine that most Parisian smokers adhere to. If you're not a smoker the bare minimum is a cup of coffee. I welcomed the absence of needing to hustle and always be busy. I felt tempted to write to one of the Americans-in-Paris bloggers that I had been following for years to let her know that everything was as they described it, glorious. They were right; Paris is a dream wrapped in a fantasy.

To me Paris felt like a mature city: the older, more confident sister of New York City. As a relatively young city compared to Paris, New York felt like it was always trying to prove something. It always had to be new and shiny, constantly evolving and adapting to every new trend that blew its way. Whereas Paris did not adapt to you, there was no bending or shaping and compromise was non-existent. It stood its elegant ground. Paris has been here for millennia, is still here, and will remain here no matter how many different types of people pass through her cobbled streets and grand boulevards. What you see is what you get, and you can either accept it or move on, but she's not changing for anyone. Without realizing it at the time, Paris was telling me, "I am who I am and soon enough, *petite fille*, you will find out who you really are, too." Paris had a few lessons up her sleeves waiting for me, but I was living in a moment of impenetrable newlywed bliss.

Everything felt new yet familiar at the same time. It was interesting witnessing the way TFM, my French boyfriend who visited me in New York City, transformed into TFM, my French husband I lived with in Paris. Most mornings I woke up to him kissing my cheeks hungrily or feeling his fingers tracing my lips or eyebrows. His appetite for me seemed insatiable and I delighted in it. Before leaving for work he left romantic notes that I found and basked in all day. He was a patient and helpful translator. He designed and built furniture for us. He was affectionate and attentive, kind and thoughtful. Those qualities didn't surprise me because they were what drew me to him for all these years. Living with him and witnessing those qualities intensify only reassured me. Our relationship felt safe from deceit, and I savored the innocence of new beginnings.

Nevertheless, the fact is that I didn't know everything about the French man that I woke up next to every morning. In the early days of our marriage I had only seen the positives of being married to someone from a different culture and living in their world—we were in a perpetual state of learning. I was learning about the different rituals, traditions and beliefs that helped to shape him into the person whom I fell in love with. He was learning about my culture and more about me but in a not-as-obvious way. Being in Paris meant that he didn't witness me in my element and day-to-day in a place of absolute comfort and familiarity, but there were other ways he learned about me and my culture, which was mostly through food.

I'm not a picky eater and I equated that quality with having a refined palate. I'm willing to try almost anything at least once, and I assumed that fact alone put me in the category of a sophisticated eater. Living in Paris made me realize that being curious about food, its origins and being willing to try something new isn't sophisticated or refined. It's simply the relationship that one has with food.

TFM's appreciation of every element that made up a meal wasn't unique to him. I noticed the same quality in many of the French people I knew personally, and in those whom I observed. They knew when fruits and vegetables were in season and tried their best to eat accordingly. Waiting for optimal ripeness was necessary in order to get the most pleasure. There was reverence around a well-cooked meal, and sharing it in good company transformed it to the main event of the day or evening. I chuckled when TFM and his friends talked about food while eating said food. Watching TFM and his friends try to decipher every element of the dish in front of us, from the combination of spices—was it ground cumin and smoked paprika?—to the ideal cooking method used to achieve the deep flavor—was it cooked in a pot on the stove or roasted?—was amusing. This was my first lesson in enjoying a meal for more than how my taste buds reacted. The entire practice of making a meal—the ingredients, method and story around it—is to be acknowledged and respected.

Once at a dinner party, before serving the main meal, the host asked if anyone in attendance had an aversion to cilantro. I raised my hand and said that I would prefer if she served me a portion without cilantro. The host kindly obliged and disappeared into the kitchen.

As soon as she disappeared into the kitchen, TFM scooted his chair closer to mine and whispered into my ear with confusion, "You don't like cilantro?"

"No, not a huge fan," I responded, not sure why this was such a big deal.

He scooted his chair away and took a good look at me then scooted back toward me and whispered into my ear again, "Since when?" he inquired.

Was he trying to start a fight? I thought to myself. I didn't expect my dislike of cilantro to cause an interrogation. "Since I was little," I responded, still whispering.

"Well, it's been a long time since you were little," he said to me with slight annoyance. "You're an adult now. Just try it again."

I didn't want to admit it, but he had a good argument. There was a possibility that my palate had evolved enough to enjoy and appreciate the citrusy freshness of cilantro. And he was right. After tasting a forkful of his beef topped with cilantro I deeply regretted my decision, and to this day I garnish almost everything with cilantro.

Over time I found myself enjoying different kinds of food that I shuddered at in my childhood—except olives, I still can't stomach those—and paying more attention to the process of cooking and the quality of the ingredients I use, not just the end result. That was all fine and dandy with me but sometimes I didn't want fresh herbs and perfectly in-season asparagus. While I didn't miss New York City life, I missed the food. There isn't a lack of restaurants in Paris, but the food landscape isn't very diverse. I was thrilled that I was able to indulge in a delicious duck breast at pretty much any neighborhood *brasserie*, but sometimes I craved a sandwich that wasn't *thon crudités*.

While at peak levels of newlywed bubble coziness we started bingeing *House of Cards*, the first Netflix blockbuster original, on the weekends. After a long week of TFM working and us spending time with his friends and family, we enjoyed spending quality time together and unwinding. We were about three episodes into the first season when I decided to make an American-style sandwich for one of our binge sessions. To me that meant a sandwich on toasted multigrain bread, no baguettes allowed. I was excited; TFM was suspicious but hungry and curious so he left me to my own devices. I decided to go down the breakfast sandwich route, a culinary experience that TFM wasn't familiar with. The end result was a sophisticated spin on the more traditional bacon, egg and cheese sandwich. On one slice of toasted whole grain bread I layered a fried egg, thin slices of smoked salmon and even thinner slices of avocado. The finishing touch was a smattering of mixed greens lightly dressed with salt, pepper and olive oil, all topped with the other slice of buttered toast. I tossed the remaining mixed greens with balsamic vinegar, olive oil, salt and pepper.

At first glance TFM eyed the sandwich with suspicion. "What's this?" he asked. "A smoked salmon sandwich," I responded. After examining it from every angle, TFM took a bite and his face instantly lit up. He paused the show, closed his eyes and threw his head back in delight while chewing. His reaction pleasantly surprised me because while making our sandwiches I braced myself to defend the simple goodness of slapping a bunch of seemingly random ingredients between two slices of bread and creating magic. Before finishing the second half of his sandwich he turned to face me, gently touched my hand and looked deep into my eyes—like he was falling in love all over again—and asked, "Can you please make this again...and other types of sandwiches?" American food, like sandwiches, is often tossed in the unsophisticated category and can sometimes cause offense to a more refined palate, but it tastes damn good and even TFM couldn't deny that.

A few weeks later TFM eagerly gobbled up a meatball sandwich dressed with silky roasted peppers, and I became convinced that I was closer to cracking the Rubik's Cube of bicultural, interracial, French-American marriages—just make sandwiches. I figured every food culture has some form of a sandwich, so the partner with the more superior sandwich culture simply needed to continuously feed the other one sandwiches from their culinary treasure chest. I started a mental list of all the sandwiches I wanted to make for TFM. However, I quickly learned that I became too confident in that theory and TFM's American sandwich consumption had its limits.

One Saturday morning after a Friday night dinner that involved too many bottles of wine, TFM rolled out of bed and left the apartment in search of croissants and baguettes. While he was away I managed to force myself out of bed and, with heavy legs and groggy eyes, began putting together brunch with bits and bobs in the kitchen. TFM returned to strawberry jam, salted butter, smoked salmon, avocado, a mix of different fruit we had left over and yogurt on the table while I was in the kitchen making scrambled eggs—a real smorgasbord brunch. When we finally sat down to eat I couldn't wait to dig in.

"What are you doing?" TFM asked when he saw me cut open the croissant.

"Making a sandwich," I said, matter-of-factly.

He didn't respond, thinking that I was going to add acceptable garnitures of butter and jam, but I didn't. Fright and confusion flashed across his face as I added a spoonful of scrambled eggs, some smoked salmon and a few slices of avocado into my croissant pocket. His jaw proceeded to drop open when I closed the sandwich and took a big bite, washing it down with a generous gulp of orange juice. The sandwich was good, but it needed something more, so I added a minuscule amount of ketchup just to the eggs.

"Do you wanna try?" I asked TFM, offering him some of my croissandwich.

"No, no, no," he said as he recoiled like he was in pain.

"Okay," I said, shrugging my shoulders. He watched me finish the entire sandwich in complete disbelief.

"How could you do that?" he asked with agony in his voice when I was finished.

"Do what?"

"That *thing* with the croissant," he answered. I looked at him blankly, genuinely confused. I didn't know what I did wrong. "You put all that *stuff* in it and then you put ketchup on it," he said.

"I didn't put ketchup on the croissant. I put it on the eggs and maybe some of the ketchup got on the croissant," I said, defending myself. "What's the big deal anyway?"

"The croissant is an institution! How could you be so disrespectful?" he angrily responded. I couldn't hold back my laughter.

"It's just a croissant," I said as I tried to regain my composure.

"It's not just a croissant," he responded. "It's my culture." He was offended that I would desecrate such a cultural icon.

I didn't quite understand why he was so up in arms or offended because the croissant isn't even French; it's Austrian in origin but I kept that to myself. Regardless of its origins, croissants have been a staple in French bakeries for centuries, and today most people put croissants in the French pastry category. It evokes a sense of pride among French people. Although other countries, like Italy, Spain and Portugal have their own version of a croissant, it's not as revered and world-renowned as the French croissant. I haven't tasted croissants from Spain but I have tried the Italian and Portuguese versions and even I, as an American who would dare defile the croissant by turning it into a sandwich, can admit that those versions didn't compare to the buttery-soft and sweet interior of the French croissant and its delicately flaky exterior.

Eventually, the croissandwich incident replaced the cheese-butter story and became one of our dinner party tales that we shared for a good laugh. He always ended the story by saying, "I watched her eat it in slow motion and when she finished it really hit me that I was married to an American. But that's okay because she's my American." I was proud to be the complementary half of a modern-day love story and romance. For me, our croissandwich story symbolized more than just a cross-cultural gaffe. It was laying the foundation for a marriage built on constant newness—we would never get bored. Our differing cultural backgrounds would always color our life together in interesting and unexpected ways. His retelling of the story and referring to me as *his American* gave me the impression that he came to the same realization and embraced it as a part of our life as a couple. I felt safe, loved and accepted.

As my first summer as a Parisian transitioned into fall, my newlywed bubble continued to expand. The constant flow of love being poured into it served to nourish and fortify what I thought I already knew. As far as I was concerned, I knew all of the thorniest parts of him, and everything else that I was to learn would either reinforce what I already knew or prove to be a positive discovery. We bickered occasionally, but not yet enough to cause worry. We argued from time to time, but not enough to make me want to flee. The thought of the bubble bursting never crossed my mind because it felt boundless.

I was his; he was mine.

Forever thine, forever mine.

Forever us.

Eight

WILL YOU BE MY FRIEND?

I was still enjoying playing housewife but besides my husband, his friends and his sister, I wasn't meeting anyone new. TFM and I were gliding toward a fusional relationship and that didn't seem smart or healthy.

A small part of me agonized about how much we both sacrificed, but I focused most of my energy on TFM and was overcome with pangs of guilt when I put myself in his shoes and thought about the crushing responsibility and pressure he must feel with his unemployed foreign wife dutifully waiting for him at home at the end of every day. I also knew that I wouldn't feel truly at home in Paris if I didn't have my own friends to confide in and also create new memories with. From my standpoint, creating my own social circle would alleviate some of the pressure I assumed he was under and give me an element of life in Paris that was entirely mine.

Meeting kindred spirits in controlled settings like at work or school is easier than trying to seek them out whenever you leave the comforts of your own home. The genesis of many of my great friendships began by asking for a pen during class or making eye contact with a colleague across the room who is also trying to stifle their laugh during a very important meeting. But how do you make a friend as an adult making your way through a foreign land? Do you just go up to them, awkwardly wave and say, "Hi, you look like you'd make a good friend?"

My friendships have always been central in my life and I find immense value in the intimacy of these platonic relationships because they give me the opportunity to live in different worlds, experience varied emotions and expand my views, for the better. I developed my first close adult friendship when I lived with Gabbie and Joli. I learned their values, what motivates them, what excites and saddens them, essentially what makes them human beings. The depth of commitment, without romantic motivations, that is required in friendships has given me the ability to think outside myself about issues and how my actions may affect others who are not a part of my immediate family.

These relationships are important to me because they are a result of a conscious and mutual decision to be a part of each other's lives, without being bound by family lineage or contractual obligation, like marriage. In the unfortunate event that a friendship ends there are no custody battles or contracts to sign that dissolve the relationship, and that is what makes them so uniquely special: they are nourished and deepened solely by mutual desire to continue. The intimacy of friendships takes the burden off yourself and your partner; there aren't too many expectations and that was why I needed it so badly.

I haven't always been the greatest friend. I've lost friends to mindless gossip that I didn't expect to get back to them, and I've since learned my lesson that if I can't share a sentiment directly with a friend, then I shouldn't say it at all. There have been times I've been hurt by comments or imagined slights and instead of communicating how I felt at the time, I allowed those friendships to fizzle out due to immaturity. This time, I vowed, things would be different when I started making friends in Paris.

I stopped myself from contacting the expat bloggers I followed because I felt self-conscious about my newness to the city and expat experience in relation to the more established Americans in Paris. I didn't want to be viewed as too impressionable, too naive or too much. My biggest problem in the early days of seeking out friendships in the expat circle was that I cared too much about what those women would think of me, preventing me from taking a crucial step and reaching out. The Americans-in-Paris bloggers that dominated the blogosphere, and that I followed, fell in the same category: very well-to-do, white and married to ideal men who were sensitive, smart, caring and cultured. They lived in breathtaking apartments on the tony Left Bank and seemingly glided through life in Paris without any discomfort, conflict or twinges of doubt. I didn't expect them to treat their blogs like intimate journals, but I naively believed that we would have similar experiences as foreigners in Paris and connect in that way. Until I built up enough courage to contact one of them, I set plan B into motion.

I had an American connection here that was outside TFM's social circle and his Paris. Cat was, at the time, the owner of the popular bakery Sugar Daze, and she made our wedding cake. Her American-style cakes appealed to me way more than the traditional *croque-en-bouche*, a tower of golden cream-filled balls that were more common at most French weddings. I rationalized that our meeting the day before my wedding justified my random appearance in her shop months later. So several months after devouring her Nutella-swirled cake with chocolate-hazelnut butter cream, I was heading back to her shop to say thank you for her delicious cake and with the ulterior motive of trying to make my first friend.

I strode confidently down the hill from Pigalle toward her

shop on rue Henry Monnier and walked right by it, on purpose. I was almost at the Saint-Georges metro station when I pulled myself together, turned around and walked back up the hill. I stopped at the window display, pretending to be a curious customer who just happened upon the shop. I eventually made my way in and was greeted with a warm and inviting smile, and a heavily accented *"Bonjour!"* Her long red hair was pulled back into a tight ponytail, and her hazel eyes twinkled when she spoke. The tattoo on her forearm was a surprising but intriguing element to this American in Paris who bakes cakes.

"Bonjour," I responded sheepishly.

"How can I help you?" she continued in French.

I wasn't even going to try to attempt to respond in French. "You made my wedding cake and I just wanted to come in and say thank you. It was delicious."

She paused, wiped her hands on the kitchen towel tucked into her apron, squinted in an attempt to recognize me before exclaiming, "Oh yes! I remember you. Congrats again!"

I'm not sure if she actually remembered me, but I was happy she decided to play along. I ordered a carrot cake cupcake, thanked her again for the wedding cake and left feeling triumphant.

I quickly became a regular. I went back three days in a row and ordered the same carrot cake while trying to learn more about Cat. On the third day, while stuffing my face with a cupcake and trying to tell a story about a recent encounter at a *boulangerie*, she stopped me midstory and asked, "So are you looking for a job or anything...?" She trailed off.

I assumed she wanted to get an idea of how much longer I would disturb her while she tried to work. After wiping crumbs off my face and shirt I said, "I'm sorta looking for a job." A look of amused puzzlement came across her face. "I worked in branding before I moved here and I want to continue in that field. I just don't know where to begin."

My full explanation seemed to relieve her. I wouldn't bother her for much longer. She offered to help put me in touch with Lindsey, a fellow American living in Paris, who worked at one of the big four advertising agencies. She didn't guarantee that meeting Lindsey would lead to a job, but was confident that Lindsey had the insider knowledge I needed to get my foot in the door. Great, I thought to myself. I went from knowing no Americans in Paris to knowing two Americans in Paris, and one of them might be able to get me a job.

A few weeks later I met Lindsey over coffee and chai tea at Café Loustic, and we hit it off immediately. I talked about my Paris journey, my husband and my career up until that point and she shared her story, too. Lindsey immediately struck me as sincere and kind, and I silently thanked Cat for introducing us. While I did want and need a job, making new friends took precedence, and I left our coffee date with instructions to send her my résumé and what I hoped was a potential friend.

That encounter was my first taste of how close-knit and intertwined the American in Paris community is. And it makes sense. As foreigners far away from home we have to create new circles of friendships and comforts. We understand small things from pop culture references to major turning points in our country's history and how they influenced and shaped us. We understand each other on a deep cultural level that our partners and foreign-born children sometimes won't, because for as long as we live in Paris they'll always be home in a way that we never will.

A few weeks after my meeting with Lindsey, TFM and I found ourselves at a housewarming barbecue in Montreuil, a close eastern suburb right outside the *périphérique*. The *périphérique* is a circular border that distinguishes Paris from everything else. All of Paris's arrondissements are housed within the circle, and everything else is considered a suburb. I was less than enthused about the barbecue. Overwhelmed with hearing French all the time, the move and being constantly on the go, I just wanted a quiet weekend, but that wasn't an option because the couple was a part of TFM's inner circle.

I knew the couple, having met them during previous trips to Paris, so while it was nice to see familiar faces, I immediately shrank upon arrival because I knew no one else. After politely introducing myself as TFM's wife, I found a seat away from the crowd and sat there with a glass of wine. TFM was off talking to his friends and I was being kept company by a bored ten-year-old who wouldn't stop staring at me. Scanning my surroundings, I noticed two groups of women. One group of around four or five women huddled together next to the table of food, whispering and giggling among themselves in the way that longtime friends do, and the remaining women, a twosome, were laughing and talking with the men. I quickly worked out that there would be no potential friends found here and signaled to TFM that I needed another glass of wine.

In addition to the wine he brought along the twosome, Sylvie and Samar, with him. Sylvie sat on my right and Samar on my left. As soon as he delivered the wine and left Samar asked, "Why do you speak English?" Sylvie looked on, also quite keen to hear my response. I was taken aback and didn't know how to respond. Did they miss my introduction, I wondered? "Um, I'm American. That guy there is my husband." I pointed to TFM. "Ohhhhh," Samar said before sipping her cocktail. With her spiky pixie cut, multicolored outfit and stiff cocktail, instead of wine like all of the other ladies were drinking, Samar stood out from the crowd. She obviously wasn't scared to strike up a conversation and let her presence be known. Sylvie was more reserved and more conventional in her appearance. She wore her hair in one very long braid, and her choice of clothing was the standard Parisian black and white. I was dressed more like Sylvie, in blue jeans and a plain T-shirt. Samar's raspy voice and mischievous laugh drew me in, while Sylvie's reserve reminded me that I was on display. The striking differences in the two made me wonder how they knew each other and why the hell they were talking to me.

Samar began peppering me with questions. "Where are you from?"

"When did you move?"

"Do you have a job yet?"

"What do you think of Parisians?" In between sips of wine I responded, "New York,"

"A few weeks ago,"

"No" and "I love them."

She cackled at the last response. "You're new," she said and took a big gulp of her cocktail. Sylvie slowly faded out of the picture and my focus was on Samar. I learned that she and her husband, Filip, were both Lebanese and had moved to Paris a few years ago. As our conversation continued, I wondered if she could become a friend. Her assured and opinionated personality didn't scare me. She reminded me of my friends back in New York City and Connecticut. By the end of the barbecue, we exchanged contact information and made promises to meet up for coffee, which we did. Over the course of weeks and months we got to know each other, and she shared what she had learned about living in Paris as a foreigner.

What I didn't know at that backyard barbecue was that I was sitting next to a woman who clearly knew who she was and wasn't going to compromise her sense of self and self-love for anyone or any culture. There's a difference between integrating into a culture and losing yourself in a culture. Integrating means being genuinely interested in the culture and showing your interest by learning the language, the rules, understanding why people do things, respecting the place you live and the people. Losing yourself in a culture means forgetting everything that makes you special and unique in order to fit in.

I met Samar at a crucial point in my Paris journey—the very

beginning. I had to decide, whether consciously or subconsciously, how I was going to live this experience. Was I going to absorb French culture and my husband's life whole and as a result lose myself, or would I try to build a life with my husband where I balanced the delicate act of integrating and respecting the French way, while remaining true to myself? I decided that I wanted to be an expat like Samar. I wanted to confidently integrate enough to feel comfortable and a part of a world I now inhabited, but not at the expense of forgetting who I was at my core. During our budding friendship she inadvertently shared lessons that would serve me as my life in Paris evolved and the delicate balance of integration, marriage and my own needs started to tremble. I couldn't have predicted the fast-approaching storm, but at least I knew to never forget what was most important: me.

Integration, even if only on my terms, was important and a part of that process included befriending French people and especially French women. There were very few people who had anything nice to say about Parisiennes, women who live in Paris, and I naively believed and internalized those preconceived notions. TFM's friends were lovely and welcoming, but I often questioned if that was because of my connection to their childhood friend. Would they have welcomed me as warmly otherwise?

The image of Parisiennes that was burned into my psyche is that of a very sultry and sexy femme fatale. Of course, the only makeup she wears is an immaculate shade of red lipstick because her skin and eyelashes are already perfect—she doesn't need anything else. The Parisienne femme fatale could switch, with the snap of a finger, from charming you with her intelligence and cultural aptitude to piercing your heart with her stiletto heel—which she magically is able to wear on cobblestone streets—then watch you bleed out and die while she smokes her skinny

Vogue cigarette and enjoys a glass of vintage red wine. Suffice it to say I was intimidated. My negative preconceived notions of French people, and Parisiennes in particular, kept me firmly in the observer role until my curiosity around the lessons that I could learn from these mysterious people got the best of me.

Initially, I tried my hand at language-exchange events hosted by various bars across the city. The language-exchange events were akin to language-acquisition speed dating. After spending a few minutes going over the basics—where you're from, the duration of your stay in Paris and your hobbies—the timer went off and shuffled along to the next participant. I wasn't expecting the events to be so overwhelmed with French men.

"Bonjour, je m'appelle Sutanya," I said to the man sitting across from me. The combination of his wavy chestnut-brown hair and blue eyes was mesmerizing, and he knew it. He couldn't stop running his fingers through his hair, and he rarely broke eye contact, not even to blink. That should've been the first warning sign that something was off with this guy. As we exchanged niceties it became apparent that he was able to correct my French in English because he spoke perfect English.

"Vous parlez trés bien anglais," I eventually said, complimenting his English, while trying to steer the conversation back to French. He acknowledged his mastery of the English language without offering up any additional information. But I needed to know why and how, so I asked.

He responded, again in perfect English, "I lived in Australia for a few years."

I was visibly taken aback and asked, "Well, why are you here?"

He raised an eyebrow and with a smirk on his face said, "To meet beautiful women like you."

"But I'm *married*," I said.

"Yes, and? Is that a problem?" he teased.

An audible gasp left my mouth; I was shocked. After his confession I looked around the room and took note of the fact that all the male attendees were French, while the women were English-speaking foreigners. I was unintentionally attending a singles event disguised as language exchanges. I grabbed my bag with unnecessary force and marched out of the bar, bursting out in laughter on my way to the metro. *How many more times will this happen?* I thought to myself. My naivety kept leading me into situations that were so plainly straightforward, but my vision was obscured by rosé-tinted glasses.

After learning the true purpose of the in-person language-exchange events I decided to go back to the internet, the source that helped me foster my most meaningful relationship with a French person to date. After some rudimentary Googling I found a website called Conversation Exchange. After creating your profile, with a photo of yourself if you wanted to, and a little blurb about why you wanted to learn the language of your choice, the language buddy possibilities became endless. It didn't feel one hundred percent dissimilar to online dating but it was easier to weed out the men who were clearly using the website as a hunting ground to meet women. After a few weeks of ignoring suspicious messages, a woman named Estelle reached out to me. She was a nurse living in Paris who wanted to improve her English for work. Our messages convinced me that she wasn't a man trying to catfish me, so we decided to meet at Rosa Bonheur, one of the recently opened bars on the banks of the Seine.

Walking toward the Seine felt like I was going on a first date. I wanted her to like me, find me interesting and funny and take me into her Parisian fold. My biggest fear that day was coming off as a bumbling idiot. Upon meeting we exchanged the traditional *bise*—I hadn't attempted to hug a French person since the incident with my mother-in-law—and off I started in my broken French. I learned that she recently moved to Paris and was a nurse at a local hospital. Her desire to improve her English stemmed from wanting to better connect with her patients. Working in the neonatal department meant that she encountered a lot of new mothers of premature babies who suffered from various ailments. She reasoned that this was already a stressful situation to be in so when she had patients who were more comfortable speaking English she wanted to be able to connect with them and communicate vital information in a language that was familiar to them and their partners. She wanted to alleviate as much stress and worry as possible. I was impressed by her compassion and thoughtfulness.

Estelle extended that thoughtfulness and compassion to our language exchange as well. She didn't overcorrect me and actually humored me by complimenting my level of French. I did the same, but the difference was that her level of English comprehension far surpassed mine in French. She understood more English than she spoke. Halfway through our friend-date we switched completely to English because it would be easier for the both of us.

"So where did you learn English?" I eventually asked her.

Sheepishly, she said, "*Gossip Girl*. You know, the show."

I found that little tidbit sweet and endearing. Coupled with her sensitive nature I knew she was definitely another potential friend and someone I wanted in my Parisian life. Although Estelle isn't Parisienne, as I got to know her and grow my circle of girlfriends I began deconstructing the stereotypes I had around the Parisienne—who she is and what she represents—and gaining agency from TFM as I started to stand on my own two feet.

While my potential-friend dates didn't become less nerve-wracking, my apprehension waned around making it obvious that I wanted, and needed, friends in my life. For me, in order to have a full and satisfying marriage I needed other forms of intimate relationships that didn't involve TFM. I needed something that was wholly mine in this new environment in order to retain a sense of identity outside of my husband and circumstances. Eventually, my willingness and honesty around making friends led to a steady flow of invitations that were hard to say no to. Unfortunately, as time went on I learned that balancing a new marriage, new friends and new life required more finesse than I had developed.

Nine

AU TRAVAIL

La réentrée is the first few weeks of early fall that signals the end of summer loafing, vacations and general idleness, except *apéros*. *Réentréé apéros* are necessary for catching up with friends you haven't seen all summer. And like everyone else, after a rosé-fueled summer and travels I had a lot to share. My coffee date with Lindsey in the beginning of the summer crescendoed into a series of interviews at the advertising agency where she worked until I landed my first job working with her on the digital team.

After sharing the job update with friends I launched into my vacation tales. Our first summer trip as husband and wife was to the seaside city of La Rochelle where we spent a long weekend with TFM's aunt and uncle. We ate seafood by the port and stole kisses while standing in line to buy ice cream. After La Rochelle we drove down to Bollène, a small town in Provence, where we spent a week with several of his friends. Our weeklong stay consisted of mostly lounging by the pool, making sure the grill was always ready to be used at any moment and drinking white wine in abundance. Then we flew to Egypt where we stayed with German friends, Hendrik and Kerstin, who were living on a houseboat in Cairo. The chaotic energy of Cairo surprised and intrigued me, and seeing the Giza pyramids in person mesmerized me. However, due to residual tensions from the June 2013 protests and coup, we ended up having to flee Cairo to the nearest desert with less than an hour's notice, and a few days later we escaped on one of the last flights out of the country. The experience left me jittery. We ended our summer travels at his family's country house in Marigny-Brizay, a sleepy village in the Nouvelle-Aquitaine region, with Annie and Emma, my mother-in-law and sister-in-law, where we read, lazed about the garden, went for runs and survived our first vacation as a new family.

The frenzied itinerary of our summer and unexpected evacuations led to several disputes—caused by stress, tension and fear. However, like the trusty Americans-in-Paris bloggers I read while in Connecticut, we always made up. But that didn't stop me from noticing that TFM angered at lightning speed and became ferocious and cold when we fought. His words cut deep and deposited small grains of worry and confusion that I attributed to the stress of what we were living—from being newlyweds to fleeing a country on the brink of civil war. I shrewdly kept the arguments and descriptions of my tears out of the retelling of our vacation adventures.

I assumed once we returned to our normal lives my mostly fluid shift from New York City to Paris, from unemployed to holder of the elusive CDI (French work contract), from single to married would only continue to encourage and embolden me. My seemingly easy transition into the cultural framework and French life, for me, solidified that I was on the proper path to becoming a bona fide Parisienne and everything was falling into place, as it should. I justified that hiccups are normal in the beginning of any marriage, and this was an opportunity to learn more about my husband. I didn't imagine that his mood swings were something that I would ever have to learn to navigate and ultimately decide if I could accept. I buried my feelings around the newly discovered side of TFM and chose to focus on my next American in Paris assignment: working with the French.

The prospect of earning money again and tapping into another facet of French culture was appealing. Becoming gainfully employed only two months after moving, with my rosé-tinted glasses still firmly in place, was the perfect way to develop a deeper understanding of French culture. My previous experience in an agency environment in New York City gave me ample experience in handling the egos and personalities that usually run amok in that world, and the strategic and cutthroat mindset needed to succeed. Before moving, I questioned my capability to morph into the type of person who could survive and thrive in that environment. I enjoyed the actual work itself—helping brands assess where and how they can stand out in their specific market and/or industry, then helping create and tell their story to their target audience—so I relied on a change of environment to help reignite my overall enthusiasm for the industry.

The agency was in the suburban southwest neighborhood of Boulogne-Billancourt, just outside the confines of the *peripherique*, not on the glitzy Champs-Elysées or sprinkled across the city center like other agencies. Paris is small and compact compared to New York City, and I didn't anticipate the one-hour door-to-door commute. I had a habit of navigating Parisian streets like a New Yorker; I expected the layout to resemble a grid. In my mind, logically, street names remained the same for its entire length but Parisian streets didn't follow that reasoning. As a result I often found myself lost and late to many *rendezvous*. To lessen the chances of being late on my first day of work TFM sat me down and we went over the directions in great detail. He quizzed me on the metro changes I needed to make and peppered me with reminders that I needed to follow a map and not just assume that I knew where I was going. And on my first day with a kiss on my forehead and a "You rock!" from TFM—a phrase of encouragement widely used by French people that I still don't really understand—I was out the door. Small acts of tenderness like this temporarily sealed the tiny fissures that were beginning to appear in our marriage.

All the coffee I drank the morning of my first day put the butterflies in my stomach into overdrive. While on the metro I looked around to make sure no one was eyeing me suspiciously. The fluttering from my stomach felt so imposing I half expected my fellow commuters to hear the flapping coming from under my denim shirt. By the time I walked through the black doors of my new place of employment my spirits were high and the butterflies finally decided to take a break from wreaking havoc on my nervous system.

Lise, my manager, welcomed me and introduced me to my new team. It was a relief to see Lindsey's familiar face as French names were being spit out at me with the owners of said names barely raising their heads to acknowledge me. I was given a quick tour of the most important places: the coffee machine, the cafeteria/dining hall where you could eat your lunch if you decided not to go out to a restaurant and the smoking spot. I expected my orientation to go beyond the spot where everyone smoked, so after my tour I sat at my desk waiting to be summoned for the real orientation where I would learn more about the client and the agency itself. But that didn't happen. It was a sink-or-swim environment, and I was doggy paddling along. I was thrown right into working on presentations and writing social media posts (all in English). My first week I had my first solo call with the client and within two weeks I was on a plane with Lise and Lindsey visiting them in Geneva.

The first few weeks I was in observation mode, so I mostly kept to myself besides my immediate team. I was interested in seeing how the French work culture differed from the United States's. I expected some similarities because the practice of advertising and branding share basic tenets no matter the country; the difference is in the execution. I was curious to see if I could connect larger cultural behaviors to certain workplace behaviors. My amateur ethnographic studies went into overdrive.

One of the first things that captured my attention was that during the hours between noon and 2 p.m. the entire office emptied out; everyone went to lunch at the same time. Phones went unanswered, emails were taken care of in due time and meetings were not scheduled during those sacred hours. The American work culture and customs were still deeply ingrained in me and dictated the way I approached work, so I didn't have the same reverence toward that two-hour window of time in the afternoon. While everyone was enjoying their *plat du jour*, I was behind my desk chomping on a sandwich and working. My expectation was that my motivation and dedication would impress my manager. Lise was the young superstar in the agency; she created the digital team and was held in high esteem by the upper management. She was under a lot of stress to perform and deliver, which explained her aloofness and hands-off management style until she showed that she was paying attention to the people on her team.

One typical afternoon, while everyone was at lunch and I was finishing my sandwich at my desk, Lise walked into the open workspace with a determined look on her face. This was out of character since she was usually one of the post-lunch stragglers.

"Hey, Sutanya, can we talk for a minute?" she asked.

"Yeah, sure." I got up from my seat, racking my brain as to what I could've done to merit this one-on-one chat. Making my way to her desk I reasoned that I had only been there a few weeks, not enough time to cause any real damage.

"So I notice that you've been eating lunch at your desk a lot," she began. I didn't reply because I wanted to see where this was going. After an awkward pause she continued, "Is everything okay?"

"Yes, everything's fine," I responded.

"Are you sure?" she began digging. "Is it because you don't have any friends yet?"

This conversation was taking all sorts of twists and turns I wasn't expecting. I let out an uneasy chuckle. "Um, no, not really," I responded. "I mean, I wouldn't say that I've made tons of friends, but that's not a problem really. I have lunch at my desk so that I can work."

She looked at me with sadness and irritation. I couldn't figure out if she felt bad for me or was appalled by my decision. I soon found out that she was insulted. "Why would you do that?" she asked.

"To catch up," I responded.

She shook her head in disbelief and released a big sigh. "There is no need to do that," she said. "It's important to take a break during the day. You must. Do you understand?" I managed to nod my head. She continued, "And if you don't have anyone to have lunch with you tell me. We can have lunch together."

Am I being hazed? I thought. In all of the years that I've been in the workforce, I've never had a manager force me to take a lunch break, much less sincerely offer to have lunch with me. Where I was from, working through lunch was the norm; taking a break was reserved for special occasions. In order to adapt to this new world, I had to eat lunch with my colleagues every day.

The relationships among colleagues intrigued me. From an outsider's perspective I was impressed by how frank and honest they were with each other. They knew each other's families and spent time together outside the office environment. Their relationships were more akin to friendship than professional. It wasn't uncommon to build those kinds of relationships in an American work environment, but after my impromptu therapy session with Lise, I quickly realized that having a social circle at work held much greater importance in France than I expected or was used to.

Pauline, a young brunette on my team, was my first target. I assumed that my status as an American from New York City would add to my cool factor and help my case, but I was quickly proven wrong. After one lunch and not a lot of spark she avoided eye contact and politely dodged my follow-up invitations. I didn't attempt to ride Lindsey's coattails since she was the more experienced and known American around the office. I had no reason to think it would've been a problem if I tethered myself to her, but she had already gone above and beyond by helping me get this job. The last thing I wanted to do was be her shadow, following her around the agency with the sad puppy-dog eyes of the lonely foreigner.

I worked hard to not draw any attention to my solo lunches by leaving for lunch before everyone else, as if I had someone waiting for me, and coming back early; I wanted to avoid another heart-to-heart about my lack of lunch buddies. My strategy failed. The few times Lise came to the café area, she would find me there alone with my sandwich, reading a book or scrolling on my phone. I didn't equate my lack of a friend group with any failing on my part; I assumed it would take time. In the same way that I was taking stock of who they were, they were probably wondering who was the strange American woman that was tied to her desk all day and seemingly enjoyed having lunch alone.

It's unclear why Lise took such interest in what she perceived to be a dreaded plight that needed to be fixed. Perhaps she felt bad for me and didn't want me to start my career in France as an outcast. Whatever her motivations may have been, one afternoon my solo lunches became too much for her and she invited me to have lunch with her and two fellow rising stars at the agency: Emilie, a shrewd account director, and Marine, a whip-smart strategist. While *en terrasse*, sunglasses on and enjoying our salads, I decided to use a lull in the conversation to share something personal about myself. "Would you like to see my wedding photos?" I asked. There was a pause and then a hesitant, "Okay, why not?" I didn't see who responded because I was already swiping through the photos, going into detail about the guests, my joy and happiness on the day and the price of my dress. At the end of my slideshow Emilie asked, "Why did you show those to us?"

I was taken aback and speechless by the candor of her question. I giggled awkwardly and stuffed my mouth with lettuce to avoid answering but they were looking at me, waiting for a response. After slowly swallowing the last bit of salad I said, "Because it was one of the best days of my life in recent memories."

After prolonged silence, Marine commented, "Well, that's very intimate."

That sentiment was true, but I had been surprised by the invitation and desperately wanted to make a good impression and I tried too hard. Sharing those photos was my graceless attempt at creating a connection. I didn't confess this to the group, but I replayed that moment in my mind for weeks. That was my first peek into how French people approach friendships. They aren't fast and furious the way that Americans tend to be. There isn't a desire to share everything about your life within the first week of meeting to solidify a connection or the desire to get to know each other. Of course, it can happen where you share more than usual but that should be organic, not your modus operandi. The belief is that if you share everything within the first week or first month, what is left to discover? You can be yourself and confident in your sense of self, but there is no need to tell everyone your entire life story from birth until the present moment.

Over the course of weeks and months I changed my approach.

Instead of being too much of an open book I allowed people to discover more about me in due time, but I needed to be visible in order to do that. The first stop on my visibility tour was to the smokers' section; their break intervals were frequent enough for them to get used to me and there was always a rotating cast of characters from other departments. The smokers introduced me to other people they knew and before I knew it I was a regular. My second stop was to the floor above me, where the client management team sat; there was another New Yorker on the team, Jennifer, so I used our common city origins as a way to wiggle my way into her work crew. I played on similar interests in order to try to form genuine connections, not by using my colleagues as my personal diary.

My strategy of allowing work friendships to develop slowly and flourish naturally proved to be fruitful when a few months after I started, Emilie suggested that we have "French lunch" together once a week. The rule was to only speak French during those lunches to help me improve my conversation and comprehension skills. I was taken aback by the suggestion, but happy that I was forming relationships the French way. Over time I started looking forward to our lunches for both the French language component and nurturing a budding friendship with Emilie. She was one of the first women who helped to demystify *la Parisienne*. Simply because she was just really nice to me.

Our personal relationship aside, the lunches had a positive effect on my French. Every week I became more comfortable speaking, began moving away from simple vocabulary and felt more confident. I still had a long way to go, but the improvement was undeniable. We tried not to talk about work; our day-to-day lives and my observations about Paris and Parisians were way more interesting and entertaining.

One afternoon I had a story on the tip of my tongue that I couldn't wait to tell her. I practiced the retelling of the story in my head all morning; I knew it was going to land spectacularly.

As usual, at 12:30 we made our way to Le Bistro de la Ferme for my French lessons. When we sat down I didn't look at the menu. I ordered the same *plat du jour* she did; only later would I realize that I didn't exactly hear correctly. As predicted, my story was a success and I wrapped it up just as our dishes were arriving. We each said *"bon appétit"* and started eating while continuing our conversation.

At one point during our meal Emilie released a satisfying sigh and said in French, "This is so good. It's been a long time since I've had *lapin*." I thought this was strange because it's on almost every restaurant menu, so in response I said, "Really? But every restaurant menu has *magret de....*" and I stopped myself because I realized that what I thought I was eating and what I was actually eating were two different things. I looked at Emilie, pointed at my plate in front of me and asked, "*Lapin* is not *canard* [duck], is it?" She could barely contain her laughter. "No, it's not." I shook my head in agreement and asked, "*Lapin* is rabbit, isn't it?" At this point she was laughing so hard she could barely speak but managed to eke out a response. "Yes, it is," she said. I instantly lost my appetite.

That story made its way back to the agency and was met with lots of laughter and friendly teasing. I was making my way into the agency social circle naturally, not by forcing intimacy but by simply being myself—an overly enthusiastic American.

As my social circle at the agency began to solidify, there were other aspects that I noticed were par for the course like the egos and competitiveness. I expected and braced myself for that. However, the more I became a part of the work culture, and began understanding what was going on around me, the things that I witnessed and heard became increasingly absurd. I had gotten used to the boundary-pushing jokes and open sexism that permeated the office. Everyone laughed at them and usually I either stayed quiet or chuckled along uncomfortably. I wasn't always ready or willing to ruffle any feathers, but the level of ego-driven patriarchal chauvinism usually left me speechless. However, the moments when a "joke" about race or gender went too far and I interjected, my objections were usually met with a chuckle and a comment about me being *trop Américaine*— way too uptight and too easily offended.

The three men who headed the agency played a significant role in fostering an environment that forced you to mouth "WTF" to your colleagues at least twice a week. One was a prankster who left distasteful messages on any unattended computer that hadn't yet gone into sleep mode and routinely told lewd jokes to an apathetic audience. The other dressed almost exclusively in The Kooples, a high-end *prêt-à-porter* French brand, and everything he wore was a smidgen too small for him. He was dogged by rumors of having an arsenal of weapons in his apartment. It was easy to believe this rumor considering the fact that he had an ax encased in a glass box hanging above his office door. When he wasn't in his office staring wistfully at his ax he was shuffling around the open space in search of snacks, asking us *"Personne n'a quelque chose à grignoter?"* Sometimes he went as far as rummaging through people's desks in search of his afternoon treat if they weren't present. The third one, obviously still making up for lost time in high school and university, had a penchant for female interns that was widely known and accepted. These interns were adults, of course, and they were consensual relationships, but one could not ignore the imbalance of power and conflict of interest.

The trifecta of desperately trying so hard to be cool, misogyny and lack of boundaries came to a head at a company-wide meeting. The entire company gathered in a new amphitheater to celebrate the recent move into the building we now occupied. There was a collective groan as our managers corralled us to the theater. It was a Friday and we all hoped it wouldn't encroach too much on our well-deserved TGIF *apéros*. A low-murmuring hum filled the room while we all took our seats, waiting for the three big men on campus to start and finish as quickly as possible. The rumored artilleryman of the group approached the makeshift podium and that was the first time I noticed that he was wearing a kilt. *I didn't know he had Scottish heritage*, I thought to myself. I didn't think that the inauguration of this building meant so much to him that he felt the need to wear ancestral garb. But whatever, to each his own.

With both of his hands firmly clasped on the sides of the podium, he began his speech. It was awash with talk of "synergies,"

"disruptive strategies,"

"innovation,"

"snackable content" and a plethora of additional buzzwords that usually don't mean much on their own, so it was even more confusing when they were strung together in run-on sentences. After the speech everyone was looking at their watches and around for the nearest exit, when suddenly the lights went off and techno music started. In the darkness I only saw the silhouetted heads of my colleagues bopping to the beat, but I imagined their faces were painted with the same confused expression as mine. Then as quickly as the lights went off they were back on and the first part of our entertainment entered the room.

Strippers.

A female stripper painted in silver with a strategically placed sash wrapped across her body and a male stripper wearing striped underwear. As they gyrated around the makeshift stage, two little people were introduced and began fighting with each other. As if it couldn't get any more surreal, a marching band arrived and the climax was the introduction of a llama. You could hear a pin drop and I couldn't believe what I was seeing. This wasn't happening. They were reenacting a scene from *The Wolf of Wall Street*. The CEO stood on the side with a big grin on his face, so pleased with himself. Before leaving I snapped a photo with the llama; I needed proof. And I left in disgust.

Things at home weren't great but after that night I had something interesting to talk about with TFM. Something that we would both find so absurd it would remind us of the few things that we did have in common.

Ten

THE CRACKS

Settling into Paris and married life involved slowly lifting the curtain to reveal our true selves. Before getting married we'd never experienced the wrath of each other's bad moods or the heights of our respective anxiety, and when we were confronted with it we didn't know what to do. Learning how to share our space and lives for more than fifteen days at a time was demanding. While distance played an influential factor in the naivety of what our marriage would be, youth played a more substantial role in not understanding the depths of patience, compassion and compromise it takes to be in a marriage with someone who is as complicated and flawed as you are. We no longer had Gmail or text messages to buffer our conflicts and give us time to craft well-thought-out responses. We were face-to-face and it was raw.

Astrologically speaking, Virgos, such as myself, and Capricorns, like TFM, are destined to be a blissful match in all aspects of life—especially love and professional, but as our marriage progressed I was learning that didn't apply to this Virgo and Capricorn pairing. Being a Virgo, I should have been a perfect match for my Capricorn partner's intellect, drive, ambition, financial savvy and stoicism. It didn't take long for us to realize that our stars were maybe, potentially, not very aligned. I never had a problem holding my own in a debate, but I wasn't quite as driven in the same way that he was. He was on a fast track to the C-suite at the consulting firm where he worked while my dissatisfaction at the advertising agency was at an all-time high and I wasn't doing anything about it.

He knew about and supported my desire to focus on creative writing. Like any supportive partner he encouraged me, either verbally or by gifting me various "how to be a better writer" books. He wanted me to write now. I wanted to daydream and stay in my head a little while longer. Where he worried about our budget, I was the fast-fashion queen. He was completely fluent in English, I was still struggling with French despite several years of studying the language. The more I settled into life in Paris and asserted my independence by going out all the time with my newfound friends the more alienated we became. We bickered everywhere and in front of everyone. We quickly went from being the cool, bicultural, interracial couple at the party to the couple at the party who stayed away from each other all night, and if we did find ourselves in same conversation it was wrought with tension. The foundation of our relationship was built on fleeting, passion-filled weeks together and sustained through the mutual feeling of missing each other. Now that we didn't have that, what did we have?

Months turned into the one-year mark of my move and marriage, and I was becoming increasingly frustrated with my French language acquisition. I reached my first plateau and was at a standstill. My social life continued to improve while my private life was secretly deteriorating. The kisses and long nights, and mornings, spent in each other's arms in bed were replaced with a symphony of yelling, name-calling and slammed doors. We reached a point where it was impossible to get along. I was still very much in love with TFM, and placed this period under the umbrella of post-wedding blues. I vowed to learn to love *all* of him, not just the sparkly and shiny bits that I was used to.

My desire to continue enlarging my circle of Parisienne friends was partially about creating an independent life outside TFM and giving each other space. The other side of that desire was exploring whether or not forming meaningful connections with French women would help me connect better with him. We still spoke English exclusively at home. Dinners and *apéros* with his friends often started in English until too many bottles of wine and beers were consumed, then the conversation naturally transitioned into French. I appreciated his friends' efforts to make me feel welcomed but that didn't stop me from feeling left out. When TFM was holding court among his friends—telling jokes and engaged in intense debates—I witnessed an ease in his body language and liberty in the way he spoke that I didn't see when we were alone. At home we circled around each other without being able to dig in. The heaviness of speaking different languages, figuratively and literally, weighed on us.

We often went to his mother's for lunch on Sundays. I loved this tradition and looked forward to it because I found immense comfort whenever I was in Annie's space and in her presence. The warmth and love in her apartment, and from her, helped to fill the void of not having my own mother in the same city.

But one particular Sunday even the comfort of Annie's apartment couldn't hide the ever-expanding strain on our relationship. It was a very bad day for TFM and me. Our conversation didn't go beyond, "Can you please pass the potatoes?" punctured with countless sighs from me and eye rolls from TFM. Annie noticed, but didn't say anything at the table. She is discreet and discerning, and bringing unwanted attention to someone didn't interest her. I always admired her ability to stay objective and not give unsolicited advice about our married life. She didn't view her son as an extension of herself or treat me as a threat to their relationship. I always felt welcomed, loved and accepted; we both genuinely admired each other and it was obvious in the ease of our relationship with each other and how much fun we had together. From shopping trips to spontaneous sing-alongs in her living room belting out Serge Gainsbourg and Jane Birkin, we wholeheartedly enjoyed each other's company, and most importantly she respected my marriage to her son and us—me and TFM—as adults. But I imagine that what she witnessed caused enough discomfort, and potentially panic, that she felt compelled to say something, anything.

After lunch I went into the kitchen where I was loading the dishwasher and aggressively clearing the countertops. I was hurting and annoyed. TFM and I were at a standstill and I didn't want to surrender because I didn't know how. I spent so much time feeling guilty about how much TFM's life changed after we got married and I moved, and I wanted my sacrifices to be recognized in the same way. While I was stewing and becoming increasingly angrier, Annie walked into the kitchen with the remaining dishes and gently placed them on the countertop, snapping me out of my trance. She tried to help me load the dishwasher, but I playfully shooed her away. She sat by the window on the metallic-gray stool, lit a cigarette and took a drag before asking, *"Ça va?"*

"Yes, I'm doing okay," I responded.

"No, between you and TFM," she said.

I stopped busying myself, wiped my hands on the kitchen towel and turned to face her, my lower back firmly against the sink. That was the very first time Annie had ever asked me such a personal question about our relationship, and I knew that she asked because she felt that something was terribly wrong. Even if everything in me wanted to unload my burden onto someone else. At this point I hadn't shared my marriage woes with anyone. How could I admit to my mother-in-law that her son and I were at an impasse so soon in our marriage?

The transition from long-distance lovers to a married couple was ripping us apart. I stood in silence, avoiding eye contact.

"I notice the way you and TFM talk to each other. It's not normal," she said. She was right. But the link between my brain and my mouth stopped functioning and I was at a loss for words. She continued, "I don't want to be rude, but maybe you should spend more time at home. You always talk about going out a lot, which is good, but maybe you don't have to go out every night. Maybe he misses you."

She was referring to my active *apéro* schedule. I spent most weeknight evenings sharing bottles of wine with my colleagues. Sometimes they were planned in advance and other times I would text TFM at the last minute, letting him know that I wouldn't be home that night for dinner, so cooking wasn't necessary. I would eat cornflakes or something when I got home much later that night. Sometimes I sent the message so late, while I was already with my colleagues, TFM would've already made dinner for us and he ended up eating it by himself.

Again, she was right. But how could I tell her that I felt that staying away from home is what kept our relationship alive? Being passing ships in the night helped to re-create the distance that we were so used to, the only thing that felt familiar in our relationship.

"I know," I finally said. "You're right."

She came over and gently caressed my face and gave me a kiss on the cheek. I turned around to continue cleaning the counter, tears spilling from my eyes.

TFM and I found ourselves in a push-and-pull power play dynamic that was hard to break out of. This was my first time living with a romantic partner, so I didn't have the tools necessary to address and fix the situation. I became so focused on my own sacrifices and life changes that I couldn't see things from TFM's perspective. I wanted some sympathy and recognition, too. Lying to TFM and not sharing my feelings with him became my go-to strategy to mitigate any arguments and keep his mood in check, but inevitably he would become aware of what I was hiding or omitting and the cycle started again. When we argued, I cried and stormed out of the apartment. I'm not proud of my behavior—the lies and how I reacted—they remain some of my biggest regrets. I wasn't well equipped in handling conflict and I couldn't find the words to express the heavy and complex emotions that loomed over me like ominous clouds. The idea that one could feel so alone and confused within their marriage scared me. I blamed myself and internalized that feeling. However, as expected, my stupid strategy only made things worse and eroded his trust in me. Although we were navigating our first rough patch, our increasingly rare breakthroughs gave me hope that one day this phase would be behind us.

Like one Saturday night after leaving a dinner hosted by friends Thomas and Clothilde. Yes, the same Thomas from Fanelli. There were no disagreements or arguments during the week leading up to the dinner, and our bickering was at a minimum. I stayed in most nights of the week prior and fell into a rhythm that seemed to set us on the promising path of finding a good groove. It was as if internally, we both waved white surrender flags and said to ourselves *"ça suffit,"* that's enough.

As the taxi made a right onto rue Jean-Baptise Pigalle, away from Thomas and Clothilde's Saint-Georges neighborhood, driving north toward the Moulin Rouge before making its way to the other side of the Butte Montmartre, I was looking out the window, taking in Paris by night. The lampposts that light the street all turn on at the same time in the evening, washing the city with a warm yellow hue that makes everything—

from the buildings to the bridges—look like the set of a theatre production. TFM scooted closer to me and put his head on my shoulder. It was a tender and vulnerable action that wasn't lost on me. I moved closer, too, and placed my hand on his thigh, welcoming him into my space.

"Did you have a good time?" he asked.

"Yeah, I always have fun with Clothilde and Thomas," I responded.

"Yeah, me, too," he said. He paused, then said, "You know, I don't want to be that couple…always bickering and arguing at home and in front of our friends. It gets old really quick."

"I agree," I said and he kissed me on my forehead and squeezed my hand. We had a mini breakthrough and it felt refreshing, but there was still the issue of my lack of ability to communicate and his temperament and how much it terrified me that he often went from zero to one hundred in .5 seconds, and how insecure in our relationship it made me feel.

There was also the matter of my abysmal French. It was a brewing point of contention, ready to implode at any moment. He felt that I wasn't putting enough time or energy into learning the language, and I forced everyone to speak English. I felt that I was already here; I was working and building my life. I was doing enough; the least he could do is lay off the French. It wasn't a problem for anyone else and I thought that he was making a big deal out of it. I was learning. He was always there to translate or someone would be there to translate for me. Everything would be okay.

My lack of French language skills came to a head when Emma and Houssame hosted lunch for his parents, who were visiting from Morocco. There was a lot of pressure around this lunch because it was the first time they would be meeting the entire family. As Morocco is a former French colony, both of Houssame's parents spoke French. Apart from the formal greetings, which I now knew like the back of my hand, I was mostly silent throughout the entire lunch. I didn't know what to say. By the time I could translate and piece together what they were saying they were already on the next topic. The possibility of employing my usual strategy of trying to be cute by chiming in with accented French was not an option because they wouldn't have any idea what I was talking about.

So I sat there stuffing my face with tangy and sweet Moroccan food until someone addressed me in English. I would pipe up and chime in, excited to suddenly be visible again. Otherwise, admittedly, I would zone out and begin daydreaming. To me that was a natural response when surrounded by people who are speaking a different language.

I thought that the lunch was a success, but Emma felt differently. A few hours after lunch she called TFM, fuming. I couldn't understand what she was saying but I could hear her through the phone as she spoke to TFM. He didn't say much except, "No, but Emma, it's not like that."

When he finally managed to get off the phone I asked, "What happened? Everything okay?"

Without skipping a beat he said, "This is what happens when you don't put any effort into learning the language of the country you're living in."

"Huh? What?" I had no clue what he was talking about.

"My sister is pissed because you hardly said anything at the lunch and as a result I didn't say much, either. She thought that we were super hungover and finds it extremely disrespectful that we would meet Houssame's parents in that state."

"But we weren't hungover," I responded.

"She knows that now, but you're missing the point," he said. He raised his voice, and I shrank. "Don't you think it's rude to not even make any effort? Everyone always bending and shaping for you?" he yelled. "Show a little respect. And it's pretty obvious when you're not paying attention, either, when someone addresses you and they have to repeat your name twice to get your attention. I'm so tired of this and you."

I tried defending myself by stating the ways in which I was trying to improve my French on a daily basis, but mostly I wanted to understand how we could have possibly ruined her lunch. We're not clowns. We didn't sign up to be the entertainment for the day. His sister expected an apology, and I made it clear to him that I wasn't going to apologize to her. He could if he wanted to but we had bigger things to handle.

Now, I understand that it was probably almost impossible for him to be comfortable and feel at home with himself and me if he couldn't speak in his native tongue. Although he was bilingual it's always easier to speak your mother tongue, especially after a long day of work or to express certain complex emotions and feelings. If I, at least, understood more French we could've created a treaty of sorts. The terms of the treaty would dictate that he speaks in French, and I respond in English. That way we would both be given the opportunity to express our feelings in the language we feel most comfortable, without risking anything being lost in translation. If we both exercised more patience and compassion with each other there was a chance that this could've been solved and worked on instead of being added to the mounting pile of grievances hovering over our relationship.

Instead of taking a forward trajectory, our relationship was taking random twists and turns. These are issues that should've been ironed out before we decided to get married and build a life together. He should've been used to my lack of French, and I should've been used to his temperament. Instead, we were merely beginning to see the raw truth of each other—the people we both really are—and it was terrifying. It was time to test whether or not our love was strong enough to withstand the pokes in our newlywed bubble.

Eleven

NOIR

One of the things that excited me the most about moving to Paris, besides TFM, was the idea of living in France. For me, living in France—especially in Paris—meant living the epitome of a bohemian lifestyle. I expected only café culture, drinking wine at lunch and with a midafternoon snack, philosophical conversations about the meaning of life, a super romantic husband that came home with a long-stem rose dangling from his mouth every night. That seemed to be the Paris that the Americans-in-Paris bloggers lived in.

Naively, I believed that racial dynamics played little to no role in society here; everyone was equal and treated as such. Only immature cultures like the United States were still grappling with that issue, I assumed. I believed that French people were the embodiment of sophistication and class. The French were romantic, not misogynistic. The French weren't racist; they had a history of welcoming Black Americans that were running from segregation in the US in the early twentieth century. My belief was that as an older more mature society and culture, France couldn't possibly have the same issues as the United States.

I was wrong. As the idealized view of my marriage began to give way so did my romanticized vision of France, Paris and French culture in general. I couldn't help but question where was all of the *Liberté*, *Egalité*, *Fraternité*? Did it get lost somewhere along the way? Was it all a lie? Maybe.

After discovering Monoprix, the French equivalent of Target, I was there at least three times a week. I enjoyed prancing around to the different independent shops with my straw bag, like any other American in Paris, but the convenience of buying everything—clothes, electronics and milk—from one store was comfortable and familiar. The comfort waned the first time I was followed in the store. Initially, I thought that the security guard popping up in the same few aisles seconds after me was a coincidence. I assumed he was doing his rounds. It wasn't until I felt his presence looming over me as I shopped that I realized he was watching me, and he wasn't being discreet about it. To make sure I wasn't being paranoid I walked all the way from one side of the store to the other and downstairs. Within minutes he was downstairs and at the other end of the aisle packed with feminine hygiene products. Now immensely frustrated, I didn't attempt to speak or defend myself in my mediocre French. I turned to look at him and asked, "Can I help you?" with annoyance in my voice. His eyes widened and shock grew across his face. He didn't expect me to address him and definitely not in English. He began stuttering and a series of "ummms" and "uhhhhs" left his mouth before he held up his hands and said "Sorry, sorry," before quickly retreating—leaving me alone to continue shopping.

This happened a few more times in various Monoprix's and Sephoras, to be specific, and over time I learned to use my Americanness as a weapon to shield myself from the racism that was directed toward me or shut it down before it received any opportunity to rear its ugly head. When I found myself in situations that forced me to question what I thought I knew about the French versus the reality, I often racked my brain in an attempt to remember if an American-in-Paris blogger shared a similar story; they never did. Almost all of the Americans-in-Paris bloggers were white women who transported their privileges to a world that welcomed them with open arms.

My Blackness wasn't something that I gave much thought to or had to come to terms with before moving Paris. Growing up in New York City, being Black was normal, and being of Jamaican heritage was quite ordinary. I never felt othered. Jamaican beef patties are just as much a part of New York City food culture as Italian zeppoles. Everything about me is what makes New York City, New York City. It's a melting pot of everyone coming together, adding a dash of this and a sprinkle of that into the stew that makes the city. But I'm not stupid. Even in New York City and being private school-educated, advanced degree-holding and raised in a two-parent household, I understood and knew that discrimination, privilege and structural racism were alive and well. I rarely had to confront it or deal with it.

That all changed when I moved to Paris. No, I didn't have white privilege, but I was experiencing privilege by association. Being American, having a white husband and a mostly white social circle led me to change my behaviors and how I viewed myself in the world in ways I never expected. Having to live with and witness white male privilege, and the arrogance that came along with it, opened my eyes to how unfair and unjust the world actually is. TFM moved through the world without having to feel the burden of race and never doubting what he thought he deserved, and I made the mistake of thinking I could do the same. I began to emulate him and wanted to take up space in the way he and his friends did. This led me to naively believe that I could walk around with my chest puffed out, demanding and expecting things in the same way a six-two heterosexual, well-off, handsome, educated white man could.

Sometimes it worked and other times it didn't.

One instance when I quickly realized that there wasn't enough progress made in our modern world that would allow me to enjoy the same privileges as my white husband was when I asked for a raise almost two years into my tenure at the advertising agency. I felt that I deserved a raise, especially after the llama incident, and TFM coached me on how to get what I wanted. I walked into the office of the director of strategy and I did exactly as I was told—I was forthright, stern and somewhat demanding—but instead of getting a raise, I was laughed at and asked to leave the agency all together.

The strategy of demanding a raise for valid reasons probably would've worked for TFM, but not for this Black woman. After the news of my dismissal made its way through the agency, I was given a second chance when a creative director I worked on several projects with went out on a limb for me and I was offered a different position, truthfully a better role, working under him. But once again, I listened to my resident white-man-who-thinks-he-owns-the-whole-goddamn-world and his second harebrained strategy that was supposed to lead me to getting a higher salary. Instead, they recanted the offer, leaving me with absolutely nothing.

I took this as my sign to leave the advertising world all together. *The Wolf of Wall Street* reenactment, the unchecked misogyny and the emotional roller coaster of being fired then not, and then having the second offer recanted was my limit. I quickly found a digital marketing role in a technology firm based in Paris's swanky sixteenth arrondissement. The ambience was a far cry from the suspended adolescent atmosphere of the advertising agency. The average age of my new colleagues increased by at least ten years, and there was less of an emphasis on being cool.

However, one instance where emulating white privilege worked in my favor was when Hannah, a white British friend, invited me to join her for dinner at The Bristol, a former palace turned five-star luxury hotel. She was writing a review of the hotel and wanted a friend to join her for dinner and to spend the night, and I was the lucky friend. The night of our dinner date I waltzed into The Bristol with my head held high like I belonged there. There was no doubt or question in my mind. I locked eyes with the tall blonde woman behind the reception desk who was elegantly dressed in all black. I didn't say anything to her until she addressed me first. It's something I'd witnessed TFM do on several occasions.

"*Bonsoir, madame,*" she said.

"Hi, I have a dinner reservation with Hannah M," I responded immediately in English. By this time I'd learned that using English as opposed to my passable French almost always guaranteed that I would be treated well.

"Oh yes, she's waiting for you in the dining room of 114 Faubourg, Madame," she said when suddenly her colleague appeared out of nowhere.

"May I please take your coat?" the equally tall but brunette colleague asked me, while simultaneously removing my coat. She handled my Zara coat that I bought on sale with more care and grace than I ever did.

"Please follow me this way," she continued after hanging my coat.

I was offered a drink and led toward the restaurant where Hannah was waiting.

As I sat in the Michelin-starred restaurant of this historical palace—where Ulysses S. Grant stayed in 1877 and that weekend was serving as Joaquin Phoenix's *pied-à-terre*—sipping champagne and reflecting on the ease with which that entire interaction took place simply because I spoke English, I couldn't help but think to myself, *damn, is this how white people live? Are they always given the benefit of the doubt that they belong and never have to justify their presence?* My American accent gave me a taste of that privilege.

That was one of the biggest differences I noticed in terms of race relations in Paris. I was treated as an American. My Americanness trumped my race and was seen and utilized as a bigger identity marker. Not being judged solely by the color of my skin gave me the freedom to just be, without thinking about where I went or whether or not I belonged. While reveling in that sense of freedom, I grappled with my own internal struggle of feeling disconnected from the Black community—both Black American and Afro-French.

France is sold and marketed as a racial utopia, with reason, and I believed it. James Baldwin, Josephine Baker and Nina Simone moved here to escape the oppressive segregation laws of the United States, and Black Americans still flock here. Racism exists in France and is, in fact, very present, but many people try to rationalize it away. I was shocked when I learned that France doesn't collect a census, or any similar data, on the racial makeup of its residents and citizens. The legislative body has gone as far as removing the word *race* from the legislation and constitution in 2013 and 2018. The reason behind this decision was attributed to science. Scientifically speaking, there is no such thing as race; we are all one race, the human race, so placing emphasis on one's race will only aid in creating unnecessary hierarchies and discrimination. While yes, it is scientifically true there is no such thing as race, in the Western world the color of your skin plays a profound role in how one is perceived and can negatively affect one's quality of life in numerous and damaging ways.

Growing up in New York City, I was used to seeing Black people of all walks of life. That was not to say that Black people are not disproportionately affected by poverty in New York City, but when and where I grew up, Blackness didn't equate to poverty, either. It wasn't uncommon to see Black women and men dressed in suits and carrying briefcases on the subway. Although there was always room for more Black people in positions of power in the corporate world, it wasn't unheard of to have a Black manager or VP. Whereas in Paris, Black people seemed to be mostly relegated to jobs of manual labor or minimum-wage roles (I can't prove this, because there are no stats, but I have eyes that can see). Nonwhite representation in corporate environments seemingly didn't exist. This is not to insinuate that if one doesn't have a corporate role they are in some way lesser than; however, a corporate job usually means a certain level of education, salary, lifestyle, integration and acceptance in society. And in Paris, Black people seemed to be on the fringes of society, and in many ways kept there. The more I noticed that I was the only Black person in many situations, the more uncomfortable I became and couldn't help but sometimes question if I was there because I'm American.

There is a cultural omission and amnesia of France's history as a colonial power and how that dynamic still plays out in society today. One way is the division that the legacy of colonialism and racism has caused within the Black community, manifesting itself in colorism, self-hate and rejection of one's Blackness. The first time I experienced this in Paris was at a hair salon.

A year into my move to Paris I was elated to find a Black hairdresser within walking distance from my apartment. It was important for me to find a Black hairdresser because the hard water wreaked havoc on my hair; my strands were dull, dry and brittle. It needed a lot of love and attention. His salon was chic, modern and upscale; it reminded me of the salons in New York City that I frequented when I lived there. Sprinkles of familiarity comforted me because I was constantly bombarded with information on how to live this new life.

I cheerily walked to the salon on the afternoon of my appointment. I was in dire need of this hair treatment, and it was also an opportunity to practice my French with a stranger. When I arrived the owner greeted me, directing me to the black leather chair.

"Would you like some tea?" he asked as I settled into the chair facing the mirror, ready to be beautified. His assistant, or so I assumed, appeared shortly after. Slim-framed and wiry, apprehension was all over his face as he stood behind me. I repeated, in broken French, the service I was there for: wash, deep conditioning, straighten and trim the ends. He nodded and just stood there, without moving, just looking at my hair. I thought he was debating whether or not to cut my hair dry before shampooing and straightening, as I know that some hairdressers dry cut kinky-curly hair in order to shape the hair the way it naturally falls. I didn't have a preference for a wet or dry cut so I told myself I would let him decide if he asked, except he never did. He wasn't looking at my hair to determine the best way to proceed. While I was browsing a magazine, he started tugging and pulling my hair, looking at it as if he'd never seen this type of hair texture in the salon before.

Eventually, with his nose scrunched up, he called over his boss, and owner of the salon, and asked him, holding a handful of my hair, *"Qu'est-ce que je suis censé faire avec ça?"* What am I supposed to do with this? he asked, with exasperation and disgust in his voice. I died in the chair. I was so embarrassed. Black hair is already so politically charged. Black salons are supposed to be our solace, our place where we can feel beautiful and feel accepted. Black women do not expect to be othered in a Black-owned hair salon. That was the place where our kinks and curls are glorified and treated with the care they deserve.

I expected the salon owner to scold him and put him in his place, but instead he responded with equal disdain, in French, "I don't know. Just do something." I couldn't believe my ears. My French had improved enough at this point to understand what was going on around me. I was surprised that a Black hairdresser and his dusty assistant were shaming me in a Black-owned salon about my Afro-textured hair. This had never happened to me before and I was frozen in shock. I was hurt, discouraged and angry. So many thoughts ran through my mind at the same time. *We're both Black, we're supposed to be together in this and look out for each other. How are you going to be racist and discriminate against me? We have the same texture hair!*

I left the salon so dejected and looking terrible with the worst blowout of my life. My hair was stiff and lifeless, and my ends were not trimmed. But again, this was something I didn't share with TFM because I assumed either he wouldn't understand, or he would question whether or not I was sure I heard and understood correctly. I held back a lot of what I was feeling and going through at the time from TFM because it was a lot for me to process, and at the time I didn't see a way in which he could help me. I was drowning, and moments of ease and joy were elusive gulps of fresh air that I hungrily took in whenever I reached the surface. But I was never on the surface long enough to fully catch my breath.

When I arrived home after my hair appointment, feeling ugly and enraged—my hair was as stiff as a carpet—TFM looked at me and said, "Your hair looks great." I rolled my eyes, went into the bedroom and slammed the door. The fissure between us continued to widen, and the wound infected by our inability to communicate festered. Our worlds continued to grow apart instead of together. I was living one Paris experience and he was living another. The team member who I thought I found all those years back seemed to be less of a teammate and more like a roommate. I didn't know this at the time but what was happening is that we weren't *seeing* each other.

Race was something TFM and I spoke about as an idea but not as a lens through which our identities were built and how we are treated in the world. We both didn't tolerate racists and condemned discrimination of any sort, but were both naive about race and the impact that it would have on my life living in Paris, and our life as a couple. Casually dating and having sex with white men is very different from being married to one. Each of us had to face our own biases regarding the race of our partner and that was a hard pill to swallow and recognize about yourself. As educated people who grew up in big multicultural cities, race wasn't supposed to be a "problem." We were "above it." But we weren't because it secretly bothered me that he didn't have any Black friends, which is one of the things I never shared with him.

I also didn't share with TFM my conflicting feelings I grappled with around the privilege I have and feel as a Black American woman living in Paris. I assumed he wouldn't understand that nuance between being a part of an oppressed group, but not necessarily feeling oppressed on an everyday basis because you're seen as a part of the group, but not really. Many times I felt that I was put in the category of a different type of Black person—a "good" one—and as a result was afforded privileges that other Black people aren't. When the truth is that I just happened to be from a culture and country that conjures positive associations. If the destiny lottery was different and I was born in a former French colony, my experience in France would've likely been very different.

I wanted to talk about this with him, but I couldn't find my words. I didn't know how to start the conversation. We had enough on our plate as a couple and I didn't want to add to it. That led to a pattern of me shrinking myself to defuse any potential blowout fights or what I considered at the time to be unnecessary tension. The essence of this relationship that set it apart from any in my past—comfort, openness, ease, respect and acceptance—was slipping away and I needed to do something to get it back.

Twelve

THE MASQUERADE IS OVER

Moments of seeing eye to eye with TFM were ephemeral, lasting only as long as a successful dinner party or *apéro*. There was always a low burning flame lingering between us, waiting to explode. When one of us was being selfish and uncompromising the other felt completely justified in releasing one of the most wretched and brutal punishments, the silent treatment. It's ridiculous that we conditioned ourselves to believe that refusing to speak to each other and sulking is the best way to express hurt or disappointment instead of simply communicating what plagued us. As much as I told myself I wouldn't do it because I knew how it made me feel when he did it to me, I always succumbed. In some ways it was easier to go inward and suppress my feelings rather than express the distress that our constant fighting caused me. We were caught in an immature and unforgiving cycle of dangerous and unrelenting spiteful behavior, and found ourselves acting in increasingly cruel ways toward each other.

My friends who were married, or in otherwise serious relationships, shared their relationship woes, but they seemed inconsequential compared to mine. None were on the brink of divorce. My friends who were divorced spoke about the ending of their marriages with great elation, and it didn't seem to bother them, ever. I didn't question their decision and trusted that a divorce was the best thing for them to do, but to myself I wondered if they ever experienced any moments of doubt. Did they not have an inkling of regret about how they allowed the marriage to deteriorate to the point of no return?

In an effort to rectify all of the wrongs in our marriage, I decided that therapy was our only solution. One evening I suggested it out of the blue. TFM was apathetic and grunted in response to my suggestion, so I moved forward with my research. I Googled "English-speaking marriage therapist in Paris" and wasn't very discerning about my first choice. After my very basic search I chose the therapist because of her name, which sounded calm and affirming.

After gathering enough courage, I called and left her a voice mail explaining that I'm an American woman, living in Paris with my French husband, and we're having a very difficult time. A lump rapidly formed in the middle of my throat as I laid everything out on the line. On one hand it wasn't supposed to be like this; we were newlyweds. But on the other, at least I was doing something about it. Two sides of the same coin, I suppose. The phone call was more emotional and draining than I expected it to be, which turned out to be a precursor to the first session.

A few days after reaching out to the therapist I noticed a missed call and voice message on my phone. The person on the other end was speaking English but their words were slurred and incomprehensible. After listening to the voice message a few times I connected the dots and realized it was the potential therapist. Apparently, she was on some heavy narcotics due to a recent surgery, but she felt it was imperative to get in touch with me. She apologized profusely for her groggy state, and her parting instructions were to call back to schedule an appointment, and I did. In retrospect her decision to call a potential new patient while under heavy narcotics probably should've been a red flag, but I was desperate for our relationship to be fixed, by any means necessary.

On the evening of our first appointment TFM and I met on the Pont Neuf, one of the bridges that connects the two sides of the city, and walked across to the *Ile de la Cité* address of the therapist. The symbolism of walking across the bridge together felt significant. We were both trying to connect our love for each other and the people we were becoming. We arrived in front of the imposing doors of the building, and I entered the code. The hallway was opulent—marble, velvet and expensive-looking oil paintings. It felt very fitting for an apartment building on *Il de la Cité*, an island on the Seine River and the epicenter of the city. Rich with history, from its role as a fortress in the fourth century to the home of instantly recognizable landmarks like the Palais de Justice and Notre Dame, it is one of the wealthiest and most exclusive neighborhoods in Paris. After making our way to her building and into the elevator, we stepped off and it opened directly into her office. Her office was in her apartment, which was the entire floor of the building. We were confined to the office section only, but I kept trying to peek to see the other side. I was curious about her. The woman in front of me was the complete opposite of how I imagined her, based on her odd voice message. She resembled a sweet, nurturing and wholesome grandmother who always had fresh baked goods waiting for an unexpected visitor. Her thick light blond hair was perfectly coiffed with curled ends that looked as soft as pillows. I wanted to touch one to see if my finger would make a dent. Her office walls were covered with wallpaper, and the chairs squeaked when we sat down. We stepped into a time machine, but she was going to fix us so the aesthetics didn't matter.

She began the session by introducing herself and sharing that she has been married to her French husband for over thirty years and they have adult children and a few grandchildren, so she understands and is sympathetic to our plight. This was reassuring because every relationship has its unique set of issues, but an intercultural relationship was an added layer. As the shininess of our differences wore off, I often felt like one of us was fighting for cultural dominance on a daily basis. We wanted to prove that our way of thinking, being and seeing the world has more merit and comes from a greater foundation. We were constantly trying to prove ourselves and begging to be fully seen without having to explain everything. There were many times I yearned to understand why TFM and his friends did certain things or shared a collective belief without a history lesson or searching "Why do French people (insert anything French people do here)" on Google.

Like an eager child on the first day of school I sat on the edge of my seat waiting to be called on, ready to lay my grievances on the table. She started off asking easy questions. "How did you meet?"

"How would you describe your wedding?"

"How long have you been married?" The kind of questions that conjure up good memories and positive responses. I saw TFM's body language relax and I began to feel optimistic about this session.

With the easy questions out of the way, it was time for the questions that made us squirm: "How often do you fight?"

"What usually triggers the arguments?"

"How do you fight?" We both shared our answers and she began dissecting from my point of view and asking TFM to understand my perspective. I expected she would reverse the roles and dissect TFM's point of view, asking me to be more understanding of his perspective either in the first session or our next, but TFM immediately clammed up and became defensive. Progress halted. What was a three-way conversation turned into a dialogue between me and the therapist. TFM completely checked out except to signal and correct any inconsistencies he believed I had shared. Exasperated with his attitude at one point, the therapist turned to him and said, "You're a piece of work, huh?" As our meeting came to a close, the therapist asked me if I wanted to come back again although we both knew the answer was no. I thanked her and walked out.

Our first trip across the bridge toward the therapist office felt hopeful; the walk back less so. TFM walked three steps ahead of me, and I broke into a light jog to keep up with his stride.

"That was pretty okay?" I questioned breathlessly as I tried to keep up with his pace.

He stopped so abruptly, I almost bumped into his back; he looked at me and spat out, "It was a fucking waste of time," before turning on his heels and continuing his stride toward the metro. I followed behind, dejected.

But I wasn't ready to give up. I wanted us to work, and I needed the right therapist to help. No more Google searches. I began to quietly ask my inner circle. This was the first time I opened up in detail about the woes of my marriage. It felt humiliating admitting that my marriage was in trouble so soon into it. But I needed help. I wondered if it was too early to confide in my new friends. I chose to ask two American women in my circle. One was still married to her French husband and the other was freshly divorced from hers. I knew I made the right decision when after asking them, the first thing they both asked was about my emotional well-being and if I needed anything. I felt a huge weight lift off my shoulders.

"Sutanya, it's normal!" one of them exclaimed. "You left everything you know and love to marry and live in France, with a French man like we all did. What we did is bold but also a bit wacky. We're wacky people! We need help!" I laughed so hard, I started tearing up. It was the first time I had laughed that hard in a long time.

Separately, both women recommended a therapist named Ursula. One friend shared that Ursula saved her marriage and although Ursula didn't help save the other's marriage, she helped her find inner peace, which sounded quite appealing at the time. Hope was temporarily reassured.

TFM joined me for the first session with Ursula. I expected more resistance after our dismal session with the previous therapist. I interpreted his willingness as a genuine effort to work on our marriage and heal both of our wounds. The day of our first appointment I sat in the waiting area in anticipation, wondering what was waiting for me behind the door. Fortunately, behind the door was a huge departure from the first therapist's office. When I walked in, sunshine streamed into the office and I instantly felt cocooned in its warmth. Her plant-filled office was fresh and invigorating. Colorful, bright, optimistic—that was how her space felt. South African with perfect pin curls, Ursula was a ray of sunshine in human form. She immediately struck me as the older sage, nonjudgmental, neutral confidante that I needed during this tumultuous time in my life and relationship.

Unfortunately, after the first session TFM made it clear that he didn't see the point in returning. At the fancy therapist's office he felt that we ganged up on him and this time Ursula's hippie vibe didn't sit right with him. I understood his point of view, but in my mind our marriage and trying to save it was worth mild discomfort. We were already living in discomfort; it wouldn't be that different from our every day. I really liked Ursula and wanted to give her at least one more try. Although, truthfully, I would've liked if she pointed out the many ways I was right and TFM was wrong, I appreciated the fact that she listened to both sides and held us both accountable for the roles we each played in creating conflict in our marriage. She didn't want us to start playing the blaming game or make one of us feel more righteous than the other. I sensed that she believed in fairness, balance and truth. I especially appreciated that she ended the session by asking, "Sutanya, what is it about TFM that made you fall in love with him?" and "TFM, what is it about Sutanya that made you fall in love with her?" We had to look at each other as we reminded each other of the feelings, ideas and hopes that created our love story. We both cried; it felt cathartic and like a step forward in the right direction. After TFM told me he didn't want to continue seeing her, I tried to remind him of this moment and how good it felt. Alas, I couldn't convince him so I decided to continue my sessions alone. I figured if I could work on myself maybe he would see a positive change in me and either decide to go to therapy himself or join me for sessions as a couple.

I went to Ursula to try to find answers around my relationship, how to fix it, how to fix myself in the context of the relationship, but Ursula wanted to know more about me before my marriage. She wanted to dig in. She wanted to get to know me, to see me. She saw how desperately I needed to go inside and connect with myself. Before attempting to fix everything around me, I needed to take stock of who I was.

During one particularly difficult session I spoke at length about TFM's good qualities and that I was becoming increasingly angry with myself because I was questioning why who he was and all that he did for us didn't translate into a peaceful relationship. At the end of the session we were wrapping up and she stated, "During this session you spent a lot of time telling me about all of the positive things that TFM brings to the relationship." I didn't know where this was going and as soon as I opened my mouth to answer her nonquestion she continued, "But what do you think you bring to the relationship?"

That question shattered me. I didn't know what I brought to the relationship. We argued so much that I didn't understand my place or role in his life. I still didn't speak good enough French. Instead of growing together we were growing apart. I lied to him too regularly and easily in a stupid and immature attempt to maintain some semblance of order and peace in our relationship. His meanness toward me had no bounds, and the venomous words he spat out at me chipped away at my core. I no longer knew who I was in our relationship. That question shook me so deeply because I couldn't answer it. I didn't know why he loved me, if he still loved me or if we were still in love.

At home after the session, TFM sensed that I was disturbed. After a few hours of seeing me pouting, looking out in the distance and sighing heavily as I moved from room to room, he finally asked me what was wrong.

I began recounting my session with Ursula and eventually shared that she had asked me what I thought I brought to our relationship. "I couldn't answer," I said, looking up at him with pleading eyes. I wanted him to see how much that affected me, and for him to tell me all of the positive things I brought to our life as a couple. Like our wedding day, I needed reassurance. I wanted him to soothe me, tell me that everything would be okay. We would work it out because our marriage was worth it. I needed him to say, "Our love is ironclad, remember? We'll get through this. It's just a rough time."

Instead, he said, "Oh," and walked out of the living room and into our bedroom where he lay in our bed and played games on his iPhone until he fell asleep.

I should've interpreted TFM's response to my cry for affection and reassurance as a telltale sign: we were at different stages in our relationship. I wanted to keep going but TFM had no fight left in him. I can't speak for him but maybe he felt too deceived by who I really was and how our marriage turned out to be. It was easier for me to continue to fight and live longer in the discomfort of our relationship because I was already living in discomfort every day just by virtue of being in a foreign country. TFM was my home whereas, I imagine, he didn't feel the same rootedness with me.

Finally, in February of 2016, almost three years to the date of our wedding anniversary, I was in a company-wide all-day meeting, not paying attention, switching between talking to my new coworker turned friend, Evelyn, and mentally planning what I would do for our third wedding anniversary. A buzz from my phone interrupted my thoughts, but not enough for me to pay attention to it. During a coffee break I read the message from TFM, but I had a hard time understanding it. It was in English but the combination of the words wasn't making sense. Everything was blurry. I shoved my phone into Evelyn's face, asking her to read the message, just to ensure that I wasn't suffering from temporary illiteracy. When the content of the message registered in her mind she looked at me with sadness in her eyes, gave me my phone and said, "I'm so sorry, Sutanya." TFM sent a seven-word text message that lit a match in my world and set it on flames, leaving me to clean up the ash and smoke of a life suddenly in shambles.

It's over. I can't do this anymore.

I read the text at least four times; my eyesight was becoming less blurry and sharpening with every glance. Threats of breaking up, although not healthy, were not uncommon for us, but they were usually made verbally in the heat of the moment, not written down and solidified by text message. The written word held more weight, and seeing the words *it's over* felt more real than anything said during an argument.

I spent the rest of the day in a haze of disbelief. I thought back to the argument we had a few days prior and convinced myself that was the reason for the text. I told myself he'd cool off by this evening, when I really wanted to delete the text message and pretend I never received it.

On my way home that evening I stopped at all of the small independent shops on my street to buy the ingredients for dinner, my peace offering. I wanted TFM to arrive home and be pleasantly surprised that I was there and that I made dinner. I imagined that our meal would begin in silence as we performed the awkward dance of being around each other and not talking, each of us waiting for the other person to address the elephant in the room. Who would break the ice didn't matter because eventually someone would, and then we would make up, have sex and continue the cycle again. Maybe it was unhealthy, but it was what I was used to and found security in. The alternative, getting divorced and being alone, seemed far more terrifying.

While cooking dinner my phone buzzed again, another text message from TFM. I'm sleeping at Emma's tonight, he wrote. This was the first time he slept elsewhere after an argument. I could no longer pretend that a dinner at home would remedy the situation. This was far too serious. I turned off the stove under the half-cooked meal and went to bed.

I tried broaching a conversation when he returned the following night, but he'd made his decision and there was no changing it. Yet, I still held out an inkling of hope because he was home every night, albeit sleeping on the couch, but he was there. But after a week of him sleeping on the couch and me sleeping in our bedroom, he did exactly what he said he was going to do. He left.

Intense panic took over as he was leaving the apartment. I began to cry—sob—begging him to stay, making him promises that I would be a better wife, a better partner, a better person. My promises were an attempt to save our marriage and myself in the process. He was my first love, the love of my life; I couldn't imagine surviving without him. I ran to the door and tried to prevent him from leaving, pleading that he not leave me. He moved me out of the way and walked out the door. The door closed behind him and I was shattered. Everything that I thought I had achieved unraveled in mere seconds. The past six years of my life evaporated in front of my eyes. Everything lost its meaning. The promises we made to each other, to our families and friends, were reduced to bullshit.

I stood in front of the closed door for a few minutes, my face hot and wet with tears. I was disoriented, not really understanding what just happened. I sent Samar a text that read, He left. Then I walked to the kitchen and poured myself a big glass of red wine. The first gulp went down easily, but it finished too quickly. I threw the glass in the sink, smashing it to pieces, and drank straight from the bottle.

ACT 3

Thirteen

SWIPING TO NOWHERE

After separating, deciding to stay in Paris was a relatively easy decision. I considered hopping on the first Air France flight back to New York City and into the familiar and comforting arms of my family and hometown friends, but I resisted temptation. As neglect and contempt weaseled their way into my marriage, Paris—the city itself—helped to keep my spirits high. When screaming matches became my and TFM's *langue d'usage* and I needed to get away, I escaped into the city. It helped soothe the sting of a marriage in turmoil. As I walked by sidewalk cafés overflowing with people, I was reminded that there was an entire world and existence outside the walls I shared with TFM.

So when TFM left I knew I couldn't just pack up and leave. I had invested so much of myself into building a life *à deux* in Paris, I wanted to see the person I would become if I managed to successfully rebuild a life of my own, alone in the city I'd grown to love. I just didn't know how or where to begin. How does one take care of themselves in a foreign country when their anchor goes off to, presumably, find another sail?

Every morning during the initial weeks of my separation I woke up silently wishing our breakup was just a bad dream. I was in so much pain. Every day felt like a nightmare come to life despite Paris trying her best to show me that waiting on the other side of despair was *joie de vivre*. As delicate and precious as the city may seem, Paris is a warrior in its own right. It's survived wars, invasions and plagues yet come out on the other end graceful, elegant and even more exquisite. As I groaned and rolled out of bed I hoped I would be granted a similar fate.

Through swollen eyes caused by nonstop crying I noticed that the city shimmered in a more receptive light. In its own way the city was offering to take me in and care for me, nourish me even, but it wasn't enough and I wasn't ready. So I turned to my personal army of warriors, the no-longer-scary Parisian women and other foreign women who were now my friends, for support. They drilled into my head *il faut vivre*, you gotta live. Over *apéro* one evening, a friend at the time, Cécile, a lawyer with a soft heart, noticed that my mind was elsewhere. At one point she said to me, *"Oui, effectivement, t'es plus mairées et c'est triste mais t'es à Paris, quand meme. C'est pas si mal que ça."* Yes, you're no longer married and it's sad but you're in Paris. It's not that bad. She was right; living in Paris under these new circumstances, while sad, wasn't the end of my world. But I wasn't sure if she'd ever been dumped. As an incredibly smart and strikingly beautiful biracial French woman with piercing green eyes and natural blond highlights in her caramel-colored hair, I assumed she wouldn't be able to relate but I was wrong. That night she shared multiple stories about unreciprocated love, disrespectful partners and men who were simply a waste of her time and how those failed romances affected her. That night I learned that heartbreak doesn't discriminate based on looks, education level or career—whenever you're brave enough to love and be loved, you're taking a risk. Cécile encouraged me to date, enjoy my freedom and the fact that I have the opportunity to get to know myself as an adult. In her opinion we were lucky to be able to live our adult lives for ourselves. She was in the category of friends whom I turned to when I needed an energy boost and a good laugh. They were the friends who knew that for me to realize *la chance* I had to be able to start over. None of them ever tried to sugarcoat the fact that I would make mistakes as I got over my divorce—I would surely stumble and fall—but the most important thing they wanted me to do was not judge myself too harshly. They didn't expect me to lead a perfect life or make all the right decisions, but they viewed guilt and regret as useless emotions that caused more harm than good. Now was the time to lean in to my freedom, which turned out to be advice I took too literally because my insatiable appetite to move on and forget would eventually bring me to my knees.

I went to my friends for advice. Before my breakup, and even more so after, Samar's kitchen had become a second therapist's office. In the corner next to the window, with a view into her neighbor's garden, was a small rattan café chair that she found and gave a second life. In the months leading up to my separation I often found myself tucked into that corner, confiding in Samar, who had been married for a few more years than I had, asking for tips on how I could make everything right again. Her firecracker attitude came in handy when I needed it the most. After one particularly nasty fight between me and TFM—when threats of divorce changed shape from shallow menaces to a last resort—she planted the seed in my head that I could survive on my own. I wouldn't have a choice. I was tucked into my corner chair, looking out the window while she poured me a glass of wine. She settled into her usual seat on the counter across from me.

"So what's up?" she asked.

"He keeps pulling the divorce card," I responded with a lump in my throat. She didn't react so I continued. "It makes me feel, so unstable…" I started to say until she cut me off by raising her finger in the air. After taking a drag of her ultra-slim Davidoff cigarette and a sizable sip of red wine, she finally said, "Oh really? He wants to leave? Let him!" My eyes instantly darted left to right; that was not the response I expected. Realizing she had to explain herself, she let out an exasperated sigh. "If he's serious, what can you do?" she said. "Just know that you have the right to stay here…and if he leaves, you keep the apartment," she finished with a smile.

She's right, I thought to myself. I'm not obliged to uproot my life again if we break up. It was easy to be rational about what-if situations because the probability of actually getting divorced was preposterous; I believed neither of us would ever pull the trigger. After we broke up I continued to squeeze myself into her kitchen corner, but with more wine in my glass, fear in my voice and a heavier heart. I was trying to find my way on my own, but it was all so much easier said than done. Samar made it her priority to remind me that I'm a fighter, even when I didn't feel equipped enough to walk bravely to the front line and collect the remnants of my broken heart.

Then of course, there were the friends I reached out to when I needed a good cry. One evening, about a month into our breakup, tear-shaped raindrops battered my bedroom window. It was the type of weather that called for a cozy night in, except there wasn't anything cozy about my apartment. I had gotten into the habit of living in the bedroom. The rest of the apartment didn't feel like mine—I felt like a house guest that overstayed their welcome. Everything about being in the space alone made me unbearably sad. I needed to get out, even if temporarily.

I decided to go to Nathalie's place since she only lived five minutes away. Our initial connection was through TFM but our friendship took on a life of its own outside him, and she was one of the few people in his friend circle who was willing to continue our friendship despite the breakup. On my way to her apartment, I held my emotions together until I rang the doorbell and her husband opened the door.

"Hey, Sue, you all right?" he asked. I burst into tears and through sobbing asked if Nath was there.

He shouted for her over his shoulder as he invited me into their kitchen.

By the time Nathalie joined us at the kitchen counter, he had opened a bottle of red wine and poured us each a glass. I didn't refuse the wine; I appreciated their kindness and his occasional comment of *"Oui, c'est la merde"* as he listened to me share my feelings of angst and pain with Nathalie, and kept my glass full.

I'm surprised that I allowed myself to be so raw in front of people whom I hadn't known for that long. At that point I'd been living in Paris for only two and a half years, yet I was sharing one of the darkest and scariest moments of my life with people I'd effectively just met. Luckily, my vulnerability didn't scare them away. Many of the friendships that I started to build in the years leading up to my breakup deepened—they became more intimate and less superficial when I was at my lowest. Not because misery loves company, but because my Parisian friends— once so seemingly perfect—shared personal details about their relationships that helped me come to terms with the ending of my own. They were my drinking partners, my shoulders to cry on when I needed it the most. I didn't feel judged or misunderstood. I felt less alone and stronger with them by my side. An army of powerful women surrounded me, and their collective feminine strength and energy gave me enough courage to at least try to face another day. Even if the sense of strength and hope my friends gave me lasted only until the next *apéro*, I was always grateful for the temporary boost.

A common thread that ran through the conversations I had with my friends in Paris, especially my French friends, was acceptance of oneself. My French friends in particular had a level of self-assurance that prevented them from falling under the spell of perfection. They didn't strive for perfection; they accepted the messy bits of themselves, and if you wanted to be a part of their lives you had to accept their messy sides, too. They didn't pretend to have everything figured out, either; they, too, fell victim to their insecurities. Self-doubt isn't relegated to only one type of woman. They experience moments of sadness and disappointment like everyone; they don't pretend to have a magic formula that guarantees an easy life. I noticed that the difference between them and me was that they weren't constantly preoccupied with fixing themselves and everything about their lives—they were along for the ride and focused on actually experiencing it. Acceptance of oneself is key to living a satisfactory life; this is something they understood and did not question. Their acceptance of themselves and people as unique individuals is what makes it so easy for them to practice unwavering loyalty to themselves.

That was a practice that I needed to incorporate into my own life. I noticed that starting from my Hartford years, through my marriage and especially in the destructive period after my marriage that my loyalty was to everything and everyone else except to myself. The self-destructive behaviors that I easily fell back into served as unwavering proof of the disregard I had for myself. I had to fall in love with myself in order to move forward and heal. I didn't know how to do that but even through the haze of wine and unbecoming men, I knew it was a nonnegotiable step I needed to make.

Despite having friends to talk to and raise my spirits, in the weeks after TFM's departure a wave of nausea swept over me whenever I crossed the threshold into what was our apartment, which I now referred to as *the* apartment—it didn't feel like mine. I lost a sense of attachment to the space because it no longer had a soul. In spite of the marriage hardship, our apartment still held life and love within its walls until TFM left. When he walked out the door the love that made it a home was violently sucked out, and left in its wake was a barren space devoid of emotion, like me. I felt abandoned and cast to the side like the old tattered toy of a spoiled child. I was no longer good enough and it was too late to return to sender, so I was just tossed in the back of the closet. In my case, the closet was the apartment in Montmartre. The idea of being alone terrified me because I had no clue who I was, or could be in this new context.

My friends plied me with wine at every chance and listened without judgement but that didn't stop the first few months of my involuntary singlehood from feeling like a perpetual Groundhog Day. I woke up every morning not believing that this was my new life. I cycled through the same emotions— disbelief, shock, pain, confusion and horror. Divorce is like an accident or illness; in theory, everyone knows that they are susceptible to it, but no one thinks it'll ever happen to them. My marriage wasn't perfect, but what marriage is? Wasn't it worth working through? Wasn't I worth fighting for? These questions ran through my head as I continuously replayed the history of our relationship. Although I posed these questions, I had no genuine interest in answering them. Probing deeper required self-reflection of why our relationship collapsed and the role I had played in its demise. So I drank. A lot. I partied. A lot. I suppressed my anguish with wine, French men and questionable decisions. Those distractions gave me temporary relief from the steady throbs of heartache.

My lessons in *apéro* culture came in handy, as I became a permanent fixture at Sunset, a New York City-style cocktail bar that became my *quartier general*—my headquarters. The blue awning that covered the *terrasse* welcomed me, and the Parisians who looked like they stepped off a movie set greeted me. It was my go-to almost every night. When you're newly single in Paris, happy hour always becomes happy *hours*. Sunset's owner was a fellow American named David whom I enjoyed flirting with. Like me, he moved to Paris for his French partner, but unlike me his marriage seemed to be just fine. I flirted with him because it made me feel desired, that someone could see me and want me. I loved Sunset for so many reasons—its proximity to my apartment, the vibe, the owner, the drinks, the waitstaff and the patrons. It was my hunting ground. Whether I wanted to drink myself into oblivion or spend the night with a waiter or a patron to temporarily ease my pain, Sunset is where I found my poison. Constant *apéroing* ensured that I didn't have to confront my new reality or find myself alone in what used to be my marital apartment.

Sleeping with someone new after a long-term partnership can feel liberating. The eagerness to explore a new body and breathe in their smell is intoxicating, but my dalliances weren't coming from a place of empowerment and owning my sexuality as a newly single adult woman. They reeked of desperation.

At the height of my Sunset period, when my self-medicating hadn't yet taken its toll, I ventured back out on the dating scene before I had any business doing so. In my grief-filled mind, throwing myself into a serious relationship seemed like the healthier way to get over my breakup. Being in a relationship was such a central part of my identity; it's the only life I'd known for years. Rather than sitting with my feelings and coming to terms with the current state of my life, I focused on proving to myself that although TFM no longer saw me as an ideal potential life partner, there were other people who definitely did.

In 2016, dating apps were still relatively new to the Parisian dating scene and, therefore, at the height of their popularity. However, I was clueless about the dating apps and reluctant to join any. Tinder didn't exist when I was in college and even in the early years that followed. Something about the immediacy of it all felt reminiscent of Craigslist casual encounters. I didn't want any part of that so I sought out a new serious partner the old-fashioned way.

My old-fashioned dating strategy was useless because I hadn't, and still haven't, mastered the skill of flirting whereas the French are master seducers. It's as genuine and natural to them as breathing. From a very young age they are taught that they must use a delicate mix of charm, persuasion and intelligence to get their way, in any situation. Charm is deployed in all situations, whether it's getting a post office employee to fall in love with you for ten minutes so that you can finally get your package after an unnecessary two-week delay, or receiving an invitation to join a potential lover back at their apartment for one last drink. Either way, their seductive persuasion powers help them get exactly what they want. My idea of flirting is simply engaging in conversation. My belief is the fact that I'm actually talking to you is more than enough proof of my intentions. It worked with TFM. Why wouldn't it work with other men?

My attempts at flirting went from bad to worse. I tried to engage in a French way, but lacked the subtlety and understated seduction. So eventually, I had no choice—I caved and joined Tinder. This was an entirely new world. There was an overwhelming amount of choice and everyone seemed too good to be true. Aspects of it were akin to being in the supermarket, trying to find the perfect avocado: squeezing, touching, holding up to the light and inspecting to make sure I picked the right one.

My feelings around my first real date with someone I met via an app were erratic and contradictory. I resented being in that situation because just a few months ago I was married; I was already emotionally naked in front of the person I thought was my life partner. I didn't want to have to do this because I didn't ever expect to have to venture into a new romantic adventure ever again. On the other hand, I was also smugly pleased with myself because I believed my own lie that dating meant I was healing. My emotions were oscillating between rage and anticipation when my date, Antoine, approached the table where I was seated.

He was two years younger than me and even cuter in person. His sandy-brown hair was neatly cut and styled, very different from the floppy-haired French men I had become used to. Behind his circular tortoiseshell glasses were nervous light brown eyes; a bit farther down I noticed his khakis and a button-down shirt. The date wasn't incredible, but it was pleasant. We laughed and talked but there was no spark. My goal was to enjoy the company of a man without going home with him.

My resolve to go home alone was still strong until our drinks continued to dinner at Le Petit Moulin, a tiny two-story restaurant that looks like it was a former home. The food was farm-to-table nouveau *terroir* fare, which means traditional French food with a twist. The restaurant changed its menu every day so you never know what you'll get the day you arrive, but it was guaranteed to be excellent. When we walked in, the open kitchen gave us a clear view of the chef, who was drinking a beer and in deep conversation with a patron on the other side, all while cooking.

The waitress led us upstairs and sat us at one of the four tables in the room; she promptly lit a candle and left us to peruse the menu. I ordered *poulet roti*, roasted chicken, fitting with the ambience, which was reminiscent of being at a friend's house. A glistening chicken thigh with golden-brown crispy skin served on a bed of pillowy mashed potatoes and drizzled with a slightly sweet but exquisitely silky *jus*, gravy, was placed in front of me when my unassuming date whom I immediately placed in the timid category surprised me. He poured me a glass of red wine, looked me straight in the eyes and asked, "Can I kiss you?" He continued, "I've been wanting to since earlier." He asked so politely, I couldn't imagine saying no, and I was curious. We kissed over candlelight and my resolve was no more.

The date didn't turn into a relationship, or anything close

to it, and it only took me a few days to be back on the app and chatting up a French-Iranian photographer. In hindsight the photographer was probably married. He was always at least an hour late to every date and mysteriously unavailable in between them. He tried to push me sexually in ways that caused me great discomfort, and when I stood my ground and refused he berated me. If I was in a healthier mental state that would've been enough for me to stop seeing him, but it wasn't. One night at his "apartment"—which also in hindsight was basically his photography studio that housed a bed—he made me "dinner" and I realized I needed to do better and respect myself. "Dinner" consisted of canned green beans and plain white rice, no salt. I'd been in Paris long enough at that point to know this meal was the height of disrespect. If you weren't gifted in the kitchen an *apéro* consisting of various cheeses, meats and dips would suffice, but you never serve a cooked meal that lacked heart and soul. That was the last straw and I moved on, but not to a place of self-reflection. I was back on the apps.

Shortly after, thanks to the apps, I had a strange encounter with a painter. By the time I arrived at the ten-seat restaurant for our date there were five empty wineglasses in front of him, his teeth were stained with red wine and he was slurring his words. I should've left immediately but politeness and curiosity around how the date would develop kept me in my seat. Whenever he opened his mouth to speak my nose got a whiff of red wine and cured meat, which in turn squashed my appetite. He dramatically ran his hands through his curly salt-and-pepper hair while staring at me, before launching into a rant about the many grievances he had with the world. I think it was his attempt at looking pensive, and I had confusion written all over my face. Eventually, between rants, he noticed that I was slowly sipping my wine and not eating. "Why aren't you eating?" he asked.

"I'm not that hungry," I responded.

He didn't like my answer. He shook his head, picked up a

piece of *saucisson*, brought it close to my mouth and demanded, "Eat, eat!"

"No, thanks, I'm okay," I said with my hands up in front of my mouth.

"No, you must eat," he said in response.

"Eat, eat, eat," he continued while trying to feed me *saucisson* and a few cherry tomatoes, added at the last minute. Tired of his antics, I grabbed the *saucisson* and tomatoes out of his hand and stuffed them into my mouth to shut him up and finally end this date. I wrapped up the date shortly after being force-fed *apéro* snacks. Standing outside and preparing to say goodbye he leaned in for a kiss and I leaned away.

"What are you doing?" I asked, startled.

"Oh, come on, just a little kiss," he begged with his red wine-stained lips puckered up.

"No," I said while backing away even farther.

"Just one little kiss, baby. Come on," he continued.

"No!" I said with more force and started walking away.

He finally got the message that I didn't want to kiss but he didn't quite understand that the date was finished.

"Where are you going?" he asked with genuine confusion.

"Home," I responded over my shoulder.

"But I live this way," he said, pointing to the opposite direction.

I left him standing in the middle of the street and was sure that I wouldn't hear from him again. I was wrong. He wanted to have a do-over date, which I declined and he didn't try to convince me otherwise. However, that didn't stop him from asking me for my underwear for a new art project he was working on. Again, I declined his request but this time I promptly blocked his phone number.

I cycled through other dates, but I couldn't shake the emptiness at the pit of my stomach at the end of each one. Dating was just another poison, another distraction from the greater, deeper, messier work that I had to do in order to heal. I filled my void with men and wine because I didn't have any strength left in me. I was wiped out. My friends suggested meeting new men as a way of reminding myself of my worth whereas I used meeting and sleeping with men as a way of proving my self-worth. Dating was just a bandage for the more deep-seated issues that I preferred to ignore. The men that I cycled through during this time weren't all terrible. I met a lot of wonderful men who served their purpose. They distracted me and kept me busy. They humored me and made me fantasize.

And for the most part, the ones worth my time cooked for me.

I observed that almost all French men could hold their own in the kitchen. Food is so ingrained in their culture, it's like they are all just magically born being able to appreciate and make delicious foods and know everything about wine, but that's not the case. It's introduced and expected at a very young age.

Once when I was having lunch at a bistro with Evelyn, I observed a little French boy, about five or six years old, having lunch with a woman I assumed to be his grandmother. While holding a very interesting conversation about his feelings and sharing in great detail the trials and tribulations of his kindergarten social life, he went to town on a bone marrow starter then devoured his second course, steak—not well-done—with a side of lightly steamed vegetables and French fries, and finally for dessert, he ate his dark chocolate mousse with innocent joy. He washed all of this down with what looked like pomegranate juice. I was impressed, but not surprised.

That little Frenchman already had a jump-start on learning and understanding the pleasure that comes with eating a delicious meal. The act of eating may be temporary, but the joy and comfort that a good meal brings becomes embedded in your heart and memory, something that I continually denied myself despite how desperately I needed it. Witnessing his delight as he ate his meal brought me back to my first meals in Paris as a newbie, the joy I experienced every day. I wondered if it would be possible to ever feel that way again.

Fourteen

THE WINE CHRONICLES

The day I got married I believed I was a fully formed adult. Sure, maybe there were a few tweaks needed here and there, but for the most part I thought I knew who I was. Over the course of my marriage and separation I realized that I'd never been more wrong about anything in my life. I didn't have a proper sense of how much the entire concept of marriage would affect my identity and sense of self. As an individual I had my own dreams, hopes and ambitions and in the new unit of husband and wife I expected to retain the essence of who I was, while creating a new life with shared dreams, hopes and ambitions with another person. I loved that my identity was tied to being the girlfriend, then the wife of TFM. I was hitting all of the major life milestones and it made sense. It seems straightforward and easy when written in black-and-white, but the gravity of the decision I made didn't hit me until TFM left. Who was I without him?

Underneath the shambles of my rapidly deteriorating identity were the pangs of rejection. I believed that I disappointed my soon-to-be ex-husband by being the person that I am and that I let down my family and friends beyond measure. We had relationship issues, but I thought they were simply growing pains—growing pains of living and loving in a different language, of being newlyweds, of living a life neither spouse had ever imagined, but I didn't expect a divorce. After a storybook romance and beautiful wedding, it was hard to view my separation, and upcoming divorce, as something that wasn't unique only to my relationship.

I was lost without a clear route back to the essence of who I was. I found solace in lying to myself and the people around me. I was sad but not too sad. I didn't talk incessantly about the demise of my marriage. I simply stated it as a fact of life, "We're getting a divorce." It was an open-and-shut case that I was managing well in the eyes of the people in my life. I woke up every day and went to work. None of my colleagues, except Evelyn, had any inkling of the turmoil I was experiencing in my personal life. But even Evelyn only knew the facts—my marriage ended and I was sad. She didn't know the horror story that my life had become. Internalizing all of my pain, confusion and anger led me to spiral out of control. Feelings of hopelessness and loss became familiar friends.

I quickly fell back into my Hartford habits of self-medicating. I was ripped into multiple pieces and didn't know how to stitch myself back together. I found comfort in the cruelty that I was imposing on myself. The self-flagellation felt familiar. I began sleepwalking through life again. My routines became a constant cycle of work, wine, gym, more wine and then back to the apartment. My goal was just to survive day to day.

My stomach flip-flopped as I walked along the wide boulevards of Paris's glitzy sixteenth arrondissement on my way to the technology company where I now worked. *The Wolf of Wall Street* reenactment at the advertising agency solidified the fact that I needed to remove myself from that environment. Working outside the advertising world guaranteed there would be fewer chances of strippers popping up at company meetings.

On my way to the office I knocked back a small bottle of freshly squeezed orange juice and two paracetamols in an attempt to quell a hangover, my head throbbing. All around me, people in impeccably tailored suits with perfectly distressed soft leather briefcases perched between their ankles whizzed by on their scooters. I always wondered how they managed to actually keep their briefcases between their ankles while navigating the chaotic Paris traffic.

As I passed through the imposing wrought iron gate and into the lobby of my office building, my musings about the self-assured Parisian scooter drivers were interrupted by an aggressive stomach growl. The orange juice and paracetamol combination was having an adverse effect, not at all alleviating the consequences of an all-night *apéro* with my girlfriends.

My stomach growled ever more insistently, and a wave of nausea surged through me as I stood in the *cafète*, the dining area, giving my colleagues the traditional double *bise*. I was attempting to finish my *café noisette* while listening to everyone share their previous evening activities and upcoming weekend plans, but was forced to stop midsip and make a beeline to the bathroom. I burst through the door and into a stall, where I began regurgitating the previous night's sins. As I battled to regain control over my body and keep down what desperately wanted to evacuate it, the bathroom door opened. After a few seconds of silence, I heard in heavily accented English, "Sutanya, is that you? Are you okay?"

It was my ultra-Parisian colleague Apolline, a statuesque brunette who moved with the precise elegance of a ballerina. Her perfectly drawn cheekbones were the creation of divine intervention. Watching her walk down the hallway was a master class in poise and confidence. Whenever I was near her my posture would mysteriously straighten, and I often found myself making futile attempts to move with more fluidity. I imagined her standing in front of the stall, one eyebrow raised, wearing her daily uniform of black pants, a loose white blouse hanging just so and Repetto flats.

Fuck, this is not what I needed, I thought to myself. In between awkward burping I replied, "Yeah, totally fine. My stomach has just been acting up lately. I'm gonna have to go to the doctor to find out what's up. Probably too many croissants," I continued, feigning laughter.

I hoped my reply and obvious embarrassment would appease her curiosity and she would leave. I was wrong.

"Do you want me to call *le docteur*?" she asked. "It sounds bad, *hein*," she added with tenderness in her voice.

Is this woman Inspector Clouseau? I thought while simultaneously wondering how she knew that I was the person behind the stall door. "No, no, all good. I think that was the last of it," I answered with a chuckle. I tried to retain a tone of American casualness in my speech, but what I really wanted to do was crawl into the toilet and flush myself down the drain with the other contents.

I left the stall and was taken aback to see that she was still in the bathroom, bent over the porcelain sink, washing her hands. She turned to look up at me and what she saw made her crumple her face, twist her lips and scrunch her nose. *"Non mais, ça va pas du tout ma chérie,"* she said in a worrying whisper. The shock of my puffy, swollen face and vacant eyes caused her to instinctively speak in her mother tongue. She quickly regained her composure and continued in English, "The first trimester is always difficult, but if you need time off don't hesitate to ask your manager. You must rest."

Great, she thinks I'm pregnant. But before I could rebuff her assumption she swiftly turned on her Repetto flats and walked toward the bathroom door.

Holding the door open she stopped, turned, looked me in the eyes and, with a mischievous grin said, "This is such exciting news! But don't worry, ma *chèrie*, it's our secret until you make the announcement." And with that, she was out the door.

"Fan-fucking-tastic," I said aloud to myself in the mirror.

I didn't recognize the reflection looking back at me, but I didn't acknowledge that. It was easier, and more entertaining, to bury my feelings, trivialize my pain and trade hangover war stories with my friends instead. As I splashed cold water on my face, I was quite pleased with myself because my well-meaning, but nosy, colleague didn't seem to smell the wine oozing out of my pores. And I looked forward to holding court later that night at another *apéro* and howling with laughter as I retold this story.

Unsurprisingly, my packed schedule didn't suppress any distress. The *apéros* were plentiful, but I was empty. The fleeting moments of laughter and ability to forget gave me a false sense of levity and relief. I became the friend who suggested having a glass of wine, which would turn into a bottle, which would inevitably end with several bottles on the table by the time we left. I ran further away from my reality, breathlessly digging myself into a deeper hole. I desperately wanted the pain to stop and knew that I was capable of doing anything to end it. In some sense, I didn't refuse any *apéro* invitations as a matter of survival.

Constant anguish made my veins throb; the pain replaced my blood and took over my soul. The only remedy seemed to be an abundance of wine. The way wine slid down my throat and temporarily relinquished the anguish that was coursing through my veins became addictive, and I didn't know how to stop or if I had the will to stop. Drinking was how I continued being "fun Sutanya," "strong Sutanya," the "amazing Sutanya" everyone was so proud of for picking herself back up again and being independent. No one saw hurt Sutanya. The Sutanya begging for reassurance. The Sutanya who would go to work while still drunk from the night before and who was slowly blowing up her life. No one saw the Sutanya whose eyes were almost constantly filled with tears. No one saw the Sutanya who felt alone and scared.

During the weekends, when work couldn't serve as a buffer and distraction between my self-destructive behaviors and myself, the *apéros* started earlier. One Saturday morning while walking home from a grueling spinning class, my thighs and legs sore from an hour of intense cardio, I wondered how I would fill my afternoon before my evening plans when my phone buzzed. Are you still coming today? read a text message from a fellow American living in Paris. She was a single mother raising her son here and we commiserated often about our status as single women. She seemed to be more at peace with her status as a divorced woman and I hung on to the words of wisdom she bestowed on me. I forgot about her brunch invitation and was relieved that she reminded me. My day was now full. I was famished when I got to the apartment but I didn't eat. I showered, threw on black shorts, my favorite gray top and brown sandals. A quick stop at my local *caviste* to buy two bottles of wine followed, then I was gladly on my way to the metro. Now I knew how my day would begin and I thought I knew how it would end.

Twenty minutes later I was on the Left Bank, in her sixth arrondissement apartment, and brunch was in swing. Wine and champagne bottles littered the table, and an interesting cast of characters from all over Europe and the United States was present. I put on the best version of the Sutanya show and when the inevitable question of "why are you in Paris?" was broached I gave the usual response, "My ex-husband," followed by a snappy joke and I quickly changed the conversation. With the Sutanya show in full swing I wasn't a desperate divorcée. I was the woman I wanted everyone to think I was, the woman who got over her divorce and immediately began living her best life.

A few hours later, after barely eating but drinking endless glasses of wine and champagne, I was heading back to the Right Bank. My second destination of the day, and where I thought I would end my night, was L'Extra Brut, my favorite champagne bar in the ninth arrondissement. The owner, Benoit, a friendly and easygoing French man who speaks English with the thickest New York accent outside Brooklyn, welcomed me as he always did; with a big smile and genuine happiness and I continued on the champagne train with another friend. We managed to finish two bottles of champagne before Benoit announced at 9 p.m., "Sorry, girls, I'm closing."

"Oh, come on, one more glass," I pleaded.

"Nope, gotta get home to the family," he responded. During my *soirée* at L'Extra Brut I was fielding text messages from another friend who wanted me to join her at a recently opened bar closer to the apartment. I didn't refuse her invitation, although I should've. I tried to convince the friend I was still with to join me at the next spot, but she wasn't unhealthy so she refused. She knew her limits and didn't want to pass them. I, too, had limits, but I was on a quest to demolish them.

We parted ways and I made the twenty-minute walk back to the eighteenth arrondissement and the bar where I would actually end my night. I believed the brisk walk sobered me up. It didn't and I continued the activity of the day. More wine was ordered and guzzled down, a downward descent fast approaching.

"So how are you?" my waiting friend asked as soon as I arrived. I ignored her and she asked again, *"Tout va bien?"* She could see the wildness in my eyes and she cared more about me than I cared about myself at that point.

I ignored her and started dancing with strangers in the bar. Answering her questions would require introspection and truth, two things I still hadn't come around to being interested in.

Eventually, I found myself at another table, talking to another group, thinking that I was charming them with my American accent, but most likely I was probably making a fool of myself and they wanted to get rid of me. But at this point I was too far gone.

The reminder of the night comes back to me in fast flashes of regret that I so badly want to forget and expunge from my memory, but I know that I never will. I need to remember this moment to make sure I never allow myself to get to this state or feel like this ever again.

I'm holding myself up from falling before opening the door of the bar and stepping into a chilly, late-spring Parisian night. I could barely walk straight, but instead of taking an Uber home I decided that I would make the ten-minute trek by foot back to the apartment. I set off stumbling and talking to myself as I walked on rue Caulincourt, the street I thought was a part of my destiny but now, like everything so far, felt like a betrayal. I tripped over my own feet and fell facedown as I made a right turn to walk down rue Mont Cenis toward my neighborhood. The next thing I knew it was the following morning and I was on the couch, our couch, TFM's couch. With one eye barely open I looked around, trying to gauge where I was and, most importantly, that I was by myself. The last thing I remembered was falling face-first on the street, my hands instantly going out to protect my face, and then I woke up on the couch.

It's not lost on me that something far more tragic could've happened on that late-night ten-minute walk through the streets of Paris while completely inebriated. But again, I slipped away unscathed from bad luck's grip. There were many nights like that—going back to the apartment completely off my face, continuously and cruelly punishing myself—and whenever I woke up safe and sound physically, but even more depleted emotionally, I couldn't help but continue. Without TFM in my life I thought I'd lost all sense of purpose and self, and I couldn't envision a way to ever get it back. Every night that I stumbled back drunk to the apartment I was tempting the universe to complete a job that had been months in the making and simply destroy me.

Fifteen

REDISCOVERING HOME

After months of debauchery and two particular back-to-back weekends of reckless behavior, the most recent being waking up at 9:30 p.m. to the aromatic smell of garlic, onions and tomatoes and thinking it was the next day when, in fact, it was actually the same night of an hours-long *apéro*. I was tired of my own behavior and the extremes of my self-flagellation. I often thought back to the evening when I was curled up on the floor and the morning I woke up not knowing how I got home. I knew that there would be *apéros* in the future, but just not right now. More than anything I needed a reset, and part of that reset meant walking to and from work.

Walking one hour each way, once in the morning and again in the evening, served as a healthier way to spend the least amount of time in the apartment as possible and pushed me to pay attention to the city around me. I had grown indifferent toward Paris as my marriage crumbled, and completely ignored it when it fell apart. My walk took me from the racially and socio-economically mixed neighborhood in the eighteenth arrondissement where I lived through less racially diverse and more affluent parts of the seventeenth arrondissement until I eventually arrived at my job in the swanky sixteenth arrondissement. Where I lived was rapidly gentrifying but the neighborhood was still trying hard to hold on to its cool factor and *décontracté*—relaxed vibe—even as the Brooklyn-style coffee shops multiplied. The neighborhood was fighting hard to hold on to its authentic Paris status. This was very different from the part of the seventeenth arrondissement that I became accustomed to on my daily walks.

Batignolles is very *bobo*—*bourgeois-bohème*—France's version of America's yuppies but with better style. Wearing their Adidas Stan Smith or Converse sneakers they control the sidewalks with their equally stylish offspring. The toddlers of French *bobos* own more scarves and wear them with more style than I ever could. On my not so fashionable days, I have been side-eyed by more than one seventeenth arrondissement *bobo* child and I am sure they were embarrassed for me. The *bobos* pride themselves on shopping locally, drink only natural wines, also locally sourced, and are appalled if you still use a plastic bag, but do not see the irony in the fact that they also shop at fast-fashion giants like Zara and live in neighborhoods inhabited by people who are just like them—not so socially leftist after all. *Bobos* are not unique to Paris; they can be found in all major cities in the world but the Parisian *bobos* wear it proudly on their feet and carry it in their canvas tote bags.

From Batignolles, my walk continued through the seventeenth and to the Monceau neighborhood, a stone's throw from the *triangle d'or*—geographically where Paris's wealthiest neighborhoods meet and the largest concentration of luxury shops can be found. Monceau is where big money lives; this is where people have maid quarters that are still occupied by maids. The architecture and urban design of the neighborhood display its affluence. *Hôtel particuliers*, the brownstones of Paris, dot the wide and elegant tree-lined streets, and stately limestone apartment buildings overlook the neighborhood's crown jewel, Parc Monceau.

Parc Monceau was the first new public park created by Baron Haussmann in 1861, as a part of his reconstruction of Paris. You enter the park through wrought iron gates embellished with gold, and a rotunda that now houses the public bathrooms immediately greets you. As you walk through the park you notice interesting oddities, such as a miniature ancient Egyptian pyramid, scaled-down Corinthian pillars and a Renaissance Arch. If I woke up early enough and found myself with extra time before making the final trek to work, I would take advantage of the sleepiness of the park to explore it even further. And I almost always stopped by again after work as a way to delay my arrival to a lonely, cold and unwelcoming apartment.

My daily walks allowed me to reflect without feeling trapped in a space that reminded me of what was and made me ache for what could have been. As I paid more attention to what was around me, I also began to focus on what was inside me. I didn't expect one week of walking to and from work and avoiding *apéros* to magically heal me, but I was surprised by the volcanic eruption of emotions that sprang from deep within me. What was simmering for so long finally had the space and permission to show its complexity. Most nights after performing the best version of the Sutanya show at work, the muscles that kept the fake smile in place all day were given a well-deserved break, and my cheery demeanor was thrown in the hamper along with the day's work clothes, replaced by sweatpants and TFM's holey white Hanes T-shirt I couldn't manage to get rid of.

I spent some of those first nights hiding in my bedroom and crying, eating whatever bullshit crackers I found deep in the recesses of my cupboard or tasteless boxed soup I bought from the supermarket. I couldn't stomach anything else. Other nights I was so giddy with optimism that I would spend a few minutes halfheartedly attempting to tidy my space by removing the shoes strewn across the living room floor, the clothes hanging on the sofa, putting the caps on the several tubes of mascara dotting the bathroom sink and too many shades of red lipstick left open to dry out on my dresser, before retreating to the bed. What was once a home had morphed into a space where I fulfilled my most basic physiological needs—sleep and shower.

Then there were the nights I stood in the middle of the living room furiously scanning the apartment, wanting to trash the entire place and burn it down. At the end of each day, I met a new version of myself. It was frightening but refreshing because I was feeling. I had a sense of overwhelming release when those negative emotions were not immediately suppressed and avoided with destructive behavior.

While I was settling into my emotionally charged hermit lifestyle, the universe wasted no time in testing me by painting the Parisian sky a beautiful shade of ocean blue one Saturday a few weeks into my *apéroing* sabbatical. The sun beamed down on me from my bedroom window as I lay in bed queuing up my Netflix programming for the day. Its powerful, intoxicating rays beckoned me to call a friend and find the perfect *terrasse* to spend the afternoon drinking wine. The *terrasse* temptation went unanswered but I couldn't miss out on a sunny Saturday. After weeks of avoiding the outside world, excluding work hours, I promised myself that I would leave my apartment and continue what I'd been doing—just observe.

Jules Joffrin, my picturesque Parisian neighborhood, was bustling with weekend activity that I rarely witnessed for months because I was usually nursing a hangover and counting down until I could start all over again. Its main street, Rue du Poteau, is a hodgepodge of small local businesses such as wine shops, flower shops, butchers and greengrocers, mixed in with limestone Haussmann apartment buildings. The charming street includes several cafés that attract different types of neighborhood characters. There's a slightly expensive café at the beginning of the street usually occupied by tourists to the neighborhood. The waiters there hardly remember a face and couldn't care less whether or not you become a regular. A little farther down the street, there are cafés like La Piscine, a neighborhood institution, where the waiters not only remember your face but if you go often enough, they'll inquire about where you've been if they haven't seen you in a few days and question whether or not *tout va bien*.

As I observed the regulars perched on La Piscine's classic Parisian rattan bistro chairs, all facing the direction of the sun and enjoying their *café allongé*, it dawned on me that for so long I failed to see and indulge in small, yet significant, acts of daily pleasure.

Farther up the street, toward the metro station, I admired the fresh produce proudly displayed by the greengrocer. I was entranced by the enormous variety of cheeses at the cheesemonger. I wanted to buy all of the elegant and long-stemmed daffodils and lush, round peonies at the florist. I popped into a bookstore and leafed through the latest French bestsellers—I didn't have any intention of reading them, but I enjoyed the movie scene that I was acting out in my mind. I soaked up the aesthetic pleasures that Jules Joffrin regularly offered its occupants and visitors, that in the past, like a petulant child, I stubbornly ignored. I fell in love with my neighborhood again—in awe of everything around me—and by early evening when I entered the butcher shop that I had passed on numerous occasions but never before stepped foot in, an old sensation crept up on me: I was hungry for real food.

For no particular reason I decided to buy a raw chicken and roast it myself. An already professionally roasted chicken and potatoes would've been the perfect dinner and ending to my day of solo urban neighborhood exploration, but I wanted to keep myself occupied and hold on to the uplifting energy of the day for as long as possible, so I decided to try making it myself.

The glass case in front of me displayed assorted cuts of meat I had no idea how to cook. Stern-looking mustached men in crisp white aprons stood behind the counter, running the show. *How were there no bloodstains on those aprons?* I wondered to myself. Something about the entire scene told me that the butchers would not be charmed by my accented French, or particularly patient, so when I heard *"Suivant, s'il vous plait!"* signaling that it was my turn to order, I said aloud in my best French, the phrase I had been practicing in my head for the past few minutes, *"Un poulet, s'il vous plaît."*

I wanted to pat myself on the back; I was so sure that my French was perfectly executed. I emphasized the *pou* and ended with confidence and Parisian nonchalance on the *plaît*. But I wasn't fooling the butcher in front of me. He saw right through me: an American who didn't know what the hell she was doing. His face broke into a sly smile; he wiped his hands on the towel hanging from the front of his apron and asked me to specify the type of chicken I wanted. In French, he asked, "Do you want a chicken with black feet?"

"A red label?" he continued, "or maybe a farm-raised chicken? You know, the ones that run wild on the farm...would that please the little lady?"

I sheepishly responded, also in French, "Um, I don't know what kind of chicken I want. This is actually the first time I'll be making a whole roasted chicken," I confessed, smiling self-consciously. I paused and made a split-second decision to my confession, "I'm pretty nervous, actually."

That led to a rapid-fire question and answer session, also in French.

"Where are you from?"

"New York City."

"Do you live in Paris?"

"Yes."

"For how long?"

"Three years."

"Do you like Paris?"

"Yes, I love it."

"Do you like Paris better than New York?"

"I can't choose. They're both great cities."

"Why did you move to Paris?"

"For work." I didn't think it was appropriate to share the emotional clusterfuck that was the past three years of my life with my new butcher friend.

Satisfied with my responses, he gave me a half smile and said, "Good luck," in conclusion.

I'm not sure if he took pity on me or if my honesty and vulnerability worked in my favor but whatever the case, he spent an extra fifteen minutes with me explaining how to make the best roasted chicken, in his not-so-humble opinion. He also made me promise that I would come back to tell him if I was successful. He was flirting, and not because I was seeking that kind of attention from him. Even if the chicken turned out to be a bust, I was already feeling successful. I didn't go back at that time, but I became somewhat of a regular there, and developed a very friendly, even flirty, relationship with him. Since that afternoon, whenever I pass the butcher shop I get a wave, smile and a wink from him, even if I am not stopping by. When I do pop in to make a purchase, he playfully reminds me that he's waiting for his dinner invitation.

I left the butcher shop that evening proud of my French language skills, excited and determined to make myself the best roasted chicken. From there, I stopped to buy two russet potatoes, one white onion and a couple handfuls of spinach from the greengrocer diagonal to the butcher shop, a bottle of red wine from the *caviste* down the street, and made a quick run to the supermarket to get a few essential bits and bobs needed for the meal—*Herbs de Provence*, smoked paprika, salt, pepper and olive oil. And just before I went home, I strolled back to the florist and treated myself to the bouquet of peonies I'd had my eye on earlier that day. I practically skipped back to my apartment. I was genuinely looking forward to my evening project, a positive distraction that would hopefully keep my mind from wandering into a dark place.

Up the blue spiral stairs and through the door, I went straight to the kitchen—this time fully clothed. I unpacked my purchases, poured myself a glass of wine and looked at it with trepidation. This was another test. Would I take a sip, immediately abandon my dinner plans and text a friend declaring, "Sutanya is back!" or would I be able to exercise self-control and only have a glass or two—allowing myself a reasonable dose of pleasure?

That evening in my kitchen, with Bossa Nova streaming from my laptop and my hips swaying from side to side, I followed the butcher's instructions—carefully mixing together the olive oil, sea salt, ground black pepper, paprika and *Herbs de Provence* into a small bowl. He recommended preparing the marinade in a bowl first, adjusting it to my preferred taste. *"Chacun a son goût,"* I remembered him saying. After achieving my desired balance of saltiness, smokiness and heat, I poured the mixture all over the chicken, massaging it in to make sure every part was covered in the liquid gold. I peeled and cut the potatoes into fours and chopped the onions in half. I had big plans for them. I lightly tossed them in a bit of olive oil, table salt and pepper, then arranged the potatoes and onions in the roasting pan and placed the chicken on top. This would allow the chicken juices to drip on them as it roasted, another *astuce* from the butcher.

With the chicken, potatoes and onions roasting away, I had nothing else to do. My usual Vogue pastel cigarettes didn't seem appealing. I didn't want to call or text anyone. I didn't drink more in order to avoid succumbing to the false promises of wine. So with my hands in the pockets of my jeans I timidly walked into the living room. I poked my head in at first, looking around as if I was about to enter a forbidden room. A room whose walls held the secrets and sins of former lovers. A room that witnessed the stages of a love that went from romance to disenchantment and ended in misery. A room where the lovers, each with their own expectations, realized that the life they hoped for and wanted to build together would never come to fruition.

I sat on the couch and tears started flowing. In the past few weeks I cried more than I did in the immediate aftermath of my breakup. They were not tears of self-pity or fear; they were cathartic. I was sitting in a room that I avoided for months and finally began mourning my marriage. Through tears I repeated to myself over and over, "I can do this. I can do this. I can do this." The self-motivational dialogue continued until the shrill tone of my iPhone timer signaled that the roast may be finished and the delicious aroma that infused the entire apartment confirmed that it definitely was. For the first time in a long time the apartment smelled like home—a cozy home you look forward to retreating to after a long day outside its comforting walls.

I pulled the chicken from the oven, cut into it and took a bite—I was obliged to taste test. Beneath the crispy, blistered skin was moist, flavorful meat. Some of the potatoes were burned but enough of them were salvageable and the onions had taken on a sweet, delicious, paste-like texture. I beamed with pride looking at the dinner in front of me. I switched the music on my laptop to jazz; I set the table with real silverware and cloth napkins, items that had been collecting dust in my kitchen drawers since TFM left. Before taking the first bite, I lit a single white taper candle, allowing light back into a space that had lately experienced far too much darkness.

"You're not a failure," I told myself. It was the first time I uttered those words out loud. I didn't entirely believe it, but felt comfort knowing that I was putting that statement out into the universe. Making a real meal and setting the table was the nicest thing that I had done for myself in months. But in reality it was more than a comforting homemade meal; it was the first step to filling an emotionless void of my own construction.

Sitting alone with jazz streaming from my laptop and a home-cooked meal in front of me felt better than deceptive drunken freedom at a bar or the excitement of falling into bed with a new body. It was surely more satisfying than overindulging in cigarettes and wine. It was nourishing from the inside out, expunging hopelessness and replacing it with a necessary *souffle de vie*.

Sixteen

THOSE RED-AND-WHITE TILES

My successful roasted chicken dinner represented more than just being able to exercise self-control and resist temptation; sitting around my dining table that evening with a homemade meal in front of me planted seeds of hope. It was the nicest thing I'd done for myself in months and over time my dinners for one became a ritual and non-negotiable form of self-care. While every evening didn't necessarily end in a feast for one, I enjoyed spending time in my kitchen. It wasn't a chef's kitchen and hadn't been recently renovated, so it wasn't its spectacular finishings that drew me in. It was the way I felt whenever I opened the door and placed my feet on the red-and-white tiles that beckoned me in, repeatedly. It filled me with joy—a long-lost feeling that colored my premarital trips to Paris and early days living here. With every meal I made for myself, the poisonous emotions that stemmed from heartbreak increasingly lost their powerful grip over me. I slowly began finding peace within myself and started setting the stage for my rebirth.

As time passed I traded my lengthy *apéros* for evenings and week-ends spent cooking in my kitchen. Without the shame or regret from the previous night's bender keeping me in bed, I filled my Saturdays and Sundays exploring the various food-shopping options that lined my street. The only corporate-owned food stores on the street at the time were three supermarkets—Monoprix, Naturalia and Franprix. Everything else was a small business and I was spoiled for choice. On my street alone there were three *cavistes*, wine shops, three *boucheries*, butcher shops, two *primeurs*, greengrocers, two *poissonneries*, fishmongers, two *fleuristes*, flower shops, one *glacier*, ice cream shop, one *fromagerie*, cheese shop, and a few cafés dotted here and there, patiently waiting for me to take a break and indulge in some people-watching after spending my morning tasting sweet and juicy in-season strawberries and laughing to myself with glee after taking a bite of the first raw green peas of the season—their zesty freshness awakening my taste buds and leaving permanent imprints.

My decision to spend as little time as possible in the big-box supermarkets was a conscious one. The small businesses, each with their own personalities and histories, were a part of my neighborhood and I wanted to remove my observer lens, just for a little bit, in an attempt to truly become a part of the community where I lived. My positive interaction with the butcher when I bought my first whole chicken gave me the courage to engage in small talk with the *commerçants*, the shopkeepers, that seemed willing to have a conversation—quite a few were not interested at all. But enough of them were curious about the American woman who spoke halfway decent French, purchased odd quantities of produce—like one potato and five sprigs of asparagus—and asked a lot of questions. My questions ranged from the best way to prepare leeks to the quantity of sugar needed to give raspberries the perfect sugar bath when making *clafoutis*, to the difference between violet garlic and regular garlic. I learned that violet garlic tends to be milder in flavor and is "fresher" than regular white garlic. Engaging in conversation with the various *commerçants* helped me in the kitchen and with my French language skills. There was no switching to English or Englishizing a French word when my French vocabulary failed me. For the first time since moving I was forced to communicate exclusively in French in order to be understood and understand.

The *boucherie*, *primeur* and *poissonnerie* were my comfort zones, the *fromagerie* not so much. The *fromagerie* was off-limits because I was intimidated; cheese purchases had always been TFM's domain because the choice was overwhelming. While all of the other *commerçants* seemed to find my curiosity endearing, I falsely believed that I would be shamed out of the *fromagerie* for being a basic American that only liked mimolette—France's version of cheddar cheese.

The butcher made sure I always remembered his dinner invitation and never failed to remind me that he needs enough notice so that *"je peux me faire beau"*—I can make myself handsome. We both knew that the invitation would never actually come to fruition, but he enjoyed making me blush, and I liked surprising myself by coming up with snippy French responses that left him roaring with laughter. I am sure many times his laughter was caused by something nonsensical, but he never made me any wiser.

The older men who worked at the *primeur* routinely popped extra treats into my bag before I left, and the young woman behind the register enjoyed quizzing my French by holding up a random fruit or vegetable and asking, *"Alors, dites-moi qu'est-ce que c'est?"*—So tell me, what's this? There was always a dazzling variety of mostly locally sourced fish and seafood at the *poissonnerie*, aptly named Les Pirates de Montmartre. It wasn't uncommon for me to walk past without any intention of buying anything and then suddenly find myself on my way to the apartment with a few shrimp in a blue plastic bag to be made for lunch with lots of finely sliced garlic, cilantro and parsley, a generous splash of white wine and butter.

One sunny day toward the end of the morning, I was walking past Les Pirates de Montmartre on my way home, as I usually do, when I heard in French, "So we're not stopping today?" I looked to my left and it was one of the pirates, a tawny Afro-Venezuelan with curly jet-black hair and a permanent crooked half smile like he was in on a naughty secret that you were dying to know all about. Without stopping I held up my tote bags and responded with a smile, "I already have everything I need." Of course, he didn't accept that response and within minutes I was examining the display, trying to make a decision about what to buy. Finding it difficult to decide what unnecessary purchase I was going to make that late morning, I asked the tenacious pirate for his opinion.

"I don't know what to buy. What do you advise?" I asked in French.

"Well, maybe salmon? You can make a *saumon en papillote*. It's one of my favorites and very easy," he responded.

I knew *saumon* was salmon, but *en papillote* threw me for a loop. I'd never heard that before. I thought to myself *did he just say* papillon, *which means butterfly*? I stopped myself from asking "what's a butterfly salmon?" and instead asked, "What's a *saumon en papillote*?" like a normal person.

"You don't know *saumon en papillote*?" he asked, answering my question with a question. "It's like a gift," he finally said. His crooked smile slightly straightening out for a millisecond. He explained that *saumon en papillote* is like a gift to yourself, or dinner guests, because it is salmon and vegetables of your choice cooked in parchment paper. I wondered what was so special about cooking salmon on parchment paper, but I liked the idea of giving oneself a gift, and I had parchment paper at home so I bought a filet of salmon and verified that the vegetables from my earlier purchases that morning could be used for the dish.

Later that afternoon in my kitchen, with my laptop perched on the counter, I Googled the meaning of *en papillote* and realized that I completely misunderstood the pirate. It doesn't mean cooking salmon, or anything for that matter, *on* parchment paper. *En papillote* is a cooking method that means *enveloping* your food with parchment paper. Whenever you *en papillote* something you place it in a folded pouch or parcel made out of parchment paper, close it and then bake it. When finished cooking you open the pouch or parcel to reveal the finished dish; that was why he compared it to a gift. I was now intent on making a food gift from me, to me.

To make my first *saumon en papillote*, I placed the salmon filet on a baking sheet lined with parchment paper then, after sprinkling it with salt, pepper, paprika, adding a generous dash of olive oil and a few other spices, I rubbed it all in. I finished by throwing in a handful of bright red cherry tomatoes, a crushed garlic clove, chopped earthy green zucchini and a few strips of sharp fennel and tangy white onion. I watched a YouTube video tutorial about making the ideal picture-perfect package that would trap steam inside, but after several failed attempts I impatiently brought each of the four sides to the center and scrunched it all up in the middle. It looked far from the sophisticated packages I saw in the tutorials, but I didn't allow any negative thoughts to take away from the pleasure I was experiencing in that moment.

After twenty minutes in the oven my gift was on my table. Steam billowed out of the top, the bottom heavy with juices, and I couldn't help but notice the smell of roasted tomato, garlic and onion—the fragrant blend that brought back sad memories of me on my knees a few months earlier. I shook that memory out of my head and delicately opened my package and received an unexpected but nevertheless thoroughly enjoyable *saumon en papillote* steam facial. Surrounding the pink flaky salmon were burst cherry tomatoes infused with garlic, onions that were now sticky and sweet, and softened fennel to round out the dish.

As I was about to dig in to the salmon I realized I forgot to make rice as a side dish, but in reality I had everything I needed right in front of me. Which is something that was becoming more apparent about my life in Paris as I began to accept my new reality, take care of myself and take crucial steps toward falling in love with myself again. My heart wasn't going to heal overnight—in many ways I was still hurting, very angry at TFM and in shock—but I had a strong network of friends, a steady job, a beautiful apartment, a newfound hobby, cooking, and my health. That was a pretty good starter pack for getting my shit together. All I needed to do was make a commitment to myself and stick to it.

My initial meals weren't always a success. Once, feeling overly confident, I invited a group of friends over to dinner and attempted to make *sole meunière*—a classic French dish—for the first time. It was a disaster. I didn't expect lightly flouring a few filets of fish then cooking them in butter to be difficult and it shouldn't have been if I had the correct ingredients. That morning when I went to buy the sole my usual pirate was nowhere to be seen, so someone else helped me. We both clearly didn't understand each other because I didn't go home with a few filets of sole; I went home with four whole fishes, unscaled, skin on and insides intact. I didn't realize the error until my friends arrived and I began cooking. With no other options I served the fish with mushy, undercooked rice. All of the guests were polite enough to pick at the fish and eat what they could, but all of the uneaten fish and rice left on their plates at the end of the night was a clear indicator that it was a fail.

I was slightly embarrassed but far from deterred. I set out to make a *sole meurnière* worthy of Julia Childs's approval. After consulting different recipes, both English and French, I noticed that many home cooks praised *Le Beurre Bordier*—a renowned

French butter. If it was anything like the butter I tasted during my first solo trip to visit TFM, I couldn't wait to cook with it. My excitement around my upcoming project grew until I realized that the butter isn't sold in supermarkets, only in specialty shops. And the specialty shop closest to me was the dreaded *fromagerie*.

The day I decided to reattempt *sole meunière*, this time for one, I set off early to avoid the crowds at the *fromagerie*. By midday the line was usually out the door and if possible, I wanted to avoid embarrassing myself in front of both the *commerçants* and customers.

The scent of the shop snuck into my nostrils before I entered the store. The abundance of different types of cheeses alongside the controlled temperature of the space produced a pungent smell that sat on the spectrum between old sweaty gym socks and cheese that had gone bad, but that was a good sign. I'd read that the smellier the *fromagerie*, the better the cheese selection.

A stout lady, wearing faded blue jeans and a nondescript dusty brown polo greeted me. She had wavy, shoulder-length hair that matched the color of her shirt and wore thick-rimmed glasses. She looked pretty no-nonsense. I was unsure if my American charm would help or hurt in this situation so I decided to play it cool.

"Hello, how can I help you?" she asked, deadpan without a smile. The lack of a smile from her, for some reason, signaled to me that I should answer her question with a big smile that displayed all of my teeth.

I responded, "Yes, I would like *beurre bordier*."

She gave me a perplexed look and said, "Euhhhh, okay." She went to get the butter and I simultaneously stopped smiling and began internally cursing myself for being such a weirdo. By the time she came back I just wanted to pay and hastily run out of there, but she asked me the question I hoped to avoid, *"Est-*

ce que vous fallait d'autre choses?"—Do you need anything else? Small sweat beads started to form around at the top of my forehead and I blurted out, *"Oui! Fromage!"*—Yes! Cheese! After a few seconds of awkward silence she let out a chuckle that was somewhere between amused and afraid, cracked a smile and said, "Well, you're in the right place."

Similar to my first time at the butcher, I was completely honest and transparent about the fact that I didn't know much about cheese, but I did know what I like. With that admission, my tasting session began. I sampled Tomme de Savoie, a nutty cheese known for its ashy rind, several different varieties of Brie and other cheese delicacies that varied in texture from ultra-hard to extremely soft. I was almost ready to buy a few cheeses that stood out when she cut me a sliver of Brillat-Savarin *truffé*. As she was cutting it she said, "You're gonna love this one," but I was skeptical. I was almost at my cheese-intake maximum, but I didn't want to risk being considered impolite if I refused.

The flavors that graced my taste buds were sublime. I couldn't speak; I just looked directly into her eyes and nodded my head. I'd never tasted anything like this before in my life. She clapped and proclaimed, "I knew it!" Brillat-Savarin *truffé* is a cheese made of cow's milk with a layer of truffle in the middle. The cheese itself is deliciously silky, its creaminess layering your tongue with a slight fruity flavor, which is intersected and balanced by the nutty, woody flavor of the truffle. There was no doubt that this was the cheese I'd be going home with that day.

In between tasting all the cheeses, she complimented my French, telling me it was *trés bien*—very good—and was pleasantly surprised when I told her I lived here. She was mostly intrigued by my decision to live in Paris instead of New York City. She told me, *"Tous les Français rêvent de vivre à New York"*—All French people dream about living in New York. I responded, *"C'est une ville incroyable mais je me sens chez moi à Paris pour le moment"*—It's a great city but I feel at home in Paris, for now.

The more I cooked for myself, put myself first and acknowledged the mixed feelings that accompanied my every waking moment, I truly did start feeling more at home in my skin and Paris. A visit to the *fromagerie* became a part of my weekend shopping ritual and I was routinely greeted with a cheerful, *"Bonjour, la petite americaine, qu'est-ce que vous voulez goûter aujourd'hui?"*—Hello, little American, what would you like to taste today? My interaction at the *fromagerie* gave me more than a lesson about different cheeses. It illustrated that the more I stepped out of my comfort zone, embraced the discomfort that was inevitable considering my situation and not being ashamed of my limitations, my taste buds and sense of self would reap immeasurable rewards.

Cooking more meant spending more time at home, which no longer bothered me. Little by little I began reclaiming the apartment by slowly transforming it into my perfect bachelorette pad. Out went the last remnants of TFM's masculine presence, like his coffee table made out of palettes and his bulky furniture that didn't leave room for air to circulate throughout the apartment. Living in the apartment on my own meant that, finally, the space could begin to slowly resemble a place I wanted to live—a colorful blend of high and low, with vintage and modern furniture coexisting peacefully.

The coffee table was the last big piece of furniture to go, and in many ways the hardest to let go of. He made the coffee table by hand the first month we lived together and it was his pride and joy. I knew that it no longer needed to be in my apartment; I just didn't have the heart to throw it away. Samar did, though. She knew that in some ways it was holding me back. It wasn't just the symbol of what it meant, it was also the size; it took up a quarter of the living room. It was as if TFM was still asserting his presence in my life, still holding court in our first Parisian apartment.

One afternoon over coffee at a local café in my neighborhood Samar randomly inquired about it. "Have you thrown out the coffee table yet?" she asked.

I hesitated before telling her the truth. "No, not yet," I responded. "But I will soon!" I quickly added in my defense.

She took a sip of her coffee and looked at me over the rims of her glasses.

"You're just like Filip," she said. "Everything is soon, soon, soon, but you never do," she continued.

"Yalla. We're throwing out that fucking table right now. Today," she declared.

"What? No, it's okay. We don't have to. I'll do it, I promise," I said, trying to get out of it, but there was no stopping her. Before even trying to convince her that I would, in fact, do it another day, the bill was paid and she was standing in front of me with her arms folded and impatiently tapping her foot while waiting for me to get up and move my ass.

We walked back to my apartment building and up the blue stairs. I let out a big sigh before we began slowly dismantling the coffee table in silence. We took the glass top off first, putting it to the side before flipping the table and removing the four wheels. I made sure we were extremely gentle during the entire process. Unconsciously, I was being delicate and attentive with the last remaining pieces of what had been a beautiful love story that ultimately collapsed under pressure. I put the wheels in a plastic bag and we disassembled the biggest part of the coffee table by breaking apart the two palettes that made up the bulk of TFM's work. We slowly took everything downstairs and in many ways it felt liberating, the last of his energy and the feelings that I was holding on to—hope, our story and denial left with it. The coffee table pieces were in front of my apartment building and should've been picked up by the sanitation department early the next morning, but by the time I went for a walk with Samar and came back, everything was gone. The remnants of my love story was, presumably, the beginning of another story in someone else's home.

I filled the empty space left by TFM's coffee table with a lively and vibrant turquoise-colored Habitat coffee table that Tiffanie gave me before she moved to London. It had been collecting dust in my bedroom. Shortly after, I began the next phase of making the apartment my own. I rearranged the furniture into different figurations until I found the one that felt right. I bought artwork that I didn't have to compromise on or ask for a second opinion. I started buying plants and nurturing and caring for them, showing them unabashed tenderness and having the pleasure of watching them blossom and grow. I started to feel hopeful in my life and began taking up space in my apartment again. With each small change—whether it was moving around furniture or buying a new *brocante* sourced treasure for my home—I was putting together the ingredients that would turn a house into my home, and I couldn't have been happier.

I was cooking more; my apartment was starting to take shape and resemble a home that was a reflection of me, but there was something still missing. Like my marriage, all of these were external markers of success, but I wanted to feel at peace within myself in order to have a real sense of completeness.

When my marriage ended my internal purpose died with it. My corporate job was serving its purpose—providing me with money to be able to pay for a roof over my head, food to eat and the possibility to live in Paris on my own—but that was all it did. I knew that I was easily replaceable and my role wasn't adding to the overall story of humanity in any way, shape or form. The question that was a constant presence in my mind was "What should I do next?" I could've restarted my sessions with Ursula to try to work through my questions around my purpose, but I wanted to tackle this myself.

When I worked at the advertising agency it was drilled into

my head that eating lunch with colleagues was nonnegotiable; eating alone was not acceptable. I was relieved to learn that wasn't the case at the technology company I now worked for. There was more autonomy around the way I spent my free hour of the day, and I took full advantage of it. The company was technically in the sixteenth arrondissement but bordered the seventeenth, both wealthy enclaves that felt worlds away from my gentrifying neighborhood. It was elegant and proper, but as usual, I was hard-pressed to find a Black or brown person who wasn't a service worker. Alas, I continued exploring. If I didn't bring leftovers for lunch I would spend my hour walking around the Ternes neighborhood in the seventeenth arrondissement, popping into stores or parking myself on a bench and losing myself, passing time in my thoughts.

One afternoon, when my post-lunch schedule was clear of meetings, I decided to take a slightly longer lunch break and walk to Parc Monceau. The sunshine, clear blue skies and mild temperature begged me to stay outside as long as possible. "I have an appointment during lunch so I'll be back a little late today," I told my manager. It wasn't a complete lie; I had an appointment with nature, I rationalized with myself. And I wasn't going to take advantage of his trust. I would only extend my normal lunch break an extra thirty minutes, maybe forty-five, but that would be my maximum I told myself as I walked down rue Saint-Ferdinand, toward Avenue des Ternes, which would then lead to boulevard de Courcelles, then it was just a straight shot to the park.

As usual, as I was walking I was taking everything in and for the first time, at the intersection of rue Saint-Ferdinand and rue d'Armaillé, I noticed a church. *This is strange, this is the first time I'm seeing this*, I thought to myself. I shrugged my shoulders and kept walking toward Avenue des Ternes, but I felt a pull back to the church. I turned around, walked towards it and went inside. I sat not too far in the back but not way up front, either. I wanted to be discreet and not draw attention to myself.

I've always found churches safe and comforting. As someone who grew up in a Christian household and went to Catholic school my entire life, it was the place where I left all of my troubles at the door and sought answers. It was where I acknowledged that I believed there was something bigger than me out there in the universe and its purpose was to help me. It was especially calming to see that I wasn't the only person who found their way into a church on a random weekday afternoon, looking for answers.

I didn't set off on my walk with the intention of going to church, but I was happy to be there. I launched into a conversation with God. I asked Him for guidance. I told Him that I felt lost and I didn't know where to turn next. I told Him that I needed Him to show me the way. I was making progress but a lot of my emotions still felt very raw. I admitted that I was still scared and sometimes I felt very alone. I wanted to know if I was making the right decisions and if Paris was somewhere I could and should be. These were a lot of questions and requests to present at one time, even to a Supreme Being, so I wrapped it up for the day. But I kept going back. I found myself in the *Paroisse Saint Ferdinand des Ternes* several times a week. I cried, I asked questions, I sat, I meditated and with every visit, slowly began feeling an internal shift. I was finding peace within myself.

The peace that I was finally finding from cooking and spending time within myself led me to not see my divorce as the end, but the beginning of a new life. It was just up to me to decide how I was going to live it and what I was going to do. For now the most important thing was to continue taking care of myself through my dinners. I was making progress and what a relief.

Seventeen

<u>JE T'AIME... JUST KIDDING</u>

I misinterpreted the *souffle de vie* I felt after my roasted chicken moment—and subsequent evenings and weekends spent in my kitchen cooking—a sign that I was ready to dive back into dating. I believed I was ready to fall in love again and put a tidy pretty bow on my story. I desperately wanted a happy ending in order to make sense of a three-year long-distance relationship and two-and-a-half-year marriage. Clearly, I was still at a loss about what actually needed to be done.

My second foray into dating French men didn't have the same lingering stench of desperation as my first post-divorce attempt. However, it was still as much of a mindfuck as the first time. This time I just didn't take it to heart. When dating in France it's not about who can pretend they don't care the longest; it's about who can go all in and be the most vulnerable while remaining reasonable. Being reasonable while dating in France means understanding that your time with the person will last only as long as you're both interested, so it's important to remain present and enjoy every moment. The relationship could last three years, three weeks or three hours, but what matters is the honesty of feelings and engagement no matter the duration of time. My French friends routinely described someone they were seeing for four weeks as an ex-boyfriend; I would say he was someone they were just dating. In my American mind you cannot create, live and end a full relationship in four weeks. Americans date first then decide to get in a relationship, once their potential partner has been vetted and approved. The French go with their feeling, and how long the feeling lasts is a mystery. But when the feeling is present it's electrifying.

I decided to be pragmatic and create a short list of criteria to help guide me to my happy ending and love. I shared the list with my friends—put it out in the universe and sat back waiting for my perfect love to appear. My list only consisted of three things: he needed to be a creative person, have a scooter and live in Paris—I wanted to keep it simple. With my criteria in mind and confident that I had control over my emotional state, a few weeks later I was tested to see if I was actually ready to embark on a new love story.

Dinner with Jen—a friend I made while working at the advertising agency and a fellow American living in Paris—transitioned into dancing at Le Carmen, a club in the Pigalle neighborhood. We lost ourselves to 90s dance music; sweat dripped off of my forehead and down my chest.

The two glasses of wine I enjoyed with dinner didn't lead to a rapid succession of several others; I was in control and proud.

At around midnight our legs started aching and we decided to call it a night. We made our way through the young gyrating bodies on the dance floor to the exit and outside. Under the club's neon signage, while Jen was waiting for her Uber, I frantically searched for my trusty pink lighter and became increasingly frustrated when I couldn't find it. After rummaging through my pockets and bag I asked the stranger closest to me for a lighter. I gently tapped the shoulder to my left and asked, "Do you have a lighter?" I spoke to this person in English because I was tired and I obnoxiously assumed that if you were in front of Le Carmen at midnight you were likely young and therefore would at least be able to understand English, even if the response would be in French.

The only way to describe the man who turned around is *beautiful*. He stood up straight, revealing his full height: at least six feet and two inches. He had the most radiant smile, a real American Colgate smile that I hadn't seen in years. He spoke perfect English and his face was splattered with golden freckles. That golden face was a disturbing mix of boyish charm and pain with a generous dash of trouble, but in that moment I decided I wanted it all. And he had a lighter.

I was instantly sucked into his universe. I couldn't stop talking to him. He couldn't stop talking to me. We were simultaneously ending each other's sentences and interrupting each other. It was like we had too much to catch up on and the universe had kept us apart for far too long. I didn't notice when Jen's Uber arrived to take her home. I was firmly planted in his world and he in mine. I was falling hard and quick. I tried to stop myself but I couldn't. I was falling deeper and deeper by the minute. I wanted to date seriously and fall in love again, but I didn't expect it to happen so soon.

As we chain-smoked cigarettes in front of Le Carmen, I became increasingly convinced that he was the man of my dreams. I learned that he was an art director at an advertising agency and just moved back to Paris after spending time abroad. Those were two essential boxes checked: creativity and city of residence. We eventually got around to exchanging names, and his name is the same as the metro station of my beloved neighborhood, my home. All of these things I interpreted as signs from a loving universe. I also learned that he was not at Le Carmen that night; he was putting his mother in a taxi after having dinner with her and was planning on going home straight after. I tapped on his shoulder at the perfect time. Had I hesitated or waited even a minute longer he would've left. I thought to myself that this was definitely another sign; fate almost. It was reminiscent of the night I met TFM. If I hadn't gone to Fenelli's I wouldn't be in Paris.

However, unlike the night I met TFM, things got physical quickly when out of nowhere he kissed me. It wasn't a shy, nervous peck on the lips. It was a full, deep, passionate, "I cannot control myself" kiss. It was an "is he going to eat my face?" kiss. He held on to my waist tightly, holding me so close I could hear his heart beating. I thought to myself, *Is this really happening*? We were kissing when I heard *"Heyyyyyy."* We both stopped and turned around. *"Salut,"* he said to a man with dark, shoulder length hair and a woman who looked like she just walked off the cover of *Vogue* magazine. He looked at me and said, "That's my brother and his girlfriend." I couldn't help but burst out in laughter. What were the chances? I exchanged pleasantries with our guests and cracked a few jokes. Eventually, they decided to leave us alone to finish what we started and I thought to myself, *This is great. I've just met the family and we hit it off. I'm definitely in.* The streets emptied around us but I didn't care. In those twilight hours I was being reintroduced to the forgotten sweetness of instant chemistry, and like a decadent serving of chocolate cake I wanted it all, to the very last crumb. Eventually, the lull around us was unavoidable and he checked the time. It was somewhere between 2 a.m. and 3:30 a.m.: time to part ways.

"How are you getting home?" he asked.

"I'm going to walk," I responded. "I need to cool off," I joked.

He wasn't amused, his face changed shape and he took on a paternal protector look.

He responded, "No, come with me. On my scooter."

I froze and asked, "Your what?" I was sure I misheard him.

He repeated himself, "My scooter. It's over there," he continued and pointed to a yellow scooter across the street from where we were standing. I couldn't believe that he met all of my criteria.

We walked hand in hand over to his yellow scooter but before hopping on, he placed his hand behind his head and pulled away, unleashing long, luscious red curly hair that tumbled down his shoulders. I didn't see the color of his hair under the dim lights in front of the club. He looked like a modern-day Viking with his red curly hair cascading down his back. I quietly squealed. He didn't comment on my burst of unexplained emotion, so I assumed he didn't hear.

"I only have one helmet," he said.

"That's okay. I only live a few minutes away," I responded.

"Maybe you do, but it's not safe," he said. I made note of, and appreciated, his chivalry. He put his helmet on me, but it was too big.

After having an internal debate he said to himself, "We're just going to have to take a quick detour to my studio to pick up another helmet." Then he included me in the conversation and asked, "It's only five minutes away. Is that okay?"

I nodded in response.

He got on the scooter first to balance it and I hopped on after, swinging my left leg over first before sitting and wrapping my forearms around his waist. I held him so close as if trying to fuse our bodies into one.

"Ready?" he asked.

"*Oui!*" I exclaimed.

Within five minutes we were in front of a gate and he was entering the *digicode* to get into the building's courtyard. We walked through the door of a ground-floor apartment. He turned on the lights and I looked around. We were not in the studio apartment I expected. We were in his music studio; he plays the bass and therefore double-checked the creativity box. I was falling deeper; this was just too good to be true.

While he rummaged around, looking for a spare helmet, I was taking in the atmosphere of the studio—looking at the vinyl album covers that adorned the walls and counting the number of the guitars in the room.

"It's pretty cool, isn't it?" he said, standing behind me with a helmet in his hand.

"Yeah, it is. It's not at all what I expected," I answered.

With further questioning he confessed that he wasn't a professional musician; his father is a music producer so naturally he and his siblings play instruments and sometimes they mess around with their father in the studio. He placed a significantly smaller black helmet on my head and affixed the chin clasp, without breaking eye contact. I didn't expect my romantic comedy to take this turn, but I decided to lean in to whatever the Viking had to offer in the same way I leaned in to TFM.

"All right, let's go," he said and snapped me out of my fantasy.

We hopped back on his scooter and cruised down Rue Caulaincourt, the street that has witnessed so much of my Paris history. Crisp air graced my face but I felt warmth permeating through my entire body. A fire was reignited—I was high on instant love drunkenness, and an old feeling of lightness came over me. We pulled up to the front of my apartment building and after a few more kisses we were finally able to, begrudgingly, pull away from each other. I glided upstairs alone.

We exchanged a few text messages after that night. Plans were made to see each other, but they were always canceled and I never saw the Viking ever again.

I wasn't as disappointed about not seeing him again as I expected myself to be. It was liberating to be present in the moment without expectations or trying to force something that wasn't organic. When I stopped using potential partners as distractions and didn't put pressure on myself to find the one, I found myself actually appreciating these experiences. If they led to a long-lasting relationship, I would chalk it up to being the right time. If they ended at least I had a great learning opportunity, while allowing myself to be courted, desired and treated with genuine affection.

I probably learned the most about myself and what I wanted and needed when I dated Antoine—another Antoine; it's a very common first name in France. A video editor by trade, he checked the creativity criteria and city of residence. He didn't have a scooter or red hair but I let it slide because there were other redeeming qualities about him.

After a successful first date he was very forthright about his interest in me and his feelings about me. He texted, called and made his presence known, but not in an overbearing way. There was no playing it cool—from leaving roses in my mailbox for me to find after a day at work to impromptu date nights he was all in, and I relished in the attention.

By the time we met and began dating, I had made considerable strides in learning French. When left on your own in a foreign country, your language acquisition accelerates beyond belief. His English was better than my French, but we naturally spoke to each other in our native languages. The lack of having to translate or think about what you want to say before actually saying it simplified a lot of aspects of us getting to know each other. I was myself and I assume that just by virtue of being able to speak in his native tongue, Antoine was himself with me as well. At times I wondered how this ease would've been helpful when I was married to TFM, but I didn't allow those thoughts to linger and take up space.

More than the comfort of speaking our native languages, we also shared a love of cooking and eating; Antoine even enjoyed baking and had a KitchenAid mixer to prove it. My skills in the kitchen improved the more I cooked for myself but his were far superior. He made the creamiest, silkiest risotto I've ever tasted. His raspberry *clafoutis* was spongy and moist, the raspberries perfectly sweet. I still dream about his tiramisu. Seeing him cooking or eating reminded me of the little boy I saw at the bistro, lost in a world of joy and comfort. I wanted to feel that, too.

In addition to his culinary prowess, Antoine was the first French man I dated whose physical living space inspired me. I found myself spending most of my time there, potentially too much, because he managed to achieve something I was still in the process of tackling—transforming an apartment into a home. Antoine's apartment was an oasis of his own making. Two red double doors opened up to his immaculate apartment. A few steps in and to your left you're greeted with floor-to-ceiling shelves full of records. He could tell you about each and every single one, from the year they were produced to the best track on the album. A little farther back into the apartment, his love of cinema was on full display. Above his couch hung three vintage posters of his favorite movies. From the couch there was a direct view of his favorite place to be and his workshop, the open kitchen. There was ample countertop space and enough room for two people to dance and drink cocktails while making their *plat du jour.*

The kitchen was perfectly equipped with everything an amateur professional home cook needed. For Antoine it wasn't about having the latest and greatest gadget; it was making sure that everything had a purpose. The pride he had in his space and the comfort he felt there was palpable and inspiring. I wanted to be proud of my space, to spend time there, to cook there, too—but I needed to do it alone. He reminded me of the importance in taking up space in your apartment by engaging in activities that bring you joy while you're there. For some people that may be in DIY projects, as was the case with TFM. For me it was becoming increasingly clear that the activity that brought me the most joy was cooking for myself. The problem was that I spent most of my time cooking with Antoine in his kitchen. Without realizing, I fell under the temptation of distraction and temporarily neglected my kitchen and space.

In the end it didn't work out with Antoine. Four months into dating, he unceremoniously broke it off with me via text. He said all the right things: "He appreciated me but the timing was off."

"He had a great time with me and has no regrets."

"He wished me the best and hoped that I found someone that would be better suited for me than he was." I would be insincere if I said I wasn't hurt. I had strong feelings for him and was sad when it ended. However, the difference this time was that I didn't go off the deep end and fall back into negative coping patterns, nor did I rush to find someone else to replace him. I wished him the best and continued on my journey without looking back. I didn't blame myself for the breakup and I didn't search for anything wrong within me that needed to be fixed. I viewed my time with him only for what it was—a lovely experience full of vulnerability, honesty and divine meals. My strong feelings for him were not fully reciprocated, but that didn't take away from my value and my potential to be the right match for someone else, when the time was right. But until then, I needed to be a better partner to myself.

I wonder if my Zen attitude around our breakup disturbed him more than he let on because two months after we broke up, he reached out to me asking me to borrow a suitcase to go on vacation with his new girlfriend, who was the woman he was in a relationship with before we started dating. I couldn't help but chuckle to myself and think. *Oh, how classically French.*

After my relationship with Antoine I took another long break from dating. My focus was still on the wrong thing—being in a relationship with someone else who wasn't me. I didn't make a big announcement to the world that I was off the market; I simply deleted the dating apps and spent more time alone in the apartment and kitchen—continuing the work of making those environments my safe space. I no longer wore my divorce on my sleeve like a badge of shame. Just because I was divorced didn't mean that my life was over. In fact, a new life was just beginning. I had the opportunity to take the lessons I learned from my marriage and apply them to all aspects of my life. I didn't need or want a man to give my life purpose or meaning. I was finding my happiness, so if they wanted to be a part of it they had to prove to me that they deserved to be in it, and that made all the difference.

My second foray into dating coincided with a greater focus on my dinners for one and rebuilding my life, which was a stark difference from my chaotic first attempts immediately after my breakup. This time around I couldn't ignore how much I'd evolved. I had an entirely new approach; what struck me as the most different and rewarding dating the second time around was that when I continued to focus on my dinners for one and building my own life, the men and their attempts at seducing me were exhilarating, and I embraced the electrification. Dating was no longer a chore; I wasn't on the hunt for a replacement or distraction. I allowed myself to be wined and dined. I accepted the compliments and knew that they were genuine, but also understood that they weren't necessarily a prelude to something long lasting. Most importantly, I allowed myself to have fun. I found my ethnography hat from my early years in Paris and put it back on. As I learned more about French men from a perspective of curiosity, rather than with an agenda of searching for a new husband, I started learning more not only about them, but also about myself.

Outside the kitchen my boldness and renewed confidence manifested in experimenting with my hair by doing things like shaving it all off and dying what remained blond, wearing colorful clothes that I shied away from, and my deep belly laughs that I suppressed for too long were coming back. I even started pushing myself even further in the kitchen by doing things like cooking Jamaican food.

The vivid memories of my mother making fried dumplings on Saturday mornings—the smell of the perfectly round and soft cloud-like balls of dough waking me up and guiding me to the kitchen where I would help myself to one while no one was looking—and recollections of my school vacations spent in Jamaica running around the countryside with my cousins, picking mangos directly from the trees, and eating everything in sight made the urge to cook the cusine that was embedded deep in my being inescapable.

I hardly ever cooked Jamaican food before because I didn't need to. When I was living in New York City, if my mother wasn't available to cook Jamaican food there were countless Jamaican restaurants to choose from if I had a craving for the cuisine that is nearest and dearest to my heart. Unfortunately, indulging in Jamaican culinary delights such as curry chicken, oxtails, jerk chicken, rice and peas, fried dumplings, etc. in Paris proved to be more difficult. If I wanted any of this I would have to cook it myself. While I couldn't find some Jamaican-specific foods, like ackee, there was a significant enough population of people from various African countries and the French Caribbean islands that I was able to find indispensable ingredients like plantains. The rest I would have to figure out on my own.

I didn't want to overly complicate the experience so I decided to make a very classic Jamaican breakfast: fried dumplings, salt fish and fried plantains. For me, making this would help me feel closer to my family and my foundation and infuse that sense of connection to my family and culture into the new life I was creating in Paris. This is a dish that isn't necessarily complex but it requires multitasking and planning and, most importantly, it was possible to find the ingredients in Paris.

After calling my mother for her recipe—which wasn't help-ful because her units of measurement are "a little of this" and "a dash of that"—crosschecking recipes and various YouTube tutorials online and stops at several stores, I had all of the ingredients for a classic Jamaican breakfast *chez moi à Paris*. All of my worlds were colliding in the best way.

I decided to cook all of the elements of the meal in order from easiest to hardest, so I started with the plantains. Cut lengthwise and fried until a deep brown, it would be difficult to screw it up. Then I moved on to the salt fish. Salt fish is the dried and salted codfish that needs to be desalted and rehydrated before cooking. Experienced cooks of Jamaican food usually leave the salt fish to soak overnight but of course I didn't do that, so I found myself boiling the piece of fish several times in order to get it to a point where it was edible—my goal was to remove some of the salt but not all. The last thing I wanted to do was end up with a bland piece of fish. Once edible the fish is broken up into flakes and cooked with red bell peppers, garlic, tomatoes, white onions, thyme, pimento seeds and ground black pepper. The result is a rich and savory thick-ish stew.

Then came the most challenging part of this meal: making the fried dumplings. Jamaican dumplings are pieces of fried dough without anything inside. A master fried dumpling maker is able to transform a ball of raw dough made with milk, butter, flour, baking powder and salt into a cooked ball of dough with a delicately flaky exterior and a fluffy and soft interior. It only took one attempt for me to understand that it would take a long time for me to become a master fried dumpling maker. The dumplings I made that morning were so hard I could hardly bite into them. I was unsure of where I went wrong but that didn't ruin my morning. I made a breakfast that was reflective of the life I was creating—I ate my fried plantains and salt fish on a piece of toasted baguette.

I'm not fooling myself; I know that my Jamaican food may never reach the same level of excellence as my mother's, but when those familiar scents are floating in the air in my Paris kitchen and I lick my lips and taste flavors that remind me of pure love, and sway my hips from side to side while listening to the reggae music streaming from my Bluetooth speaker, I truly feel like I'm *à la maison*.

There were many other successes and failings in the kitchen. I almost sliced off the top of my index finger when trying to use a mandolin to slice carrots and there was the time while attempting to make *crème brûlée* my dishcloth caught on fire and I set off the fire alarm in my apartment. I promptly gave away the torch and mandolin; I decided to keep things simple. However, on the other hand, I was so pleased with myself the first time I made a successful fried chicken that was juicy and tender on the inside and crunchy and crispy on the outside. I wanted to personally call Emmanuel Macron and request French citizenship when I made duck confit and *gratin dauphinois*. Whenever I was in my kitchen, whether the end result of my experimentation would lead to an edible dinner or me eating cornflakes and wondering where I went wrong, I was finally putting my own needs and desires at the forefront of everything that I was doing. I was accepting myself, and the universe seemed to be rewarding me because inner peace and joy began eliminating feelings of worthlessness and failure.

The meditative act of cooking for myself gave me the time to reflect. In those reflective moments of stirring, tasting, searing and roasting I realized that my life was mine to design, and my success in Paris depended on genuinely believing that I belonged and deserved to be here. I was slowly coming home to myself and the opportunity that I held in my own hands to make this experience worthwhile was practically blinding me.

The repetition and practice of cooking for myself brought an immeasurable amount of good to life—it's an act of giving to and serving to myself. When I could easily go to a restaurant and surround myself with people or continue my hunt for a TFM replacement, I was using this time to reconnect with myself. My dinners for one went far beyond putting food in my stomach; they nursed my body, heart and spirit and propelled me into action. Making dinner for one was saving me.

Eighteen

A TALE RETOLD

As my dinners for one started to take shape, two elements of my life were at odds: on one hand my confidence in the kitchen was growing but on the other I was still floundering emotionally. To some extent I had confronted my divorce and the effect it had on me, but not really. In an attempt to practice more self-compassion I told myself that it isn't entirely unreasonable for my emotions to fluctuate during a difficult transition. After all, over the course of several years I've gone through several identity transitions that had a profound effect on my sense of being in the world, and they were all attached to one person. I went from the American girlfriend of TFM living in New York City to the American wife of TFM living in Paris, to the American ex-wife of TFM still living in Paris. But deep down I knew that there had to be something else, a life and story about Paris outside my identity as a married woman.

The topic of identity is a tricky one because it is shaped by the sum of one's lived experience and choices. There isn't one thing, one sentence, one word, that anyone can say that defines your identity. I'm talking about true identity not something that people, or society, bestow upon you without your consent. This is about something deeper than that; it's about how you see yourself in relation to the world and how you want people to think of you and interact with you. It's multifaceted and influenced by so many different elements. After having my identity tied to someone else for so long I wanted to be Sutanya in Paris and that was it. I wanted people to see me without all the baggage masking the essence of who I am as an individual.

I wanted, and needed, to reclaim my identity and make it my own. Don't get me wrong; I enjoyed these identities and was delighted that those identities were formed through mutual and genuine love. They were cozy identities that painted an easy picture of who I was and what mattered to me the most. It gave people something to work with and a box to easily slip me into. I was checking all of the right boxes and that made my life decisions—like getting married and moving to Paris—more palatable and easier to digest. I wasn't asked to justify any choices made within the confines of those identities; my choices seemed to be universally understood and accepted. But the truth is, I lost myself in those identities, and in many ways my attempts to grasp and reclaim the small inklings of myself that remained led to the breakdown of my marriage.

Although I initially rejected my pull toward Ursula to help me work through my post-divorce feelings, I thought that I did need her. I rationalized that I needed her help and expertise. I started seeing Ursula again to help guide me as I attempted to form and come to terms with my new identity; it was too messy and chaotic to do on my own. But it only took a few sessions for me to realize that they weren't helping me. I wasn't using our sessions to find an appropriate treatment plan that would help me heal from the trauma of divorce. I didn't digest or give further thought to anything Ursula said during those sessions. I used them to either purge my anxieties of the day or just have a chat. Instead of indulging in *apéros* she became my distraction.

After one particular session, where we just chitchatted for an hour, on my way back to my apartment, as I walked past cafés filled with people enjoying their *apéro*, I felt a twinge of jealousy that was swiftly overshadowed by a revelation: I needed to continue the transition into my new identity on my own. I was thankful that Ursula was my therapist, and I secretly wanted her to be my friend, but by continuing to see her I would be using someone else, yet again, to help me form an identity when I needed to do it on my own.

Though I vowed to tackle this without the help of my therapist, I still yearned for stories similar to mine to help me better understand what I was living through, so I turned to Google in search of divorce stories. Most of the search results yielded women who were older and usually they had children. Their stories felt far removed from the reality I was living—divorced in my early thirties and still living in the foreign country where the divorce took place while trying to move forward.

I knew for a fact that I wasn't the only divorced American woman living in Paris. There were a few in my own social circle but they rarely spoke candidly about their experience. I wanted to hear someone else's story about the first time they had to confront an administrative issue without their personal Emmanuel Macron by their side, stepping in and taking over. I wanted to know if anyone shared the feeling of double loneliness that comes with being divorced and living abroad in your ex-partner's country and how that feeling can sometimes warp your sense of self. I was sure that someone penned a funny blog post about dating French men post-divorce. I couldn't wait to stumble upon the essay of someone waxing sentimentally about their decision to continue to build a life in Paris despite being bombarded with valid reasons why they should go back to their home country.

My searches were futile so I turned to my trusty Americans-in-Paris bloggers for guidance. But of course, after endlessly scrolling and searching, I realized that they had none. Everything about their lives and Paris, at least according to their Instagram posts, was just as perfect eight years later when blogs were at their height of popularity. They still lived in big, spacious apartments with *double sejours* and most of them had acquired second homes in the countryside. Their husbands adored them and the rare times they did argue it was about something cute like a misunderstood word, never anything dramatic that called their marriage into question.

I noticed that many bloggers didn't touch on the less exciting aspects of living abroad. No one wrote about homesickness, how it felt to constantly be an outsider and the yearning for familiarity. No one wrote about the discomfort you sometimes feel in a social situation where you're the only non-French person. No one wrote about how dumb you felt because you weren't seemingly as cultured as all of the Parisians around you. Didn't they, like me, sometimes just wish everyone spoke English? Personally, I didn't like sounding like a two-year-old learning how to form a complete sentence.

My envy grew the more I dug into the updated lives of the bloggers I followed when I lived in Connecticut. Their love and relationship seemed so solid—ironclad in the same way I thought mine was. Via their social media I went along with them as they rode tandem bikes in Vallée de la Loire, lazed in the sun in the South of France and shared croissants from their local *boulangerie* in Paris. Often, I found myself lying in bed, endlessly scrolling through their posts and wondering *what are they doing right that I did wrong?*

During one of my deep-dive scrolling sessions I received a notification that a hometown acquaintance commented on one of my recent posts. The comment read, "I love seeing your photos of Paris! You're living the life. I'm so jealous!" I laughed to myself because if she only knew I was lying in bed, looking at the photos of people who also "live the life" in Paris and thinking the same thing. Immediately following that thought I realized that this person knew nothing about the reality of my life in Paris. She had no idea that my marriage ended. My social media posts didn't highlight my lowest and saddest moments here. Based on what I shared on social media she would have no idea that for months waking up and going about my day was a test of my strength.

In the same way many people in my life were oblivious to the issues TFM and I faced in our marriage or about my post-marriage self-destructive phase because I hid it so expertly. It's possible that the highlights that various Americans-in-Paris bloggers chose to share on social media weren't accurate portrayals of their day-to-day and experiences living here. I didn't know the truth of their interior lives and struggles and they weren't obliged to share that part of themselves with the world. In the same way that there was nothing in my social media that hinted at my life being in turmoil.

However, I remained disappointed that much of what was shared about Paris and living here as a foreigner didn't truly explore the full scope of the confusion, joy and heartache that it encompasses. I understood how much easier and profitable it is to perpetuate the idealistic American-in-Paris narrative. The fantasy is real, but so are the disappointments. Who wants to hear about feeling like you have to put on an armor of protection whenever you leave your apartment? It's easier to share pictures of croissants and talk about Provence trips. I also didn't see myself in a lot of these expat stories; they were usually white women whose experience in Paris was very different from mine. For me, more than anything, proved that the American-in-Paris story needed a refresh. The narrative needed modernization, in terms of the actual story being told and its format. I became determined to add my two cents to the American-in-Paris narrative.

I tried many "American in Paris" projects—a YouTube channel and several blogs—but none of them stuck because they didn't feel authentic to me. I wasn't expressing myself in the way I wanted to on those projects nor was I sharing the story I wanted to tell. I knew that in order to do it right I needed to be vulnerable and invite strangers into my world in a way that I never had before. Telling my story the way I wanted to required experimentation, boldness and a little bit of spice—the same basic ingredients I used over and over in the kitchen. While trying to pinpoint the most authentic way I could share my perspective on this common but not widely discussed American-in-Paris experience, I realized that first I needed to change my approach.

I was an American in Paris going through a divorce but the story and feeling is one that people can resonate with whether or not they live in Paris. Most people have been single at some point in their lives, and the single young woman demographic is steadily rising; we need our voice heard, too. Everything I read about being single sounded sad, miserable and that it was a status that needed to be changed immediately. I sat in a puddle of misery for a while, and I think that was normal at the end of any relationship, but I eventually found my form of self-care in cooking. Cooking is a form of care that tends to be bestowed on others but rarely on oneself. My dinners, no matter how simple or extravagant, came from a place of generosity to myself. My desire to cook for myself didn't come from a place of duty; my dinners became an expression of love. With every meal I was showering myself with much-needed attention and care. I approached every meal by thinking if I can do this nice thing for myself I can fall in love with myself again and I will survive. And when I stepped into my red-and-white-tiled kitchen I wasn't opening barren cupboards or removing mold-covered food from the refrigerator; now I entered the same space with cheery anticipation. My kitchen became a space where I felt capable, strong, in control and hopeful.

Nevertheless, the immense sense of peace of mind that I experienced cooking for myself as a single woman was in direct opposition with what I was reading. I didn't see the benefit in searching for a partner just to have someone in my life. Through cooking I was giving power to my singleness. Just because I was alone didn't mean that I was inherently lonely and distraught. Being able to feel—and be—satisfied and find happiness within myself was actually a strength that should be acknowledged and rewarded.

I also used my dinners for one to ensure that people didn't pity me. I was young and divorced, but my life wasn't ruined. TFM did the right thing by pulling the trigger on our marriage. If he didn't I would've continued to try to make the relationship work because I loved him and because so much of my identity—who I thought I was and how I believed my life should continue— was tied up in our story. I felt compassion for people who were unhappy in their relationships but couldn't remove themselves from its grip because the relationship is crucial to their identities. I felt kinship with them. I wanted to talk to those people and show them that there could be so much more to life.

With the thought that food, cooking and being single were universal experiences I decided to talk about cooking dinner for one in Paris. I decided to create a podcast that talked about the healing power of food and how I used my solo dinners to nourish my spirit, body and soul as a way of overcoming the trauma of divorce. I wanted to document the journey of rebuilding my identity and a home in Paris, and from that desire the Dinner for One podcast was born.

Initially, I envisioned a blog but I didn't have the discipline or desire to update a biweekly-blog and the format struck me as dated. Around the same time I was listening to podcasts religiously and found them to be such great company while I was cooking, cleaning or running errands around the city so I began toying with the idea of telling my story in podcast format.

I thought that my podcast would stand out for two reasons: as a single narrative podcast presented by one person in a kitchen, and a new way to experience food. Everyone is used to using their sense of smell, sight and taste when interacting in food, but what happens when you rely on just your ears to give you the same sensation? I liked the idea of potential listeners hearing me pour wine, chop vegetables, taste test and crackle pepper. The possibility of heightening a sense that people don't usually associate with food excited me, and the fact that I would invite people into my world via my kitchen and create an intimate relationship by talking to them drove me forward.

I didn't expect my podcast to become such a source of joy in my life and give me such a strong sense of purpose but it has. I'm not the first person, and certainly won't be the last, to move to Paris for love and find myself on the other side of love trying to pick up the shattered pieces. So I decided to open my big New York mouth to talk about that experience. I just had to dig deep and not be afraid to confront myself and embrace what came out on the other end.

But how would I begin? I didn't know how to start a podcast.

A post on a Facebook group dedicated to expats in the creative industry introduced me to Lory Martinez, a Colombian-American fellow New Yorker and daughter of immigrants who lives in Paris with her French husband. She's a podcast producer and one of the first people to believe in my project. I was one of her first clients. Every two weeks Lory came to my apartment, fitted me with my mic and we would walk into my kitchen where I recorded an episode and cooked at the same time. I chose a topic and corresponding meal that spoke to either the divorce experience or American-in-Paris experience, or both. And Lory took the raw footage home and stitched it all together.

Expressing the thoughts, feelings and experiences that were

roaming around in my head felt cathartic and arrogant at the same time. It felt freeing to just talk, without a filter or being observed. However, there were moments when I questioned whether or not anyone would actually be interested in my story; a woman from New York City whose marriage to her French husband ended and now she's trying to live her best life in Paris by herself in a charming apartment in Montmartre doesn't necessarily sound like a sob story. Nevertheless, I continued and with every recording I felt the push to be more candid and raw. The podcast helped me put words to my emotions and sometimes I cried; occasionally I drank too much wine while cooking and overshared; I retold hilarious stories of cultural gaffes and outright embarrassing situations; and there were other times I couldn't focus and would jump from topic to topic. But I didn't give those less-than-perfect recording moments any attention because at that point the podcast felt more like an audio log that was listened to mostly by my family, friends and acquaintances until I received my first message from a listener. That was when it was confirmed that I was reaching beyond my own circle.

A listener named Colleen who lives in the Midwest area of the United States was the first person whom I didn't know from my personal life to send me a message. She shared that she lived in Europe, why she listened to the podcast and how she felt about it. Her message was encouraging, warm and positive. Although we are at different stages in our lives—she is the mother of adult children and married—my stories and experience resonated with her and knowing that encouraged me to continue and see where the podcast led me. As the podcast continued it became a true source of delight, in addition to cooking for one. It helped me destigmatize my divorce and made me feel like I had a purpose and true reason to stay in Paris. More than anything, the podcast made it clear that my experience mattered; my story and I mattered.

Nineteen

THE NEXT EPISODE

This isn't a typical or traditional happy ending. I'm still making dinner for one in Paris, very single and enjoying it. I thought that by now, the five-year mark of the end of my marriage, I would be in another relationship and possibly have a child of my own, or at least be pregnant. That is not the case as of the writing of this book and that's okay. I truly feel that everything is as it should be. There were lessons that I needed to learn and ways in which I needed to grow in order to not fall back into unhealthy and self-destructive habits and comforts. I feel more prepared than ever to tackle all that life has to throw at me. I know that this will not be the first or last time I will have to confront hardships, but now I have the only tool I needed all this time—self-love.

I envision Paris as my forever home, but I don't know if that is what life has planned out for me. But for now I'm here and content in Montmartre, still living in the apartment I shared with TFM. My apartment isn't perfect in any sense of the word; sometimes I get the impression that it's slowly falling apart because of the repairs that are an almost constant. The furnishings are a mix of highbrow and low, IKEA and vintage hand-me-downs and plants that don't exactly fit their pots. The art that hangs on its walls brightens the space and makes me smile every day.

My apartment was my refuge throughout my divorce when everything became a bit too overwhelming and my world felt like it was caving in. We've been through many ups and downs together, from various furniture configurations to a moment of mild neglect from me, but it remained my sanctuary when I needed it most and always welcomed me back. It has been my home, my ride or die, since June 2013, and today it's an unquestionable reflection of who I am after the storm.

My other sanctuary—France—is not without its challenges, many that plague most modern societies today—racism, classism, climate change, sexism, etc. I am not apologizing for the harm that France has caused as a colonial power or excusing the way many Black and brown French people are ignored and kept on the margins of society and discriminated against; I'm not asking for that to be ignored. However, that doesn't take away from my personal experience, which has been more or less positive due to the generosity, loyalty, humor, openness, care, concern, warmth and overall *joie de vivre* that I have had the opportunity to experience with French people and through their culture.

Despite all of the uncertainty and fear I choose to stay in Paris. It's not perfect—it can be frustrating, confusing and just bizarre, but I still wouldn't want to be anywhere else. For a long time I couldn't explain why, but then I realized that even when Paris is bad, *elle n'est jamais si mal.* Even on my low days—when I felt like staying here was a big mistake, that my life is one big joke and a series of unfortunate events—something keeps me going. Something that is unique to Paris. It was difficult for me to articulate what that "Paris factor" was. It wasn't necessarily satisfaction or joy—both feel too simple and overdone—it was deeper. It influences my feeling of satisfaction and heightens my joy.

It's pleasure.

Pleasure is an art form and way of life that the French have perfected, and I have wholeheartedly adopted. I find that the French, the Parisians, seek out and expect life's simple pleasures in everything that they do. Whether it's a meal, wine, clothes, or a lover, it should *donner envie*, meaning it should give one desire to partake in whatever activity or thing that is placed in front of them. In French, there is no such thing as "guilty pleasure." It baffles them as to why something so good as pleasure would have a negative connotation attached to it. I've learned that pleasure doesn't have to have a sexual connotation. Pleasure is being grateful for life and enjoying it! Pleasure is taking care of you—mind, body, soul and stomach. And that's the only problem with Paris, really. It turns everyone into a cigarette-smoking, wine-drinking, cheese-eating hedonist.

Initially, accepting and expecting pleasure as my human right was difficult but that didn't last very long. Now I'm a proud pleasure seeker. I enjoy my alone time. I indulge in food that sends tingles down my spine and awakens my taste buds. I give potential lovers a fraction of attention only if I feel that what they're offering me comes with care and attention in return. Accepting and expecting pleasure in all forms wouldn't have been possible if I didn't live in Paris. Finding myself through mistakes, growing from them and falling back in love with myself was only possible because Paris was on my side the entire time, even when I thought she abandoned me.

Love and affection from Paris come in different shapes and forms. For me, summertime in Paris is when the city sparkles the most and I cannot get enough of it. But that wasn't always the case.

For a long time I thought that there was nothing better than summer in New York City. It's electrifying when the snow melts and the city wakes up—the city itself and its inhabitants are bursting with sensuality. The block parties evoke a sense that the entire city is just one big party. Every possibility is on the table and you can never quite put your finger on where the summer night will lead. Your night could start on the stoop of a friend's apartment in Fort Greene, Brooklyn, transition into dancing to Afrobeats with sweat beads forming and dripping off your body and the bass of the beat and pulse of your heart become synchronized, and it ends with a sunrise motorcycle ride on the West Side Highway. It's hard to know. The air is thick and ripe, waiting for that intense summer romance. Inviting in the stolen glances that you may catch across a crowded hot subway. Impromptu barbecues give the sensation that every weekend is Thanksgiving. I didn't think that I could ever experience a similar summer anywhere else until I began spending more time in Paris during the summer when my marriage ended.

I was familiar with and addicted to the hot and sticky summers of New York City that felt familiar and titillating. When I started staying in Paris during the summer the Parisian summer vibe grew on me and I've come to look forward to and appreciate that time of the year here. Where the energy of New York City summers is raw, intense and, more often than not, chaotic, the summer in Paris energy is sweeter. It's the moment to take a break and enjoy the tenderness of long days and even longer nights.

The unexpected happens in Paris, too; the difference is that the activities of a summer night come from a place of deep desire with a focus on what is going to be the most pleasurable. The emphasis is not on trying to cram the most into one night by frantically jumping from place to place. The pink-and-purple cotton-candied skies that stay light until 10:00 in the evening, sometimes even pushing to 10:30 p.m., keep people outside *en terrasse* until well past midnight. The conversation flows naturally; no one wants to move or go home. In the daytime it's not uncommon to walk by a flock of Parisians sitting outside *en terrasse* facing in the direction of the sun, soaking up every ray they can. The behavior of the sun worshippers leads you to pause and think to yourself *I should be doing the same thing*, so you sit down and join them—enjoying the splendor of having the sun caress your face. There isn't a thought given to what you should be doing or where you should be because you're doing what is most important—relaxing and enjoying a beautiful moment.

Live jazz at restaurants turns sidewalks into dance floors. French kids whiz by on their *trotinettes* squealing with laughter, but never forgetting to say *"pardonnn!"* as a gaggle of them rush by. The summer picnics that consist of juicy nectarines, fleshy tomatoes, wine-dark cherries, deliciously sticky figs, unholy but oh so necessary cheeses, the best bread and of course wine fit for the gods also add to the sensual sweetness of Paris summers. Scooter rides on Vespas through the city at night make you feel like you're living in your own movie, but this time with a better ending.

The relationship that I have with Paris is complicated. Sometimes I love it, like in the summertime, and sometimes I can't stand it. There are times when I curse the fact that I'm still here and wonder why I'm torturing myself. Is being so far away from my family and friends worth the sacrifice? It's the most frustratingly bizarre place that you don't ever want to leave. I won't make any big declarations about the future. I don't know what it holds or where it will take me, but Paris will always have a special place in my heart. I wouldn't want to have experienced these chapters of my life anywhere else, and I owe Paris more than I could ever pay her back in return.

Cooking dinner for one in Paris played a crucial role in shaping my womanhood in more ways than I could have ever imagined. In the span of six and a half years, from end of 2009 to

2016, I met my future ex-husband, embarked on a three-year transatlantic relationship, got married, moved to Paris, experienced the breakdown of a marriage and went through a divorce, stayed in Paris and embarked on the journey of rebuilding my life. My journey has shifted and changed gears more than I ever wanted it to, but I am grateful that I lived, and experienced it with the City of Light as my beacon.

Living alone in Paris forced me to confront myself and sit with my uncomfortable feelings in ways that I doubt I would've if I had returned to New York City after my marriage ended. I imagine that my family would've coddled me and as a consequence I would've felt pressure to fix myself by quickly getting into another serious relationship. The significance of my marriage and experience in Paris would've been treated as a small parenthesis in my life—its weight and importance only acknowledged through whispers with undertones of embarrassment and shame. Paris forced me to be still and to think—pushing me to create my own sense of self and future. Her beauty gave me hope and her melancholy showed me that it was not only okay, but also courageous, to embrace my emotions. No matter how manic, no matter how unsettling they were. Paris is not an easy place to live and you have to work for it, but when she shines on you, you feel appreciated—flaws and all. It's almost like the city is on your side, and you feel special. I was allowed to be messy and come to terms with the unexpected tectonic shift that happened in my life without fear of judgment. It is a culture that sees beauty in what would be considered flaws in the United States. Here, my flaws, my complexity, my humanity, are what make me beautiful. I am no longer afraid to confront the depth of my emotions, needs and desires.

Now I'll have a completely different story to tell any future daughters and granddaughters I may have. I'll tell them that although I loved purely, wholeheartedly and unabashedly it wasn't enough to withstand the waves and crashes of my marriage to TFM. There are no broken pieces of any one person to be put back together with the Krazy Glue of love. I am, and will remain, a deeply flawed human being. I simply saw a light in someone else and walked toward it, with hope. Although my love story didn't continue as I expected it to, through the agony of divorce and finding peace through cooking for one I've learned the true meaning of caring for myself.

I blossomed into a flower in Paris and finally found home within myself.

Epilogue

I hope to fall in love again one day and if I do I'll make sure to keep everything that cooking dinner for one in Paris has taught me near to my heart. I've grown and learned so much from this experience. These lessons will live with me forever.

1. Making a nice meal for yourself is *always* worth the time and effort.

2. There's no such thing as too much butter.

3. Being open to life and experimenting is often more rewarding in the long term.

4. Trust yourself, and your intuition, above all. Knowing when to add, remove or modify elements of your life that are no longer serving you is key.

5. The end is rarely actually ever the end; it's almost always just the beginning. I like to think of it as another door being opened toward a better path.

6. Your journey is yours alone; don't judge yourself too harshly because no one knows what they're doing. We're all putting one foot in front of the other and trying to figure it out day by day.

7. Breakups suck. They chip away at your self-esteem and you have to relearn a lot about yourself and your expectations, but they don't have to destroy you.

8. To love and be loved is a brave and courageous endeavor. If it doesn't work out the way you envisioned, feel some satisfaction in the fact that you gave it your best shot.

9. Just because you're single, or alone, doesn't mean that you're automatically lonely. Being able to feel, and be, satisfied by your own company is actually your strength.

10. Falling in love with yourself is one of the most profound and special love stories you'll ever experience.

★ ★ ★ ★ ★

LOVE AFTER LOVE

The time will come
when, with elation
you will greet yourself arriving
at your own door, in your own mirror
and each will smile at the other's welcome,
and say, sit here. Eat.
You will love again the stranger who was your self.
Give wine. Give bread. Give back your heart
to itself, to the stranger who has loved you
all your life, whom you ignored
for another, who knows you by heart.
Take down the love letters from the bookshelf,
the photographs, the desperate notes,
peel your own image from the mirror.
Sit. Feast on your life

—Derek Walcott

Recipes

The following recipes are pulled from different parts of my life and various influences, with the strongest and most profound influence coming from cooking dinner for one in Paris. The meals I made, and continue to make, in my small red-and-white-tiled kitchen are an unwavering source of comfort and joy in my life. For me this collection of recipes represents a significant turning point in my life journey and I wouldn't be the person I am today without it.

I'm thrilled that I am able to share these recipes with you. I hope that if you find yourself cooking one or two or several of them, your taste buds dance with delight as much as mine do when sitting down to indulge in your very own dinner for one.

Pasta Salad

This was a staple during my Hartford years. Gabbie still remembers it. For me it symbolizes the naivety and beauty of being in one's early twenties. You're old enough to live independently but you still have a few years to figure life out and the consequences of your decisions and actions don't seem to hold that much weight. You can wing it and get by.

Ingredients

DRESSING

1 tablespoon and 2 teaspoons olive oil
2 teaspoons Dijon mustard
1 teaspoon lemon juice
2 teaspoons cilantro
Salt
Pepper

PASTA

1 cup (100 grams) penne or orzo pasta
2 tablespoons crumbled feta
1 tablespoon sundried tomatoes, finely diced
A handful of cherry tomatoes, sliced
¼ cucumber, cubed
½ red onion, finely diced
½ an avocado

Preparation

DRESSING

1. Whisk together olive oil, lemon juice and Dijon mustard. Salt and pepper to taste.

PASTA

1. Bring heavily salted pot of water to boil.

2. Add pasta and cook according to directions on the package; you want the pasta soft not al dente.

3. When finished, drain and rinse under cold water, put to the side and allow to cool while you prep the vegetables.

4. Toss the vegetables with the pasta, then add the dressing, feta and cilantro. Taste and adjust accordingly.

Chicken Sausage Salad

In hindsight, I recognize that in the period between November 2009 and September 2010, when Hartford stopped being fun and I wanted out but didn't know how to leave, I experienced my first bout of depression and self-medicating. I had to continue to be "fun Sutanya." I exercised to feel in control and worthy enough to actually change my life. I believed if I could achieve the goal of losing weight and getting into shape, I would be confident enough to move back to a bigger city. During that time my local Whole Foods supermarket (I *really* miss Whole Foods) sold a variety of chicken sausages that were low enough in calories and high enough in protein that they aligned with my manic eating regimen and exercise routine.

Ingredients

DRESSING

1 ½ tablespoons olive oil
1 tablespoon balsamic vinegar
Salt
Black pepper

SALAD

1 ½ chicken sausages, sliced
1 romaine heart lettuce, chopped
4 mozzarella balls, halved
6 cherry tomatoes, halved
½ an avocado, diced

Preparation

DRESSING

1. Whisk together olive oil, balsamic vinegar, add salt and pepper according to your taste.

SALAD

1. Sautee sliced chicken sausage in a skillet or pan on medium heat until brown.

2. Place romaine on plate and top with the other salad ingredients.

3. If salad dressing has separated simply mix again, recombine and drizzle over salad.

Vegetable Hummus Sandwich

In the beginning of my transatlantic relationship with TFM, before either of us was thinking about marriage but knew we wanted to be together, I moved back home with my parents and was working at a branding agency in New York City. My mother made most of my meals and I didn't object. Because I was living at home I usually brought my own lunch to work and when it wasn't my mom's leftovers, this sandwich was one of my favorites. In between working on pitches and brand strategies, I would find a quiet spot to reread a conversation or an email between TFM and me while eating my vegetable and hummus sandwich.

Ingredients

Two slices of bread (I like sourdough or whole grain), toasted

2 tablespoons hummus

6 thin slices of cucumber

½ an avocado, sliced

1/3 cup shredded carrots

4 teaspoons crumbled feta cheese

Salt

Ground black pepper

Red pepper flakes

Preparation

1. Spread a layer of hummus onto each slice of toasted bread.

2. Top one slice of bread with cucumbers, avocado, shredded carrots and feta cheese. Sprinkle with a pinch of salt and a crackle of black pepper. Finish with a dash of red pepper flakes.

3. Complete the sandwich by placing the second slice of bread on top.

Mini Burgers;

DUCK *and* CARAMELIZED ONION TARTLETS

TFM and I did not have a traditional seated wedding dinner. We wanted to do something that reflected the ease and nonstuffiness of our relationship, so we had a cocktail reception. That meant a menu of finger foods that represented both of our cultures, and lots of wine. The menu at our wedding mirrored the fusion of cultures that we hoped to create in our new life as husband and wife.

MINI BURGERS

Like many of the tart recipes in this book, this recipe is impossible to make for one, or at least I haven't figured it out yet. This recipe should make about 8-10 that you can make for yourself, freezing half for a later date or to share with an upcoming lunch or dinner guest.

Ingredients

500 grams lean minced beef
2 red onions, sliced in semicircles
1 egg
20 grams butter (salted or unsalted)
10 grams bread crumbs
15 grams grated Parmesan
¼ teaspoon salt, plus a pinch if using unsalted butter
Pepper
Olive oil

Preparation

1. Preheat oven to gas mark 7/425°F/220°C.

2. Melt butter in a small pan; add red onions and a pinch of salt (if using unsalted butter) and cover. Stir occasionally;

the goal is to get them as caramelized as possible while you make the burgers.

3. Beat egg in a large bowl, add Parmesan, bread crumbs, salt, beef and a good crackle of black pepper and mix together until combined.

4. Form 8-10 small burgers.

5. Place burgers on a parchment lined, or lightly greased (with olive oil), baking sheet.

6. Bake for 17 minutes, or until cooked through.

7. Top with caramelized onions and any other favorite toppings.

8. Serve on mini hamburger buns.

DUCK *and* CARAMELIZED ONION TARTLETS

Ingredients

1 confit duck leg, store bought or homemade

1 puff pastry sheet

35 grams salted butter

2 white onions

Brown sugar, a pinch

Salt and pepper, to taste

Preparation

1. Slice onions and put in a warm pan with melted butter, sprinkle a dash of sugar and stir. Turn heat down to low, cover the pan and cook for 20-30 minutes until golden brown. When golden brown transfer to a bowl and allow to cool.

2. If using store-bought confit, cook according to directions on the package. When finished, remove the meat from the bone and shred. If using homemade duck confit there is no need to reheat before shredding.

3. Preheat oven to gas mark 6/400°F/200°C.

4. Use a round cookie cutter to cut the puff pastry into smaller circles. Cutter sizes between 3 and 4 inches work best.

5. Place each individual small round of puff pastry into the lightly greased pockets of a tartlet or muffin tray.

6. Spoon caramelized onions into each pastry-lined pocket and top with shredded duck.

7. Put in oven and bake until golden brown, about 10-12 minutes.

Tarte Tatin;

CONFIT DE CANARD *with* CRISPY POTATOES; ALGERIAN FELFLA SALAD

TARTE TATIN

TFM's favorite dessert. According to him, his grandmother made the most amazing tarte tatin. Mine never did reach that mythical status but it was pretty decent and I enjoyed making something that brought back memories of happy times with his grandmother whom he loved dearly. Making this tart was my attempt at telling him, "I love you and I understand what's important to you."

Ingredients

6 medium apples, Pink lady or Gala are ideal

1 puff pastry sheet

1 teaspoon flaky sea salt

2 tablespoons lemon juice

1 vanilla bean halved and scraped or 2 teaspoons of vanilla

1 cup (200 grams) white sugar

10 tablespoons (150 grams) unsalted butter

¼ teaspoon cinnamon

¼ teaspoon nutmeg

⅛ teaspoon ground ginger

Preparation

1. Preheat oven to gas mark 6/400°F/205°C.

2. Peel and core apples, cut into wedges and toss with lemon juice to prevent browning and put to the side.

3. Melt 50 grams of butter in skillet and add apples rounded side up; precook for 10 minutes then remove with tongs and put to the side.

4. Add salt, butter, sugar and vanilla to the skillet on low-medium heat, stir continuously until the butter and sugar dissolve and the mixture begins to brown—this is your caramel.

5. Once the caramel is brown and not hard, begin adding the apples in the circular form, purposely crowding them together.

6. Sprinkle cinnamon, nutmeg and ginger on apples.

7. Place puff pastry over the sautéed apples; the apples should be touching the puff pastry.

8. Tuck the edges in tightly all around and make a small cut in the center; this will serve as a vent.

9. Bake for 25-30 minutes, until the puff pastry is golden brown.

10. Use butter knife to loosen the edges and let the tarte cool for 20-30 minutes.

11. Invert by topping the skillet with a serving plate; holding the skillet and plate together tightly, flip quickly. Remove the pan; if any apples are stuck to the pan, remove and place them in the missing slot(s).

12. Eat warm with a dollop of ice cream or crème fraiche.

CONFIT DE CANARD *with* CRISPY POTATOES (DUCK CONFIT *with* CRISPY POTATOES)

The first time I met my mother-in-law, she made this for lunch and I loved it so much that it became *my* dish. She made it fairly regularly and every time was better than the last. It is a warm and comforting dish that feels and tastes like the ultimate "mom meal"—a dish that is a labor of love, and as the aroma makes its way out of the kitchen and throughout the entire house, it envelops you in that love. Whenever she made it I felt like a part of the family.

I recommend making the duck in advance because it's easily reheatable in the oven when you're toward the end of roasting the potatoes.

Ingredients

DUCK CONFIT

1 duck leg

1 teaspoon salt

½ teaspoon ground black pepper

½ teaspoon coriander

½ teaspoon cumin

½ teaspoon dried thyme

½ garlic clove, sliced

1 rosemary branch, finely chopped

Preparation

Duck confit

1. The process starts the day before you actually start cooking. Mix the salt, ground black pepper, coriander, cumin, sliced garlic, dried thyme and rosemary together. Rub mixture all over the duck leg. Wrap tightly in plastic wrap and place in the refrigerator overnight.

2. The next day when you're ready to cook, preheat the oven at gas mark 3/325°F/165°C

3. Wipe the marinade off the duck leg with a paper towel; don't wash. Then place skin down in an ovenproof skillet on medium heat until the duck starts to produce its own fat. When there is close to half an inch of fat in the pan, which takes about 15-20 minutes, flip the duck, cover the skillet with aluminum and place it in the oven.

4. Roast for 1 hour 30 minutes then remove the aluminum and continue to roast until the duck is a nice golden-brown color and crisps up; that should take another 45 minutes to 1 hour.

5. Remove the duck from the fat but don't throw away the duck fat; you're going to use it for the potatoes!

Ingredients

CRISPY POTATOES

4 fingerling potatoes; if not available 1-2 Yukon or new potatoes will do
2 garlic cloves
1 tablespoon fresh rosemary
1 tablespoon duck fat
½ teaspoon salt, or to taste
1 teaspoon pepper
Big pinch paprika

Preparation

1. Preheat oven to gas mark 7/425°F/220°C.

2. Leaving the skin on, wash and cut the potatoes lengthwise.

3. Put the potatoes in a large pot of salted water; the water should cover the potatoes. Bring to a rolling boil for about 7-9 minutes, until the potatoes are tender but not falling apart.

4. While the potatoes are boiling, mince the garlic cloves and roughly chop the rosemary.

5. When the potatoes are finished, drain and immediately put them back in the empty but hot pot.

6. Cover the pot and shake for about 45 seconds; this will rough up the edges and also help them steam at the same time.

7. Lay the potatoes on a parchment-lined baking sheet and toss with the duck fat, garlic, rosemary, salt, pepper and a pinch of paprika. If the duck fat has congealed, melt so that it's pretty warm. You want a small sizzle when they're tossed with the potatoes.

8. Since the potatoes are semicooked, you can break off a tiny piece of one to taste and adjust.

9. Before roasting turn all of the potatoes skin side up, roast for 15-20 minutes or until they become nice and brown and even more tender.

10. Flip so that the skin side is down and roast for another 15-20 minutes until the potatoes are evenly brown all over. Wrap the duck confit in foil and put back in the oven for the last 10 minutes or so to reheat.

ALGERIAN FELFLA SALAD (BELL PEPPER SALAD)

TFM is of Algerian-Jewish heritage on his maternal side so he grew up eating his fair share of North African food. The first time his mother made Algerian food for me I felt honored. She was introducing me to their culture by sharing a simple but loved dish. I've tried to re-create it; mine will never be as good as hers (is any dish as good as when a mom makes it?), but I gave it my best shot.

Ingredients

4 bell peppers (any color or color combination)

2 tomatoes, chopped

1 garlic clove, minced

1 tablespoon olive oil

Salt

Pepper

Preparation

1. Preheat oven to gas mark 8/450°F/230°C.

2. Put peppers on a baking sheet lined with aluminum and bake for 30-45 minutes, until the peppers are soft. Black spots on the skin are normal.

3. Remove and allow to cool. Once cooled peel off the skin, remove stem and seeds and cut peppers into strips.

4. Heat olive oil in a pan over medium heat, add garlic, tomatoes and peppers.

5. Cook until tomatoes are soft and all of the vegetables are well incorporated. Add salt and pepper to taste.

6. This salad can be enjoyed by itself, on toast or over rice.

Bouillabaisse;

PISSALADIÈRE; MOULES "FRITES"

These dishes represent a time when my appetite for Paris and French food was insatiable. Yes, the picture-perfect image that I had of the city was starting to fade, but I was also learning so much. The smells still excited me. The flavors floored me. The pastries sang to me. The recipes that follow represent a sweet spot in my time in Paris. A time when I wasn't 100 percent new to the city so I felt more comfortable being on my own, but there was still so much to discover. I first had each of these dishes in restaurants. The recipes that follow are my re-creations of these culinary delights.

BOUILLABAISSE

Ingredients

7 tablespoons (100 grams) unsalted butter + more if necessary

2 scallops, 1 of which should be roughly chopped

150 grams fresh shrimp, half with shell and head removed and the other half with the shell and head on

200 grams fresh mussels, washed and cleaned

2 medium tomatoes, diced

2 carrots, chopped

1 snapper filleted and cut into 4 parts

1 large Yukon potato

1 strand thyme

1 fennel bulb, roughly chopped

1 celery stalk, roughly chopped

1 white onion, diced

1 small leek, the white and light green parts roughly chopped

1 bay leaf

½ tablespoon tomato paste

½ bulb of garlic, roughly chopped

¼ teaspoon saffron threads
Pinch fennel seeds
Pinch red pepper flakes
Zest of ½ lemon
Salt
Ground black pepper
1 liter of water
½ cup of dry white wine

Preparation

STOCK

1. Melt butter in a big casserole on medium heat and add all of the vegetables, garlic and fennel seeds. Cook, stirring occasionally until soft. When the vegetables have softened add the tomato paste and cook, stirring until completely cooked down and incorporated. Transfer the softened vegetables to a bowl.

2. If necessary, add more butter, then add the roughly chopped scallop, and 75 grams of shrimp with head and shell still intact. Cook until soft, on medium heat.

3. When the fish is soft put the vegetables back into the casserole and mix everything together, still on medium heat.

4. Add wine, bay leaf, thyme, fennel seeds, red pepper flakes, citrus zest, salt and ground black pepper.

5. Cover and cook for about 10 minutes, stirring often to prevent as much sticking as possible, still on medium heat.

6. Add enough water to cover the vegetables and seafood mixture and bring to a rolling boil.

7. Once at a rolling boil reduce to a simmer, add the saffron and taste, adjusting accordingly.

8. Cover and turn heat down to a simmer for 1 hour-1 hour 30 minutes, the longer the better for the flavors to infuse.

9. After 1 hour-1 hour 30 minutes remove as much of the solids as possible from the pot. Blend remaining bits and bobs directly in the pot using an immersion blender or with a countertop blender or food processor. If using food processor or blender transfer broth back to the pot.

SOUP

1. Chop potato and put in broth, bring to a boil and cook until tender.

2. Add scallop and remaining shrimp, then add mussels, give it a few good stirs and cover for about 5-8 minutes. When the scallop and shrimp are opaque and mussels opened it's ready to plate.

3. Enjoy with thick, crusty whole grain bread, or bread of your choice.

PISSALADIÈRE

My version of the pissaladière doesn't have any olives simply because I don't like olives. It's a matter of personal taste, but feel free to add olives to yours if you're a fan.

Ingredients

1 puff pastry sheet

7 yellow onions, cut into strips

8 tablespoons (125 grams) salted butter

8 anchovy filets, whole

Salt, to taste

Black pepper, to taste

Preparation

1. Melt salted butter in a pan or skillet on medium-high heat.

2. Add onions and mix; the goal is to cover as many onions with the melted butter as possible.

3. Cover and turn the heat down to low and cook for about 50 minutes-1 hour, stirring occasionally. The goal is to cook the onions low and slow in order for them to caramelize and become soft. About 30 minutes into cooking add 2 anchovy filets to the onions and mix; they will dissolve in the onions.

4. When the onions have reduced in size by half and have transformed into a brown color, taste and add salt and pepper accordingly.

5. Heat oven to gas mark 7/425°F/220°C

6. Lay puff pastry in a tart mold dish and transfer onions to the puff pastry in one single layer.

7. Place the anchovy filets on top, trying to cover as much of the surface as possible. The filets don't have to be very close to each other.

8. Bake for 15 minutes, or until the puff pastry is cooked and golden.

MOULES "FRITES"
(MUSSELS *and* "FRENCH FRIES")

I haven't quite mastered French fries yet, so I almost always roast my potatoes if they are not mashed. I recommend roasting the potatoes first because the mussels cook rather quickly. The "frites" recipe is a variation on a similar roasted potato recipe found in this book.

Ingredients

"FRITES"

2 potatoes cut into wedges (Yukon or russet potatoes are great
options)
½ tablespoon olive oil
1 teaspoon salt
1 teaspoon ground black pepper
¼ teaspoon onion powder
¼ teaspoon paprika

MUSSELS

1 lb (500 grams) fresh mussels
2 teaspoons (10 grams) butter
3 garlic cloves, thinly sliced
1 shallot, thinly sliced
1 cup dry white wine
1 parsley branch, roughly chopped
¼ teaspoon red pepper flakes (optional)

Preparation

"FRITES"

1. Wash potatoes and leave the skin on.

2. Add enough water in saucepan to cover the potatoes.

3. Bring potatoes to a boil until they can be easily pierced; this
   usually takes about 7-10 minutes.

4. Remove the potatoes from the pot and immediately dunk
   into cold water to stop the cooking process.

5. Pat dry with paper towel then slice them lengthwise.

6. Mix olive oil, salt, pepper, paprika, onion powder in a decent-sized bowl, taste and adjust accordingly and then add potatoes in the bowl. Mix to ensure that the potatoes are covered with all of the marinade.

7. Place potatoes on a baking sheet lined with parchment paper.

8. Roast at gas mark 8/450°F/230°C for 25 minutes, flipping halfway.

MUSSELS

1. Thoroughly clean the mussels and discard any that do not close after applying pressure to them.

2. Melt the butter in a large pan and add garlic and shallots on medium heat. Cook until soft.

3. Add the mussels to the pan then white wine and mix well.

4. Cover and let cook for 5 minutes; give the pan a little shake to encourage any mussels that haven't opened. Sprinkle with parsley and mix before covering again for another 5-7 minutes.

5. Remove from heat when most of the mussels are opened; discard any unopened mussels.

Classic Parisian Apéro Dînatoire

During the period of time when I was cooking at home, or spending much time at home, TFM took over the kitchen duties while I *apéroed* with my new friends and focused on building my own community in Paris. Most of my friendships in Paris began, and sustained themselves, over *apéros*. An *apéro*, or an *apéritif,* is an early-evening drink enjoyed before dinner, often accompanied by a small snack like nuts, olives and a few chips. It is meant to open one's appetite for the proper sit-down dinner that usually follows.

However, my friends and I would take it to the next level with an *apéro dînatoire*—especially if one of us was hosting. An *apéro dînatoire* is a more elaborate affair. It replaces dinner because it includes real food, appetizer-type food, but real food nevertheless. The recipe that follows is everything one would need to have a typical Parisian *apéro dînatoire* at home.

All of the other recipes were written and presented with the thought that you would prepare it for yourself and enjoy for a solo dinner (or two), but *an apéro dînatoire* is too much of a festive event to enjoy alone. I highly recommend sharing this with a friend or two.

A proper *apéro dînatoire* consists of the following:

- Wine
- Saussion or dried meat
- Cheese (at least one hard and one soft)
- Butter (for the bread)
- Smoked fish (usually salmon)
- Bread
- Dips
- Fruit
- Raw vegetables

Your *apéro dînatoire* can and should consist of any combination of your favorite items on the list, but here are my favorite that I use at almost every *apéro dînatoire* that I host.

- **3 different types of dried meat:** jamon serrano, coppa and chorizo (extra spicy)
- **3-4 different types of cheeses**: Brie with truffle, mimolette, goat cheese with herbs and peppercorn
- Smoked salmon
- 2 baguettes
- **Dips**: hummus and tzatziki
- Strawberries and red grapes
- Baby tomatoes and baby carrots

After you've washed everything that needs a quick rinse (the veggies), you simply arrange all the ingredients on pretty plates and have a sip of wine (and sneak a bite or two) while you wait for your guests to arrive.

Tatin De Légume (Vegetable Tarte);

SESAME CHICKEN

I rediscovered these dishes as I was consulting old emails between TFM and me. We communicated via email a lot even when we lived together because our relationship was built on that mode of communication and that was the only way we could actually talk openly to each other. These recipes were my last-ditch efforts at being a "good wife"—they were meals TFM liked and that I cooked because I wanted our relationship to work. I wanted to show him that I still loved him and cared.

TATIN DE LÉGUME

Ingredients

1 puff pastry sheet

2 small courgettes (zucchini)

1 medium eggplant

1 medium white onion, minced

1 garlic clove, minced

6 basil leaves

1 tablespoon olive oil or knob of butter

Salt

Pepper

½ teaspoon ground coriander

A few slices of sundried tomatoes, roughly chopped (this is optional but I find that this adds nice color and a bit of pep but it is also simple and delicious without)

Preparation

1. Wash eggplant and courgettes, remove both ends and cut into ½ inch semicircles.

2. Peel and mince the onions and garlic.

3. Preheat oven to gas mark 6/390°F/200°C.

4. Heat oil/butter, add vegetables, salt, pepper, garlic and ground coriander to sauté pan or skillet and cook for about 10 minutes on medium heat. Stir often to ensure the vegetables cook evenly.

5. When softened, taste and adjust accordingly, adding more seasonings depending on your palate.

6. Place vegetables in tart mold, spread evenly across the surface. No additional greasing or liner needed.

7. Place puff pastry over the vegetable mixture; the vegetables should be touching the puff pastry. Tuck the sides down and prick the tip of the pastry all over with a fork.

8. Bake for 25-30 minutes, until the pastry top is golden brown.

9. Remove from the oven and let rest for about 10 minutes. Remove the tart from the mold by placing a plate on top of the pastry and flipping it over. The vegetables should be on top and the pastry underneath.

10. Garnish with basil and enjoy. Best eaten warm.

SESAME CHICKEN

Ingredients

SAUCE

2 teaspoons soy sauce

1 garlic clove, finely minced

1 tablespoon sesame oil

1 teaspoon honey

½ teaspoon salt

½ teaspoon powdered ginger

¼ teaspoon ground black pepper

CHICKEN

1 skinless boneless chicken thigh, cut into cubes
1 tablespoon sesame seeds
¼ cup cornstarch
1 tablespoon sesame oil
Salt
Pepper

Preparation

SAUCE

1. Mix all the sauce ingredients in a bowl, taste and adjust accordingly and put to the side.

CHICKEN

1. Pat dry chicken thigh with paper towel then chop into cubes and sprinkle with salt and pepper.

2. Toss the cubes in cornstarch, making sure every bit is covered.

3. Heat 1 tablespoon of sesame oil in a frying pan or skillet.

4. When the oil is hot, fry the chicken cubes until done.

5. Transfer the chicken to the bowl with the sauce and coat.

6. Add the sesame seeds; if necessary add more sesame seeds to ensure that every morsel is covered.

7. Serve with warm rice.

Hard-Boiled Eggs;

GROWN-UP GRILLED CHEESE SANDWICH; SARDINES *on* TOAST

The recipes that follow highlight the point in my Paris journey where cooking for myself was put firmly on the back burner. During this time, if I did cook for myself it wasn't for pleasure; it was merely a means to an end. I have slightly jazzed up these recipes but the foundation of what they are made of and their purpose—quickest and easiest route to put some food into my stomach—holds true.

HARD-BOILED EGGS
TOPPED *with* FETA *and* RED PEPPER FLAKES

---

*I like my hard-boiled eggs well-done, no runny yolks welcomed here, and the recipe will reflect that. If you decide to make this very simple but delicious meal please cook the hard-boiled eggs to your preferred level of doneness.

Ingredients

2 large eggs

4 teaspoons (20 grams) feta cheese, crumbled

Dash of red pepper flakes

Salt

Ground black pepper

Drizzle of olive oil

Preparation

1. Put eggs in a pot of cold water; there should be enough water to cover the eggs.

2. Bring eggs to a rolling boil on high heat and leave to boil for 15 minutes.

3. After 15 minutes remove eggs from boiling water and either run under cold water or transfer to a bowl of ice-cold water.

4. Remove the shell then cut in half.

5. Sprinkle with salt and pepper first, then the feta and finally the red pepper flakes.

6. Drizzle with olive oil.

GROWN-UP GRILLED CHEESE SANDWICH (OPEN-FACED)

Ingredients

2 thick slices of bread
½ medium courgette (zucchini), cut on the diagonal
½ red onion, thinly sliced
6 thin slices of scamorza cheese
½ tablespoon sunflower oil (1 tablespoon unsalted butter can be used as substitute)
½ teaspoon butter, for spreading
1 small garlic clove, minced
¼ teaspoon salt
¼ teaspoon pepper
½ teaspoon cayenne pepper
½ teaspoon cumin
½ teaspoon smoked paprika
Fresh cilantro and red pepper flakes, for garnish

Preparation

1. Turn on the oven broiler to preheat.

2. Put courgette and garlic in a bowl and toss with salt, pepper, cayenne pepper, cumin and smoked paprika; mix.

3. Add oil, or butter, to a skillet or small pan on medium-low

heat. Add onions and cook until tender. Pour the contents of the bowl into the skillet or pan and stir. Continue stirring occasionally until the vegetables are cooked through and tender, about 10 minutes.

4. Taste and adjust according to your palate.

5. Remove vegetables from the skillet, or pan, and wipe it clean with a paper towel. The goal is to remove the excess spices.

6. Butter both sides of both slices of bread and put in skillet, toasting one side until golden brown.

7. Place both slices of bread on a baking sheet lined with parchment paper, toasted side down.

8. Add three slices of scamorza on top of each slice of bread and put under the grill/broiler. Toast until the cheese is melted and bubbly, only a few minutes. Keep your eye on the toast.

9. Remove from the oven, and top with vegetable mix. Garnish with cilantro and a sprinkle of red pepper flakes.

SARDINES ON TOAST

Ingredients

2 thick slices of bread (I prefer multigrain or sourdough, but you can choose your favorite)

1 can of sardines

1 big garlic clove

¼ red onion sliced in circles

½ avocado

¼ teaspoon lemon juice

Red pepper flakes

Salt
Pepper
Olive oil
Parsley

Preparation

1. Cut garlic clove in half and rub on the slices of bread.

2. Slice the onion.

3. Toast bread.

4. While the bread is toasting, put avocado, lemon juice, a sprinkle of red pepper flakes, some salt and pepper in a bowl and roughly mash together. You want the mixture to be slightly chunky.

5. When the bread is finished toasting spread the avocado toast on one side, then layer the sardines on top, followed by the red onions, a generous sprinkling of black pepper and a drizzle of olive oil.

6. Garnish with parsley.

7. Place the other slice of bread on top and enjoy.

Leek Anchovy And Goat Cheese Tart;

SPICY SHRIMP and RICE

My girlfriends! Where would I be without them? I'm a girl's girl through and through. I've never viewed women as competition. We're sisters going through life together. We cry together, laugh together and lift each other up. When I was at my lowest low, they stood by me and helped me, never deserted me, and loved me even more. The following recipes are some of my girlfriends' favorite dishes that I've made for them.

LEEK, ANCHOVY and GOAT CHEESE TART

Ingredients

2 leeks, white and light green parts roughly chopped

2 small spring onions, diced

2 eggs

4-6 anchovy filets (depending on how much of an anchovy fan you are), finely chopped

½ cup crème fraiche

½ cup (100 grams) fresh goat cheese, crumbled

20 grams salted butter

1 puff pastry sheet

¼ teaspoon salt + pinch

1/3 teaspoon paprika

Ground black pepper

Preparation

1. Preheat oven to gas mark 4/350°F/170°C.

2. Melt the butter in a pan over medium heat.

3. Add leeks and onions to melted butter. Add a pinch of salt and a little bit of pepper; allow to soften about 5-8 minutes.

4. In a bowl whisk together eggs, crème fraiche, anchovies, ⅓ teaspoon salt, black pepper and paprika.

5. Put puff pastry in a tart mold and add leek and onion mixture in a single layer.

6. Pour egg and cream mixture on top, then liberally sprinkle crumbled cheese as the final layer.

7. Bake for 25-30 minutes until golden brown.

SPICY SHRIMP *and* RICE

Ingredients

SPICY SHRIMP

60 grams shrimp—peel and devein if necessary
1 ½ tablespoon olive oil
1 tablespoon butter
2 teaspoons red pepper flakes
1 tablespoon dried herbs (coriander, oregano or parsley will do. I usually like using a dried herb blend but it's not absolutely necessary)
1 big garlic clove or 2 small- to medium-size cloves
1 teaspoon salt, or to taste
½ teaspoon of ground black pepper, or to taste
½ teaspoon of paprika, or to taste
Fresh coriander for garnish

RICE

½ cup of Basmati or long grain rice
2 cups water
½ teaspoon salt
Knob of butter

Preparation

SPICY SHRIMP

1. Season the shrimp with salt, ground black pepper, dried herbs and paprika, then put to the side.

2. Thinly slice garlic cloves, then put to the side.

3. Begin to heat the pan under low heat, and then add olive oil. Wait for the pan to slightly warm up, but not to the point where it is smoking, then add butter.*

4. Add garlic and allow to soften.

5. Add red pepper flakes.

6. Add shrimp.

7. Make nice big circular stirring motions so that everything blends well.

8. Allow shrimp to cook for 5-10 minutes maximum until they are nice and pink, and slightly firm and plump.

9. Once all cooked, serve over white rice.

If the sauce begins to get less saucy as the shrimp is cooking feel free to add more butter, but the more butter you add be sure to top it up with some garlic powder, or more fresh garlic if you have any, and red pepper flakes because you don't want to lose the spicy garlic flavor.

RICE

1. Rinse and drain rice, add to a small pot. Add water.

2. Add salt and butter.

3. Mix and bring to a boil.

4: At boil cover the pot and turn down to a simmer; the rice will steam cook.*

*The rice should cook in about 10 minutes, but you should periodically check the rice to make sure it's not getting too dry before it's actually finished cooking. If you like your rice soft like me and you notice the water is all dried out but the grains are still crunchy just add a tiny bit of water to continue the steaming process. The addition of the water should help to continue to steam the rice.

Burrata With Toasted Noisettes And Olive Oil;

TATAKI DE THON ROUGE *with* CRÈME D'AVOCAT; CARROT SOUP TOPPED *with* FRESH GOAT CHEESE, LARDONS *and* SUNFLOWER SEEDS

I wish I could take credit for creating these recipes but I can't. I neglected my kitchen during this time, and luckily Sunset was there to provide most of my meals. The menu at Sunset changed regularly but these were my favorites and I hope that my re-creation of these sensory delights has done them justice.

BURRATA
with TOASTED HAZELNUTS *and* OLIVE OIL

Ingredients

1 small burrata (about 120-125 grams)

3 teaspoons roughly chopped skinless hazelnuts (about 10-12 grams of whole hazelnuts)

1 teaspoon olive oil

Dash of salt

Preparation

1. Remove burrata from container or plastic wrap, shaking off excess liquid before putting it on a plate or in a bowl. This first step is very important; straight out of the refrigerator burrata is not the way to go. Room temperature is ideal.

2. Heat a skillet on medium-low heat; once hot add hazelnuts in a single layer. Nuts burn easily so don't walk away. Stir occasionally for about 5-6 minutes until fragrant.

3. Remove from heat and put to the side.

4. Soft slice in the middle of burrata. Soft slice means cut in the middle just enough to open the cheese, without slicing in half.

5. Sprinkle salt all over the cheese.

6. Sprinkle the hazelnuts on top of the salt and cheese.

7. Drizzle with olive oil.

TATAKI DE THON
with CRÈME D'AVOCAT

Ingredients

TATAKI DE THON

90 grams raw ahi tuna

2 teaspoons soy sauce

1 teaspoon mirin

1 ½ teaspoon grated fresh ginger

½ tablespoon sesame oil

½ teaspoon sesame seeds, the color doesn't matter. I prefer white sesame seeds, but you can use black or a mixture

1 tablespoon of neutral cooking oil, reserve for cooking

CRÈME D'AVOCAT

1 small ripe avocado or 1/2 large avocado

1 teaspoon lemon juice, or to taste

½ tablespoon crème fraiche

1 teaspoon of olive oil

Salt

Pepper

Paprika

Red pepper flakes

Cilantro for garnish

Preparation

TATAKI DE THON

Part 1

1. Mix the sesame oil, soy sauce, ginger and mirin together in a bowl.

2. Cut the tuna into semithick slices.

3. Add the tuna to the bowl, making sure all sides are coated in the marinade. Cover and let sit in the refrigerator for 2-3 hours; you can leave it for up to 8 hours to get the maximum flavor. I've tried both marinating times and while there was a slight difference in the depth of the flavor, it wasn't significant.

Part 2

1. Heat the neutral oil on a medium-high heat.

2. Remove the tuna slices from the marinade and roll each side in the sesame seeds.

3. When the oil is hot sear each side of the tuna. The exterior should be slightly cooked and the inside raw.

4. When finished searing, cut each slice into 4.

CRÈME D'AVOCAT

1. In a food processor or with a hand mixer pulse together avocado, lemon juice, crème fraiche and olive oil.

2. Add salt, pepper, paprika and red pepper flakes to your taste.

3. Pulse until smooth and creamy; if gritty add more crème fraiche until the texture is smooth and silky.

4. Plate and garnish with cilantro or fresh sprouts.

*I like plating this dish with the tuna on top of the crème d'avocat and drizzle with a tiny bit of sesame oil, but you can have fun with it and plate it as you wish.

CARROT SOUP TOPPED *with* FRESH GOAT CHEESE, LARDONS *and* SEEDS

Ingredients

3 medium-size carrots, peeled and roughly chopped

2 cups water

1 tablespoon salted butter

1 cube of vegetable stock

1 garlic clove, minced

½ small white onion, chopped

½ teaspoon fresh ginger, minced (if you don't have fresh, ground ginger will be fine)

Salt

Pepper

Paprika

Ground coriander

Ground cumin

Chili powder

Black pepper

25 grams smoked lardon

25 grams crumbled fresh goat cheese

1 tablespoon crème fraiche

Sunflower seeds

Preparation

1. Melt butter in a saucepan then add garlic, onions, ginger and carrots and a pinch of salt. Cook and stir occasionally on medium-high heat until tender, about 10 minutes.

2. Add the water and vegetable stock cube. There should be enough water to cover the carrots; add more if needed.

3. Bring to a boil, then cover and reduce to a simmer for another 10 minutes while the carrots cook.

4. While the carrots are cooking start on the lardons. Add lardons to a cold skillet in a single layer; the goal is for the skillet and lardon to heat up at the same time. Cook on medium heat until the lardons are fragrant, brown and cooked but not super crispy. This should take about 6-8 minutes. Remove from pan and add to paper towel-lined plate.

5. The carrots should be cooked by now; pierce with a fork to check.

6. You can puree the carrots directly in the pot using an immersion blender or puree in a regular blender then return soup to pot.

7. Stir in crème fraiche and start with small pinches of the remaining spices, including salt and pepper. After each pinch taste and adjust accordingly.

8. Pour into bowl and top with lardons and crumbled goat cheese. Garnish with a sprinkling of sunflower seeds.

Leek Risot to;

RASPBERRY CLAFOUTIS

The men that I cycled through during my Sunset days didn't last and some memories of them are fading, but not the delicious meals they made for me. Some of them were great cooks. It was a part of their seduction technique and it worked every single time. With them, I feasted on their homemade versions of these dishes.

LEEK RISOTTO

Ingredients

1 leek, trimmed and finely chopped into semicircles

2 spring onions, chopped

1 garlic clove, minced

½ cup (100 grams) Arborio rice

2 tablespoons (40 grams) butter

½ glass dry white wine

35 grams finely grated Parmesan cheese

1 tablespoon olive oil

½ teaspoon salt, or to taste

3 cups of hot vegetable or chicken stock

Preparation

1. Add 15 grams of butter, the minced garlic and vegetables to a large pot on medium-high heat; stir until vegetables are soft.

2. Add rice and 15 grams of butter and stir over high heat until it becomes translucent.

3. Pour in the white wine and stir continuously so that the rice doesn't stick; the wine should completely evaporate before moving on to the next step.

4. Add salt, then start to add your warm stock a ladle at a time, at a medium-low heat. Allow most of the liquid to absorb before adding more stock. Repeat ladle and evaporation process until rice is al dente, about 20-30 minutes, then you can move on to the next step.

5. Turn heat down very low and add the remaining butter and Parmesan cheese; stir vigorously for a few minutes until everything is incorporated.

6. Turn heat off and garnish with extra Parmesan cheese if you're a cheese lover; if you're not a cheese lover skip this step and simply drizzle with a small spoonful of olive oil.

7. Eat immediately while still warm.

RASPBERRY CLAFOUTIS

Ingredients

2 cups (250 grams) raspberries

1 cup (200 grams) white sugar

1 cup (125 grams) flour

1 cup (240 ml) whole milk

8 tablespoons unsalted butter, melted and cooled (98 grams)

1 teaspoon vanilla extract

½ teaspoon almond extract

Pinch of salt

3 large eggs

Dusted sugar (optional)

Vanilla ice cream (optional)

Preparation

1. Heat oven to gas mark 5/375°F/190°C

2. In a medium bowl, toss raspberries with ¼ cup (50 grams) of sugar and put it to the side.

3. Whisk the flour, sugar and melted butter together until fully incorporated.

4. Pour the milk into the batter, add the eggs and combine, then whisk in the vanilla and almond extracts.

5. Sprinkle with pinch of salt.

6. Place the raspberries in a porcelain or ceramic baking dish.

7. Pour the batter over the fruit.

8. Bake for 20-30 minutes until brown and the edges curl.

9. Let it cool before serving.

10. Add dusted sugar and a dollop of vanilla ice cream on the side, if you'd like.

Roasted Chicken With Fingerling Potatoes;

STUFFED DORADE; SALMON ROASTED IN BUTTER; SALMON EN PAPILLOTE

The first time I made roasted chicken it was good, but it has, fortunately, gotten better over time. These were the first real solo meals that I made for myself when I decided I needed to start taking care of myself and they hold a very special place in my heart. They warmed my heart and nourished my soul when I needed it the most and helped make my apartment feel like a home again, and they're still on regular rotation in my kitchen.

Ingredients

ROASTED CHICKEN

1 (600-700 gram) Cornish hen (coquelet)

2 tablespoons (40 grams) melted salted butter (if you use unsalted butter add more salt to the marinade)

1 tablespoon olive oil

1 ½ teaspoon salt

1 teaspoon ground black pepper

1 teaspoon smoked paprika

2 crushed garlic cloves

POTATOES

3 fingerling potatoes

½ tablespoon olive oil

1 teaspoon salt

1 teaspoon ground black pepper

¼ teaspoon onion powder

¼ teaspoon fresh garlic, chopped

¼ cup of parsley, chopped

Preparation

ROASTED CHICKEN

Ideally, you want to marinate the chicken overnight.

1. In a bowl mix olive oil, salt, black pepper, smoked paprika and garlic cloves. Taste and adjust accordingly. These measurements worked for me, but maybe you like a bit less paprika and more pepper, *fais-toi plais*!

2. Pour the mixture all over the chicken and rub it all in. Get under the skin, in the crevices; get very comfortable and familiar with your chicken.

3. Let it sit for 5-7 minutes then pour the melted butter over the chicken. The butter should be completely cooled, but not resolidified.

4. If you're cooking the chicken the same night, leave it out for 15-20 minutes until it gets to room temperature.

5. If you're cooking the chicken the following evening, place it in your favorite Tupperware or other food storage and store in the refrigerator overnight. Be sure to remove it from the refrigerator at least 30 minutes before roasting.

6. Place chicken in baking dish lined with aluminum; if necessary, brush a very thin coat of olive oil on the aluminum to ensure that the chicken doesn't stick.

7. Roast at gas mark 8/450°F/230°C for 45-50 minutes in total. The first 23 minutes or so roast with the chicken breast up then flip and finish the cooking process with the chicken breast down. *This is the temperature and cooking time that worked in my Parisian kitchen and with my gas stove. Depending on your stove you may need more time or less. Please use your own judgment when determining whether or not the chicken is finished roasting. In my experience deep brown crackling skin usually means that the chicken is finished.*

<u>POTATOES</u>

1. Wash potatoes and leave the skin on. Add to a saucepan.

2. Add enough water to saucepan to cover the potatoes.

3. Bring potatoes to a boil until they can be easily pierced, this usually takes about 7-10 minutes.

4. Remove the potatoes from the pot and immediately dunk into cold water to stop the cooking process.

5. Pat dry with paper towel then slice them lengthwise.

6. Mix olive oil, salt, pepper, garlic and onion powder in a decent sized bowl, taste and adjust accordingly and then add potatoes to the bowl. Mix to ensure that the potatoes are covered with all of the marinade.

7. Place potatoes on a baking sheet lined with parchment paper.

8. Roast at gas mark 8/450°F/230°C for 25 minutes, flipping halfway.

9. When finished, sprinkle with fresh parsley.

STUFFED DORADE

Ingredients

1 whole dorade (head on), scaled and insides removed, sliced open on one side (the fishmonger usually does this for you but be sure to ask)

1 tablespoon olive oil + a drizzle

½ tablespoon salt

1 teaspoon ground black pepper

Dash of paprika

2 garlic cloves, roughly chopped

¼ yellow onion cut in rings

½ bunch of fresh parsley

½ bunch of fresh cilantro

Preparation

1. Wash and pat fish dry with paper towel.

2. Preheat oven to gas mark 4/350°F/180°F.

3. Put olive oil, salt, pepper and paprika in a small bowl and mix, taste and adjust accordingly.

4. Transfer fish to parchment-lined cookie sheet.

5. Spoon the marinade on each side of the fish and inside; really get in there.

6. Us the parsley, cilantro, onion and garlic mixture to wipe up any marinade left in the bowl, then drizzle a tiny bit of olive oil and add a bit more salt and pepper.

7. Stuff herbs, garlic and onions into the fish; place the stuffing that didn't fit underneath the fish.

8. Wrap fish with the parchment paper and let sit for 10 minutes.

9. Place on the middle rack of the oven for 30 mins.

10. Enjoy with rice or a crunchy green salad.

SALMON ROASTED IN BUTTER

Ingredients

2 tablespoons butter

1 tablespoon minced fresh herbs (chervil, parsley or dill)

1 salmon fillet, skin on

Salt and freshly ground black pepper, to taste

Red pepper flakes

Preparation

1. Preheat the oven to gas mark 9/475°F/245°C. Place the but-

ter and half the herbs in a roasting pan and place it in the oven. Heat about 5 minutes, until the butter melts and the herbs begin to sizzle.

2. Add the salmon to the pan, skin side up. Roast 4 minutes. Remove from the oven, and then peel the skin off. (If the skin does not lift right off, cook 2 minutes longer.) Sprinkle with salt and pepper and turn the fillet over. Sprinkle with salt and pepper.

3. Roast 3 to 5 minutes more, depending on the thickness of the fillet and the degree of doneness you prefer. Cut into serving portions, spoon a little butter over each, garnish with the remaining herbs and sprinkle a little bit of red pepper flakes over the fish.

POTATOES *with* HERB BUTTER

I made my own herb butter for this part of the meal. I was very proud of myself, if you don't mind me saying. The herb butter recipe is from *Bon Appétit* and it's essentially idiot-proof. The best thing about this is that it goes with everything.

Ingredients

HERB BUTTER

1 cup (packed) fresh herb leaves (like parsley, chives, and tarragon)

½ small garlic clove

½ cup (1 stick) unsalted butter, room temperature

¼ teaspoon finely grated lemon zest

1 teaspoon fresh lemon juice

Kosher salt, freshly ground pepper

POTATOES

2 Potatoes

Salt

Pepper

Preparation

HERB BUTTER

1. Pulse herbs and garlic in a food processor until finely chopped. Add butter, lemon zest and lemon juice and process until smooth; season with salt and pepper. You will make more than enough for two potatoes, so you can cover and save the rest and add to anything you cook that would benefit from a little herb butter.

POTATOES

2. Cover potatoes in a pot with cold water and then bring it to a boil.

3. When the potatoes can be pierced with a fork they are pretty much finished.

4. Remove potatoes from hot water, add salt and pepper.

5. Take a tablespoon of herb butter and slather all over the potatoes.

SALMON EN PAPILLOTE

I love this dish because it's like I'm making a little salmon gift for myself. *En papillote* means putting something in a parcel, which is literally what is done in this recipe. Once you get the hang of it, you can use any vegetable medley you want. If you want to use mushrooms, go ahead; if you want to add whole garlic cloves, do as you wish. You can customize to your heart's desire.

Ingredients

1 salmon filet
1 ½ teaspoons olive oil
1 knob unsalted butter

1 teaspoon table salt

1 teaspoon black pepper

1 teaspoon paprika

A handful of cherry tomatoes

½ courgette (zucchini)

½ fennel bulb

½ white onion

½ teaspoon of red pepper flakes

½ teaspoon of ground coriander

½ teaspoon of ground cumin

½ fresh garlic clove, crushed

1 sprig of fresh thyme (if you don't have fresh thyme, you can leave this out)

Preparation

1. Preheat the oven to gas mark 6/400°F/200°C.

2. Combine olive oil, salt, pepper, paprika, red pepper flakes, coriander, cumin and garlic powder in a bowl and mix. Adjust to taste and set aside. Cut the fennel and courgette lengthwise, the onion crosswise and the tomatoes in half.

3. Use either parchment paper or aluminum to create the parcel. Personally, I like using parchment paper. Keep in mind that you want the parcel to be big enough to fit the fish and vegetables. Place the salmon in the center of the parchment paper or aluminum sheet and arrange the vegetables around and under. Pour the marinade all over. You may have to get your hands in there to make sure that the marinade is evenly distributed. Add the knob of butter on top of the salmon and if you have a fresh sprig of thyme, add that on top of the butter before creating the parcel for your salmon and vegetables.

4. To create the parcel, think of wrapping a gift—you want all the

corners to be closed and protected. The heat from the oven will create steam and that moisture will cook the salmon.

5. Place the wrapped parcel on a baking sheet or a cookie sheet and bake for 20-25 minutes.

THE *Dinner For One*
GLOW UP RECIPES

The following recipes represent the sweetness of life and how good it can be when you start to take care of yourself and love yourself. I remember this time very vividly because it was the first time that I felt like I was really shedding my post-divorce skin. The idea of starting a podcast was bouncing around in my head and I had an inkling that I had finally found my "thing." I walked with my head a little higher and I was slowly rebuilding my confidence. I was selfish, but in a good way. I was my number-one priority and the way that I cooked reflected that.

Cooking for myself became a real source of pleasure; I didn't want to be numb to the world around me. I wanted, and needed, to fully experience the world around me and the beautiful city I lived in. As I continued to make dinners for one I grew more comfortable using elements of experimentation, boldness and spice in my meals and I continue to sprinkle them throughout my daily life.

Chocolate Mousse

Ingredients

3.1 oz (90 grams) dark chocolate, chopped
1 large egg, separated
1 tablespoon salted butter
2 tablespoons powdered sugar
¼ cup heavy cream, cold
½ teaspoon vanilla extract
Pinch of salt

Preparation

1. In a cold bowl whip cold cream with icing (powdered) sugar until you have soft peaks.

2. In another bowl beat the egg white, adding a pinch of salt, until foam bubbles form.

3. Melt chocolate and butter together in a bowl and let cool. When completely cooled whisk in the egg yolk and vanilla extract until smooth.

4. Gently and carefully fold the egg white into the chocolate mixture; when it's all incorporated, repeat the same with the whipped cream. You must fold, do not stir.

5. Cover with plastic wrap and refrigerate for at least two hours, but preferably overnight.

6. When ready to eat top with chocolate shavings or your favorite fruit.

Pistachio Apricot Tart

Ingredients

1 puff pastry sheet

8-10 apricots, halved and pitted

1 ½ tablespoons sugar

3 tablespoons honey

1 teaspoon ground cardamom

1 teaspoon ground cinnamon

1 teaspoon vanilla

1 ⅕ cup (150 grams) pistachios, roughly chopped

1 egg

Lemon zest

1 tablespoon (10 grams) pistachios roughly chopped, for garnish

Preparation

1. Preheat oven to gas mark 6/400°F/200°C.

2. In a bowl stir apricots and sugar, put to the side.

3. Transform pistachios into a fine powder in a food processer, blender or a handheld mixer. Add honey, egg, cardamom, cinnamon and vanilla to the pistachio powder until you've achieved the consistency of paste.

4. Place puff pastry in your tart mold and spread a layer of the pistachio paste over it.

5. Arrange apricots cut side down on top of pistachio paste; it doesn't matter if they're a bit close.

6. Bake until apricots are cooked through and tender and puff pastry is golden brown, about 30-40 minutes.

Cassoulet

The traditional French way of cooking this meal takes hours. This is the quick and dirty version that I like to use when I have a craving for something hearty and filling. The two biggest untraditional things about my recipe are that I replace andouille with chorizo and I use canned beans instead of dry.

Ingredients

FOR THE BASE

100 grams canned haricot beans, drained and washed

10 grams smoked lardons

5 grams duck fat

1 celery stalk, chopped

1 small yellow onion, chopped

1 bouquet garni (A herb mixture of fresh parsley, thyme and 1 bay leaf tied together with butchers twine)

1 carrot, roughly chopped

2 garlic cloves, peeled

1 chorizo sausage

½ teaspoon salt

Dash of black pepper

FOR THE CASSOULET

1 confit duck leg

5 grams duck fat

1 garlic clove

10 grams bread crumbs

Preparation

1. Heat oven to gas mark 1/250°F/120°C.

2. Melt duck fat in a deep oven-safe pot on medium-low heat. Add celery, carrot, garlic and onion, cook until soft.

3. Add the beans, lardons, sausage and bouquet garni and pour in just enough water to barely cover the vegetables and meats.

4. Bring to a rolling boil; skim off any fat that rose to surface and add salt and pepper.

5. Put the uncovered pot into the oven and cook for 1 hour, stirring halfway through. The beans are already cooked so usually any longer will turn the beans into mush. By this point some of the water should have evaporated and the liquid thickened; if not return to oven for another 15-30 minutes.

6. When the liquid is thick remove the pot from the oven and tuck the duck leg into the bean mixture. Liberally sprinkle over the bread crumbs, duck fat and garlic. Put back into the oven and cook for another 40-50 minutes.

7. This dish is traditionally served in a shallow bowl and garnished with an herb of your choice.

Steak "Frites"

As with Moules "Frites," the potato recipe here is a slight variation on another roasted potato recipe instead of French fries. I recommend roasting them first as the steak cooks rather quickly.

Ingredients

"FRITES"

2 potatoes cut into wedges (Yukon or russet potatoes are great options)
½ tablespoon olive oil
1 teaspoon salt
1 teaspoon ground black pepper
¼ teaspoon onion powder
¼ teaspoon fresh garlic, chopped

STEAK

½ rib eye steak
1 tablespoon unsalted butter
½ tablespoon vegetable oil
1 rosemary branch
1 thyme branch
1 garlic clove, whole
Salt
Pepper

Preparation

"FRITES"

1. Wash potatoes and leave the skin on.

2. Add enough water in saucepan to cover the potatoes.

3. Bring potatoes to a boil until they can be easily pierced; this usually takes about 7-10 minutes.

4. Remove the potatoes from the pot and immediately dunk into cold water to stop the cooking process.

5. Pat dry with paper towel then slice them lengthwise.

6. Mix olive oil, salt, pepper, garlic and onion powder in a decent-sized bowl, taste and adjust accordingly and then add potatoes in the bowl. Mix to ensure that the potatoes are covered with all of the marinade.

7. Place potatoes on a baking sheet lined with parchment paper.

8. Roast at gas mark 8/450°F/230°C for 25 minutes, flipping halfway.

STEAK

1. Pat dry and season liberally and generously with salt and pepper; let it sit for 30 minutes before cooking.

2. After 30 minutes heat dry cast iron pan or skillet until hot. When hot, add oil and allow oil to heat up.

3. When the oil is also hot add the steak; cook each side by constantly turning every 3 minutes for about 10-12 minutes then baste.

4. Add butter, rosemary and thyme and garlic then tilt the pan toward you so that it all gathers on one side of the pan. Take a spoon and scoop up the herb-and-garlic-infused butter and pour it over the steak until the butter begins to brown; this only takes a few minutes.

5. Remove the steak from the pan and let it rest for 8 minutes before slicing.

Canard à la Jamacaine

JAMAICAN JERK DUCK WITH RICE AND PEAS

Ingredients

<u>JERK MARINADE*</u>

3 scotch bonnet peppers

6 scallion stalks

7 garlic cloves

1 yellow onion

¼ cup soy sauce

2 tablespoon brown sugar

1 tablespoon fresh ginger, grated

1 tablespoon ground black pepper

½ teaspoon salt

2 teaspoons all-spice

1 teaspoon cinnamon

1 teaspoon nutmeg

1 teaspoon lemon or lime juice

5 fresh thyme springs

½ cup neutral oil

<u>DUCK</u>

1 duck breast, cold

Salt

Pepper

*You will not use all of the marinade on one duck breast; there will be lots of leftovers to use on other meats, fish or vegetables.

Preparation

JERK MARINADE

1. Roughly chop all of the vegetables then add all of the ingredients to a blender or food processor and blend until fully combined and you're left with a thick marinade.

2. Reserve 2 tablespoons of the marinade, store the rest in an airtight container or jar.

DUCK

1. Remove duck from the refrigerator and score the skin; be sure not to cut all the way to the flesh.

2. Pour the reserved tablespoons of marinade over the duck and rub in. Get friendly and comfortable with the duck; you want to cover every inch with the marinade, especially the skin that was scored.

3. Cover and return to refrigerator and marinate overnight.

4. Remove the duck breast from the refrigerator about 1 hour before cooking to get it to room temperature.

5. When ready to cook preheat oven to gas mark 6/400°F/200°C.

6. Place duck skin side down on a hot nonstick pan with no oil until golden brown, about 6 minutes. Remove the fat as you cook. When the skin side is brown, repeat on the other side.

7. When both sides are brown, transfer duck to the rack of a roasting pan. Roast skin side up for 17-20 minutes, or until done to your likeness. Allow duck to rest for 5-8 minutes before serving.

8. Serve with Jamaican style rice and peas or favorite side dish or salad.

Jamaican Rice and Peas

Ingredients

1 cup long grain or Basmati rice (rinsed and drained)

½ cup kidney beans

2 cups water

1 clove garlic, chopped

1 teaspoon butter

¼ cup of coconut milk

1 scallion

1 teaspoon salt

¼ teaspoon black pepper

1 sprig fresh thyme

Preparation

1. Place garlic, kidney beans, water and coconut milk in a pot and bring to a boil.

2. Add scallion, salt, butter and black pepper to saucepan and stir in thyme.

3. Stir in rice and bring to a boil.

4. When at a rolling boil turn the temperature down to low, cover the pot and cook until all water is absorbed (about 15 to 20 min).

5. Remove thyme and scallion before serving.

Braised Lamb Shank

Ingredients

1 lamb shank

1 tablespoon olive oil

½ tablespoon of salt

1 teaspoon ground black pepper

1 teaspoon each dried herbs—parsley, oregano, paprika

1 fresh tablespoon rosemary, finely chopped

3 garlic cloves, crushed

½ cup of red wine, a dry and hearty red wine is ideal. No sweet red wines

2 medium carrots, cut in circles

1 big yellow onion, cut into wedges

2 cups warm beef stock

1 tablespoon unsalted butter

Preparation

This is a two-part process.

Part 1

1. Season lamb shank with salt, pepper, spices, garlic and rosemary.

2. Pour wine over the lamb shank, cover and let marinate overnight in the refrigerator.

Part 2

1. The next day remove lamb shank from the refrigerator 30-45 minutes before cooking, until it's at room temperature.

2. Chop carrots and onions.

3. Preheat oven to gas mark 4/350°F/180°C.

4. Pour olive oil into an ovenproof casserole dish and heat up on the stove, medium heat.

5. When the lamb is at room temperature remove it from the marinade and blot dry with a paper towel.

6. Once the olive oil is warm but not smoking sear the lamb on each side until brown, about 3 minutes each side.

7. Remove lamb from casserole and place on a plate or in a bowl.

8. Tip carrots and onions into the casserole and sear on each side, about 4 minutes each side (add a teaspoon of olive oil if needed, then remove carrots and onions from casserole and place on a plate or in a bowl.

9. Put lamb back into the casserole and whatever juices were released into the bowl or plate.

10. Pour wine marinade into the casserole and stir then add carrots and onions and stir.

11. Pour beef stock into the casserole; it should cover the lamb. If it doesn't add warm water until the lamb shank is covered.

12. Cover and bring to a boil.

13. Once at a rolling boil, remove from the stovetop and place in the oven. Turn the oven temperature down to gas mark 1/275°F/140°C. Cook until shank is completely tender, should take about 3 hours; feel free to check at around the 2 hour and 30 minute mark.

14. Remove the casserole immediately from the oven when the lamb is finished; if you leave it in the oven the lamb will continue to cook and dry out.

15. Remove lamb, carrots and onions from casserole and cover with aluminum while making the sauce.

16. Over medium-high heat bring the remaining liquid in the casserole to a boil, reduce heat to a simmer until reduced and thickened about 8-10 minutes. Stir in a tablespoon of unsalted butter. Taste and add salt and pepper if necessary.

17. Serve lamb and its gravy with your side of choice. My personal favorites are rice or creamy mashed potatoes.

Moroccan-Spiced Rainbow Salad

Ingredients

100 grams halloumi cheese, sliced into thick strips

115 grams chickpeas

½ red onion, sliced

2 handfuls fresh spinach

½ avocado, diced

½ tomato, diced

1 cup red cabbage

1 ½ tablespoon olive oil

2 teaspoons mustard

½ teaspoon red wine vinegar

3 teaspoons vegetable oil

1/3 teaspoon Ras-el-hanout seasoning

Salt

Pepper

Preparation

1. Preheat oven to gas mark 6/400°F/200°C.

2. Toss ½ teaspoon olive oil, chickpeas, onion, Ras-el-hanout, salt and pepper together in an oven-safe pan and roast for 15-20 minutes until the chickpeas and onion are brown and cooked through.

3. In the meantime, make the salad dressing by whisking together the mustard, red wine vinegar and remaining olive oil; adjust taste by adding salt and pepper.

4. Heat vegetable oil in a skillet or pan until hot then add strips of halloumi cheese. Fry each side until it has achieved a very

deep brown color. When completed drain excess oil on plate lined with paper towel.

5. In a large bowl mix the spinach, avocado, tomato and cabbage together.

6. When the chickpea and onion mixture is finished roasting, let it completely cool before adding to the bowl of vegetables.

7. Add dressing to the salad and top with the strips of halloumi.

The Green Delight Salad

Ingredients

6 cherry tomatoes cut in half

4 asparagus stalks

1 tablespoon fava beans

2 handfuls arugula

10 grams shaved Parmigiano-Reggiano

½ avocado, diced

½ tablespoon olive oil

3 teaspoons lemon juice

Salt

Black pepper

Preparation

1. Remove and discard the woody ends of the asparagus then cut the remaining stem in half.

2. Blanch the remaining halves of the asparagus and fava beans by gently lowering them into a pot of boiling salted water for about 2-4 minutes depending on their thickness; the goal is to have tender asparagus.

3. Transfer the asparagus to ice-cold water for a few minutes so that it stops cooking.

4. Drain on paper towel while making the dressing.

5. Using a fork, whisk olive oil and lemon juice together until combined, then add salt and pepper to taste.

6. In a large bowl toss arugula and dressing and top with cherry tomatoes, Parmigiano-Reggiano, avocado, fava beans and asparagus.

The Fearless Tarte
with SHAVED ASPARAGUS AND FENNEL SALAD

THE TARTE

Ingredients

1 puff pastry (homemade or store-bought, as you want)

1 medium-size eggplant

1 courgette (zucchini)

1 small shallot

2 garlic cloves

2 eggs

½ cup of heavy cream

Feta (1 usually use 200 grams)

Olive oil

Ground black pepper

Salt

Paprika

Preparation

1. Cut the courgette and eggplant into semithin circles.

2. Add salt, pepper, paprika and olive oil to the courgette and eggplant and put to the side.

3. Add olive oil to your pan and add thinly chopped shallots and garlic until softened.

4. Once the shallots and garlic are soft, add the courgette first until light brown.

5. Remove the browned courgette from the pan.

6. If needed, add more olive oil to the pan; if no additional oil is needed just start to cook the eggplant until lightly brown like the courgette.

7. Remove the eggplant and let everything cool.

8. While the vegetables are cooling, roll the pastry onto a tarte pan and start to layer the ingredients. I started with the eggplant since the circles were quite big. Then add some crumbled feta and then the courgette and repeat until everything is in the pan.

9. When the veggies and cheese are layered, in a separate bowl mix two eggs and the cream. Add a bit more salt and pepper. Whisk together until everything is blended and the mixture is smooth, then pour over the layered veggies.

10. Pop into the oven at gas mark 4/350°F/177°C for about 20 minutes.

SHAVED ASPARAGUS *and* FENNEL SALAD

Ingredients

5 asparagus stalks
½ fennel bulb
1 fresh lemon
A pinch of lemon zest
Leftover feta
Salt
Ground black pepper
Olive oil

Preparation

1. Blanch the asparagus by placing them in a pot of boiling water for 2 minutes then immediately transfer to ice-cold

water to stop the cooking. Let it sit in the water for about 1 minute or so until it is fully cooled down then remove and let it dry a bit.

2. While asparagus is cooling, shave the fennel. If you don't know how to do that you can simply cut it lengthwise into medium slices.

3. Once the asparagus is cooled you can start to shave it using a peeler; again, if you don't know how to do that you can just cut it lengthwise into fairly thin slices. I remove the top bits before peeling/cutting because I use it to decorate the dish.

4. Mix the asparagus and fennel together.

5. Sprinkle feta on top.

6. To make the dressing add olive oil, salt, pepper and juice from half of the fresh lemon and the lemon zest to a bowl and aggressively whisk together. Depending on how thick you like your dressing you can add more olive oil. But not too much because you don't want the olive oil taste to overpower the lemon citrusy flavor.

7. Once the dressing is finished drizzle over your salad and toss.

Don't Lose Your Softness Pasta

Ingredients

100 grams spaghetti or linguine
Salt
Black pepper
3 tablespoons extra virgin olive oil
4 garlic cloves, peeled and roughly chopped
½ white onion, roughly chopped
8 anchovy filets, rinsed and roughly chopped
½ teaspoon red pepper flakes, or to taste
Parmesan for grating, optional

*I use a lot of anchovies because I love them and believe that one can never have too many anchovies.

Preparation

1. Put the spaghetti in a large pot of well-salted boiling water and cook until firmly al dente. I would recommend you start checking the pasta's al dente-ness at around 7 minutes. If it is not al dente at 7 minutes, keep checking every 30-50 seconds.

2. While the pasta is cooking, warm the olive oil in a small skillet over medium heat.

3. Add white onions and cook until translucent; they shouldn't be brown.

4. Add the garlic and cook for about 1 minute; it shouldn't be brown.

5. Stir in the all the anchovies, add the red pepper flakes and ground black pepper.

6. Cook until the anchovies are most dissolved. It should take

about 1 minute or so; if the anchovies aren't mostly dissolved but the onion and garlic is beginning to burn, turn down the heat under the skillet.

7. Turn off the heat, but keep the anchovy-garlic-onion goodness in the skillet.

8. Drain the pasta and return it to the pot.

9. Pour the garlic and anchovy mixture into the pot of pasta and toss well to coat.

10. Serve with grated Parmesan, if desired.

Citrus Fennel Salad

Ingredients

DRESSING

2 tablespoons olive oil
1 tablespoon red wine vinegar
1 teaspoon lemon
1 garlic clove, finely minced
Salt and pepper, to taste

SALAD

Watercress
1 fennel bulb, cleaned and shaved
1 blood orange, peeled and sliced
1 clementine, peeled and sliced
¼ cup red onion, thinly sliced
¼ cup sliced almonds, toasted
Fresh mint, for garnish

Preparation

DRESSING

1. Place all of the dressing ingredients in a small bowl and stir; taste as you go and adjust accordingly.

SALAD

2. Sprinkle a tiny bit of salt and pepper and a drizzle of the dressing on the watercress then toss together. You want to season it a little bit before adding the rest.

3. Put watercress on a plate; this will serve as the base for the salad.

4. First layer are the two types of citrus, blood orange and clementines; drizzle with a bit of dressing. Second layer is the shaved fennel.

5. Liberally sprinkle the red onion.

6. Top with the toasted sliced almonds.

7. Spoon the remaining dressing on top and garnish with fresh mint leaves.

Scallop Macaroni and Cheese

This recipe is for more than one person. Enjoy the leftovers!

Ingredients

250 grams of scallops

500 grams of elbow macaroni pasta

1 cup butter

½ cup all-purpose flour

1 teaspoon kosher salt

½ teaspoon freshly cracked black pepper

½ teaspoon of nutmeg

½ teaspoon of paprika

½ teaspoon of garlic powder

1 ½ cups whole milk

1 cup of shredded Gruyere

1 cup of shredded comté

1 cup of shredded emmental

1 cup of breadcrumbs

Preparation

1. Cook macaroni to al dente and put it to the side.

2. Heat ¼ cup of butter in a saucepan; when hot add the scallops.

3. Cook the scallops two minutes on each side then put to the side; they will finish cooking in the oven.

4. Make the roux by melting ½ cup of butter in a saucepan and whisking in the flour.

5. Whisk in the salt, pepper, nutmeg, paprika and garlic powder.

6. Continue stirring for 3-4 minutes until the roux becomes a bit darker in color.

7. Slowly stir in the milk until mixture is thick and creamy; this will take a few more minutes of stirring.

8. Once thick and creamy, add cheeses.

9. Allow the cheese to melt and turn off the heat; *voila*, you have your cheese sauce.

10. Pour cheese sauce over macaroni; you want the cheese sauce to cover all of the macaroni.

11. Roughly chop the scallops and add to the cheese sauce and macaroni.

12. Transfer to a baking dish.

13. Mix butter and breadcrumbs and sprinkle across the top of the scallop macaroni and cheese mixture.

14. Bake at gas mark 4/350°F/177°C for 20 minutes.

15. Garnish with fresh herbs of your choice.

Champagne Lavender Cocktail

Recipe adapted from Martha Stewart

Ingredients

½ cup sugar
1 tablespoon dried lavender
1 bottle dry champagne, chilled
Fresh lavender sprigs, for garnish

Preparation

1. Bring sugar and ½ cup water to a boil in a saucepan, stirring to dissolve sugar.

2. Stir in dried lavender.

3. Remove from heat and let cool completely.

4. Strain out lavender.

5. Refrigerate syrup until ready to serve (you can keep it in the refrigerator for up to one month).

6. When ready to serve, pour about 6 ounces champagne and 1 ½ teaspoons syrup into each flute.

7. Garnish each with a lavender sprig.

Acknowledgments

This book wouldn't have happened without my family propelling me forward every step of the way. Thank you all for your support, whether you're near or far. In particular, I'd like to thank my parents for always encouraging my love of reading and writing. All those Scholastic Book Club orders really paid off! And thank you for instilling a belief in God and faith in me. I may be an ocean away, but I call on God and rely on my faith often, and it strengthens me. I love you.

Annie, you helped me make the transition to life in Paris so much easier and less stressful. I didn't feel like I was losing a family when I was welcomed with open arms into yours. I deeply admire your kindness, compassion, empathy and generosity. Thank you for the ways in which you've been there for me over the years and for being the fabulous woman you are.

My agent, Leigh Eisenman, you plucked me out of the kitchen and from behind the microphone, giving me the confidence to tell my story and reassuring me that my voice mattered. The year 2020 was very rough and in many ways isolating, but having you in my life during that time made it so much more bearable. Thank you for taking a chance on me and for your continual support and encouragement.

My first editor, Natalie Hallak, it only took a few minutes into our first call for me to know that I wanted you to help me shape my story. Thank you for your patience, kindness, care and thoughtfulness throughout the entire process. Erika Imranyi, thank you for taking over the reins and continuing the task of refining my manuscript. You were an integral part of why I made it to the finish line.

Lory Martinez, *gracias, mi amiga*, for believing in the *Dinner for One* podcast from the very beginning when I slid my idea to you across that café table in the thirteenth arrondissement. You saw the *el cacumen* in me before I did.

To my friends! *My friendssss!* I love you all so, so, so, so much and you mean the world to me. Thank you for putting up with my weird sense of humor, my continual onslaught of inappropriate GIFs in our group chats, for supporting me and the podcast since day one, and for always being so encouraging. I feel very lucky to have a group of kind, wonderful, supportive people in my life that I consider family. Unfortunately, I can't name all of you, but you know who you are *et je vous aime.* However, I would be remiss if I didn't specifically thank Alice Smith, Chantal Drost, Camille Joux, Evelyn So, Gabbie Barnes, Kristin Frederick, Nathalie Bonnet Conchon, Samar Trad, Tiffanie Delune and Tina Harris for either listening to me, talking to me, drinking with me, dancing with me or crying with me at some point between 2016 and 2018 when I needed it the most. Those were the two of the hardest years of my life, but having my army of women behind me helped me survive. I am much better now and there is no doubt that it is in large part thanks to all of you.

Monique Benoit, I wouldn't have been able to finish the first draft of the book without your generosity. Thank you so much for having me in your beautiful home in Aix-en-Provence. My months in Aix not only helped me finish the first draft of this book, but my time there also did me a world of good.

Dr. Luke, Lauren Arcache, your love of and passion for food made both of you the perfect people to test the recipes that made it into the book. Thank you for your time, patience and effort in helping me with this integral part of the story.

Lauren Collins, thank you so much for your support around this manuscript, taking the time out of your schedule to read it and championing everything about *Dinner for One*.

A special shout-out to the Trad family: Samar, Filip, Joylynn and Loann. My life in Paris wouldn't be the same without you. You're my home away from home, and I am so grateful to have you here. My Jojobear and Lolobean, the both of you are such bright lights in my life. It is truly an honor watching you grow up, and I hope you'll still want to hang out with me when you're both taller and cooler than me.

I had three very influential teachers in my life. They never dimmed my light; they accepted the fact that I talked a lot in class, entertained my stories; and always championed me and my writing. My very first teacher when I lived in Jamaica, Mrs. Stevens, my kindergarten teacher after moving to New York City, Mrs. Wills, and my high school senior year English lit teacher, Ms. Cordill. Although I was in a somewhat strict and constrained environment of private school, I can't thank you all enough for simply letting me be myself. I am the confident, forthright and curious woman I am today because of you. Ms. Cordill, I remember on the last day before graduation when the bell rang and I was running out of class, you pulled me to the side and said, "You must write." I brushed it off, but it stayed in the back of my mind. Thank you.

Merci à Gabrielle Barnes, Hannah Meltzer, Hattie Crisell, Jillian Hobbs, Kristin Frederick, Lauren Arcache, Lauren Collins,

Laurianne Melierre, Léonard Diga, Lindsey Tramuta, Manal Alsaleh, Marie Chalamet, Natasha Nyanin, Nathalie Bonnet Conchon, Samar Trad, Rebecca Plotnik and Tanish Townsend for appearing as guests on the podcast and sharing your stories and recipes with me and the larger *Dinner for One* community. It was a pleasure having you in my kitchen.

To all of the *Dinner for One* listeners, what a wild ride, huh? I literally wouldn't be where I am today if you hadn't accepted my invitation to join me in my kitchen and listened to me talk about *n'importe quoi*. You've been a huge part of my healing journey, and I cannot express enough gratitude for your well wishes, vulnerability when sharing your own stories and humor around this wild experience called life. I appreciate each and every one of you. *Merci beaucoup.*

To everyone who purchased this book, thank you for your support and for giving me a place in your heart and homes.

À Paris, quand nous nous sommes rencontrés, je me cherchais encore et tu m'as aidé à devenir la femme que je suis aujourd'hui. J'ai hâte de découvrir ce que notre histoire d'amour va m'apporter.